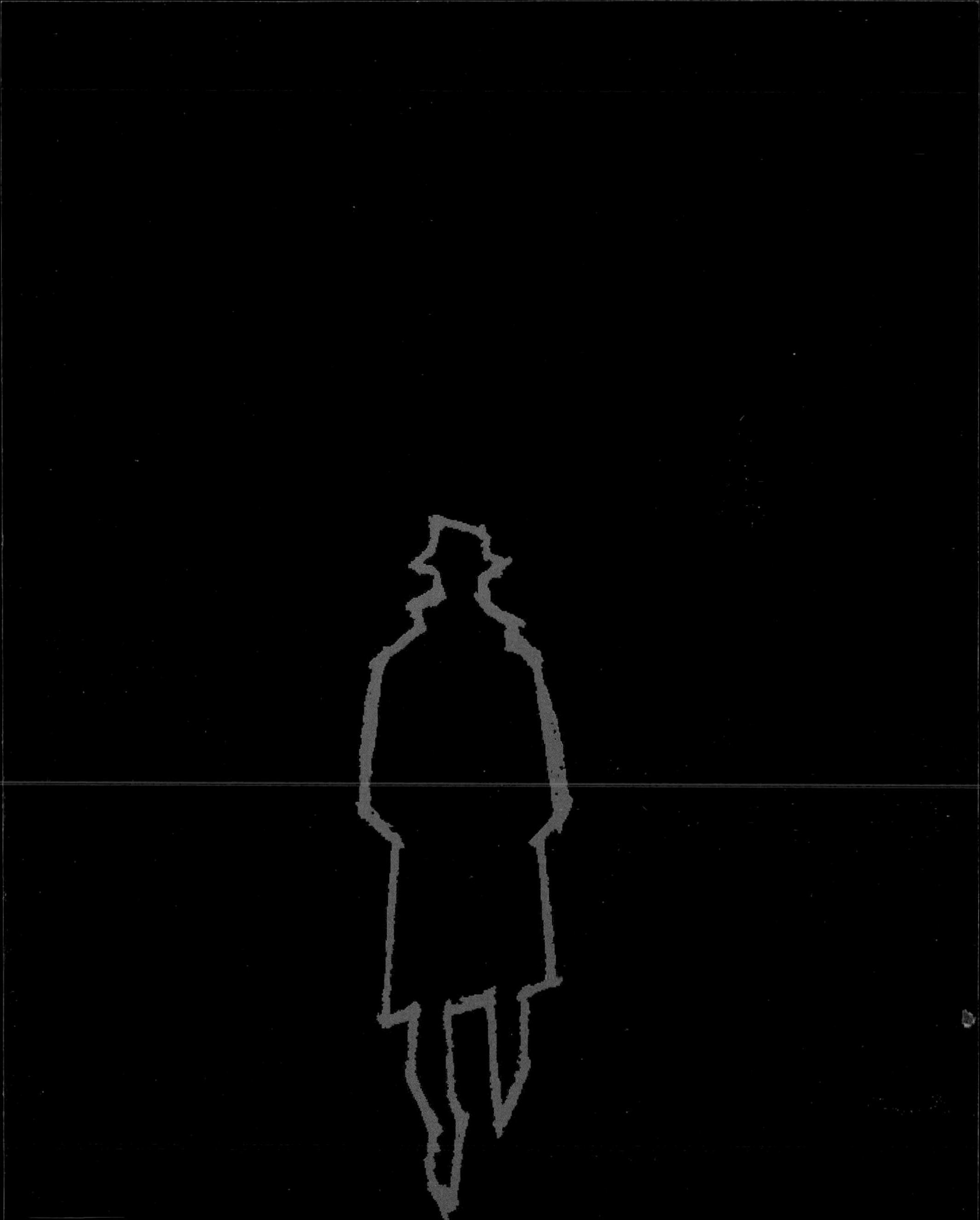

IDW

Facebook: **facebook.com/idwpublishing**
Twitter: **@idwpublishing**
YouTube: **youtube.com/idwpublishing**
Tumblr: **tumblr.idwpublishing.com**
Instagram: **instagram.com/idwpublishing**

COVER ART BY
JOHN K. SNYDER III

EDITS BY
TOM WALTZ,
JUSTIN EISINGER,
AND ALONZO SIMON

DESIGN BY
JEFF POWELL

PUBLISHER
GREG GOLDSTEIN

ISBN: **978-1-61377-884-5**   21 20 19 18   1 2 3 4

Greg Goldstein, President & Publisher
Robbie Robbins, EVP & Sr. Art Director
Chris Ryall, Chief Creative Officer & Editor-in-Chief
Matthew Ruzicka, CPA, Chief Financial Officer
David Hedgecock, Associate Publisher
Laurie Windrow, Senior Vice President of Sales & Marketing
Lorelei Bunjes, VP of Digital Services
Eric Moss, Sr. Director, Licensing & Business Development

Ted Adams, Founder & CEO of IDW Media Holdings

For international rights, contact licensing@idwpublishing.com

LAWRENCE BLOCK'S

Eight
Million
Ways to
Die

Adapted and Illustrated by
JOHN K. SNYDER III

Lettering by
FRANK CVETKOVIC

I wrote *Eight Million Ways to Die* in a first-floor apartment on Haven Avenue in Washington Heights.

It was a stone's throw from the block where Matthew Scudder, some years earlier, had fired his gun at a pair of killers. One bullet took a bad hop and killed a child, burdening Scudder with a load of guilt that lingered through quite a few books. Then I guess he got over it, or perhaps I got tired of writing that paragraph.

But we first heard about Estrellita Rivera in Scudder's debut, *The Sins of the Fathers*, written in 1974, and I didn't move to Haven Avenue until the fall of 1981. Once I'd settled in I got to work on the fifth book in the series. I hadn't been working on it for very long before it became clear to me that the new book—I hadn't yet come up with a title for it—was going to be more ambitious than the first four. Longer, too.

The length bothered me, for both artistic and commercial reasons. Like all of its predecessors, *Eight Million Ways to Die* was told in the first person. That had worked fine in the early books, which ran to perhaps 55,000 words apiece. It worked in the fourth, *A Stab in the Dark,* which came in a little longer. But it was going to take me well over 100,000 words to do the story justice, and that's a long time to have a single voice droning in your ear.

That was the artistic part. On the commercial side, the standard definition of a mystery still applied; it was a work of fiction in which a crime was committed and solved, all in no more than 65,000 words. Crime fiction was ghettoized back then. It never got much promotion from its publishers, it never appeared on bestseller lists, and while it might be the guilty pleasure of half the intellectuals in the country, it got no more respect than Rodney Dangerfield.

So what would Arbor House make of this one? At the time, it was very much the creature of Donald I. Fine, and I knew that nobody could ever predict what Don Fine would do. So I shrugged off my artistic and commercial concerns and gave myself up to writing the book.

When I turned it in, around the time 1981 was turning into 1982, nobody even mentioned the length. My editor, Arnold Ehrlich, liked it just fine. Don Fine thought it was dandy, and rushed it into print.

And I figured I was now out of a job.

And why was I out of a job?

I can best explain that by answering another question: Why was this book twice as long as its fellows? Answer: it was trying to tell three stories.

First, it was telling the story of Matt Scudder's investigation into the murder of Kim Dakkinen, and the several events that followed in its wake. And that story had to be gripping or you, Dear Reader, would put the book down unfinished.

The book's second theme was the perilous nature of life in New York—and, by extension, of life anywhere. "You know what you've got?" Joe Durkin rants. "You've got eight million ways to die." (And that's where I got the title. Joe Durkin gave it to me. On the other hand, I gave him the line.)

Scudder is very conscious of the many ways death can reach out and find a person. He reads the paper, and people tell him stories, and they weigh on his mind. One of those stories, that of Mrs. Rudenko and the free television set, came from a friend. His name wasn't Rudenko, and the woman in question was not an elderly Ukrainian woman but an elderly Jewish woman, living out her days on East Tenth Street. She was my friend's mother, and I figured any book called *Eight Million Ways to Die* ought to have her story in it.

The other awful tales came one after another. I'd

moved to Haven Avenue to live with a woman with whom I already had a lengthy and complicated history, and cohabitation did not make it any less complicated. She was out working during the day, while I worked on the book, and then she'd come home and we'd have dinner and then, more evenings than not, I'd ride the A train downtown, to get together with friends on Perry Street, in the West Village. On my way to the train, I'd pick up a tabloid—usually the *News,* but sometimes the *Post*—and by the time I reached my destination the city had supplied some new outrage for Scudder to meditate on during the next day's writing. New York never failed me.

And, of course, the third thread or theme or story is that of our hero struggling to come to terms with his alcoholism.

Now when I wrote the first books I never thought Matt would wind up spending time in church basements. I mean, the guy seemed okay to me. No reason to think he had a problem. And, problem or no, why should he change? Fictional detectives didn't change or grow. They stayed the same, even as I took it for granted Matt would, sitting at a corner table at Jimmy Armstrong's and drinking until his liver quit on him.

But in the fourth book, quite without any conscious intent on my part, Matt begins to get the idea that his relationship to alcohol might be, um, problematic. His new girlfriend starts going to AA meetings, and at the book's end he slips into a room in the basement of a church, looks around, reads the slogans on the walls—and wisely gets the hell out of there and heads for the nearest bar.

But the jig was up. I knew it, even if Matt didn't, and that aspect of his story had to be a key element of the fifth book. So throughout *Eight Million Ways to Die* we see him trying to get sober and trying not to get sober, going in and out of meetings and in and out of bars.

But once I'd told that story, then what? What future was there for a sober Matthew Scudder? We'd followed him through five books, and each was a complete novel in and of itself, but in another sense they were all chapters in a longer novel that ended in the basement of a church. His overall story had had its arc, and now his *d'etre* had no *raison.*

And for a couple of years that seemed to be the case. But really, what the hell do I know? There was a flashback novel, *When the Sacred Ginmill Closes,* with the hard-drinking Scudder we'd all known. And then, a little later, there was a book that starred a sober Scudder, and I've since found quite a few books and stories to write about him.

Eight Million Ways to Die was filmed, with the first word changed to a numeral. Jeff Bridges and Andy Garcia did good work in *8 Million Ways to Die,* but I've never made any secret of the fact that I didn't think much of the film. (Neither did the critics, or the handful of people who actually saw it and told their friends not to waste their time.) It would be ungrateful of me to bad-mouth the movie, as it paid off a mortgage for me, but I can't in good conscience good-mouth it either.

Scudder and the movie-going public got better treatment from writer-director Scott Frank and actor Liam Neeson in 2014's *A Walk Among the Tombstones.* That was a film that pleased me greatly, and when the graphic novel of *Eight Million Ways to Die* started to come together, I hoped it would be more like the second movie and less like the first one.

I never dared to expect it would be as good as it is. John K. Snyder III has been faithful to the original novel as no film has ever been to its source. Snyder's New York has the look and feel of Scudder's New York, and the whole three-pronged story of the novel is fully realized, superbly told, and beautifully illustrated.

— Lawrence Block
March 2018

NEW YORK CITY

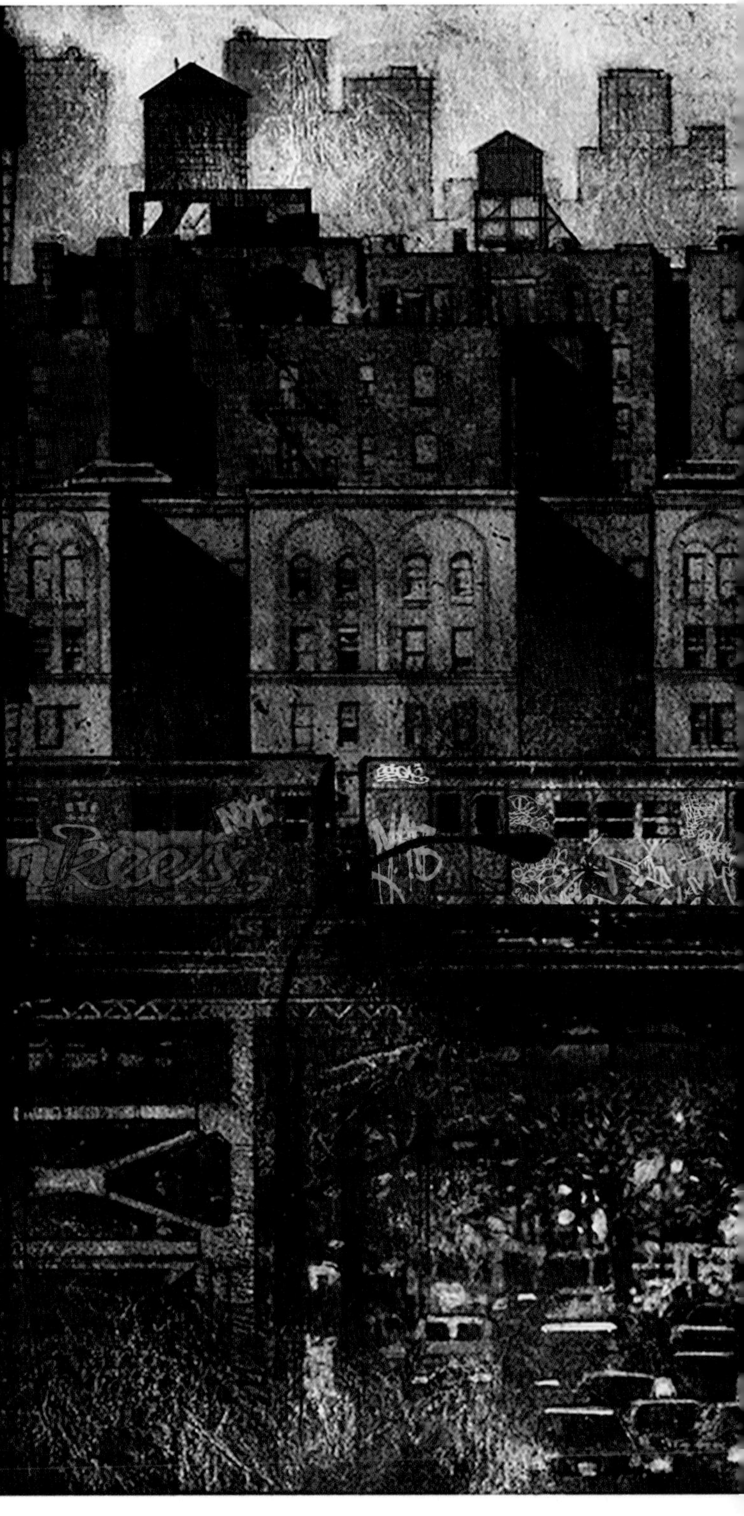

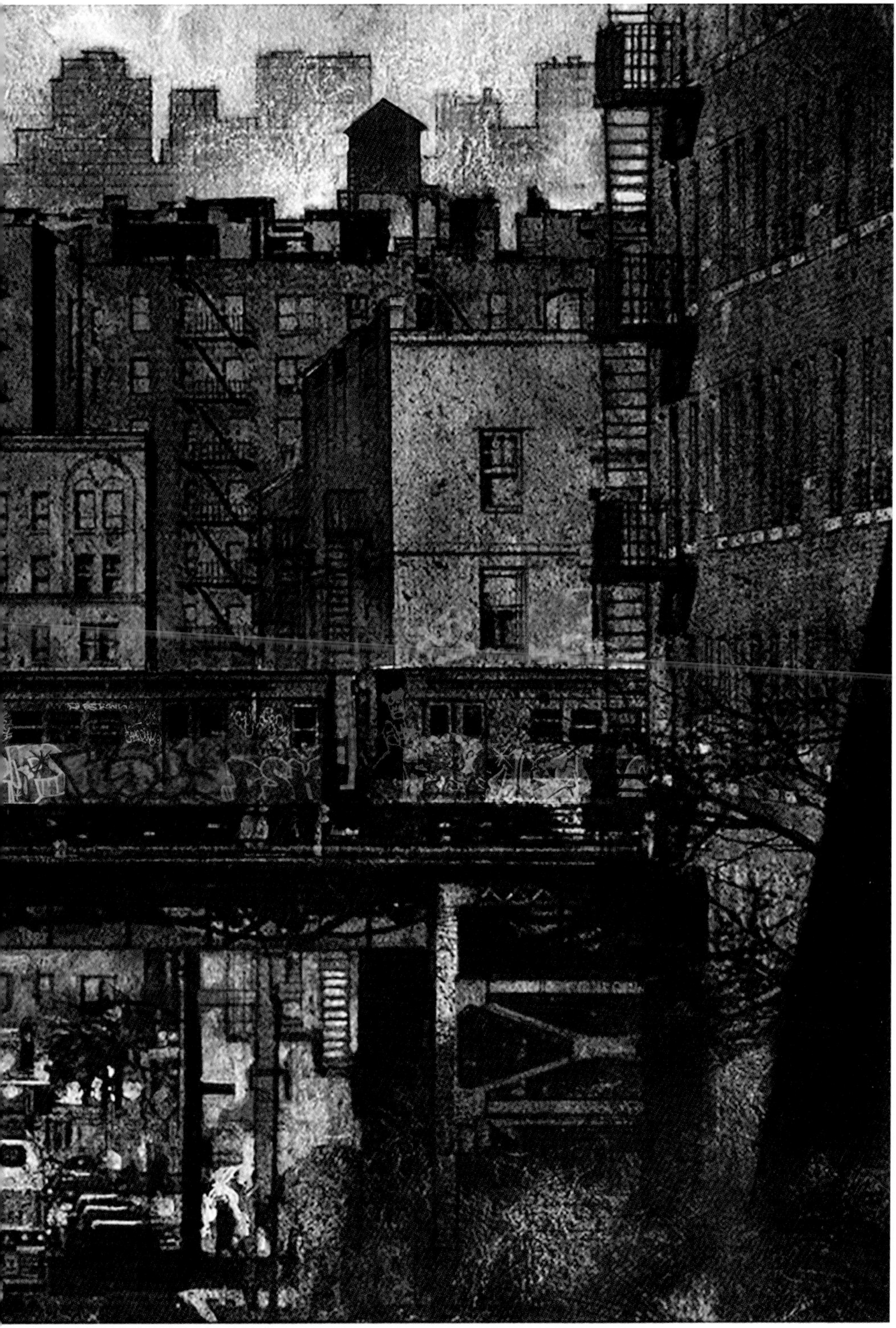

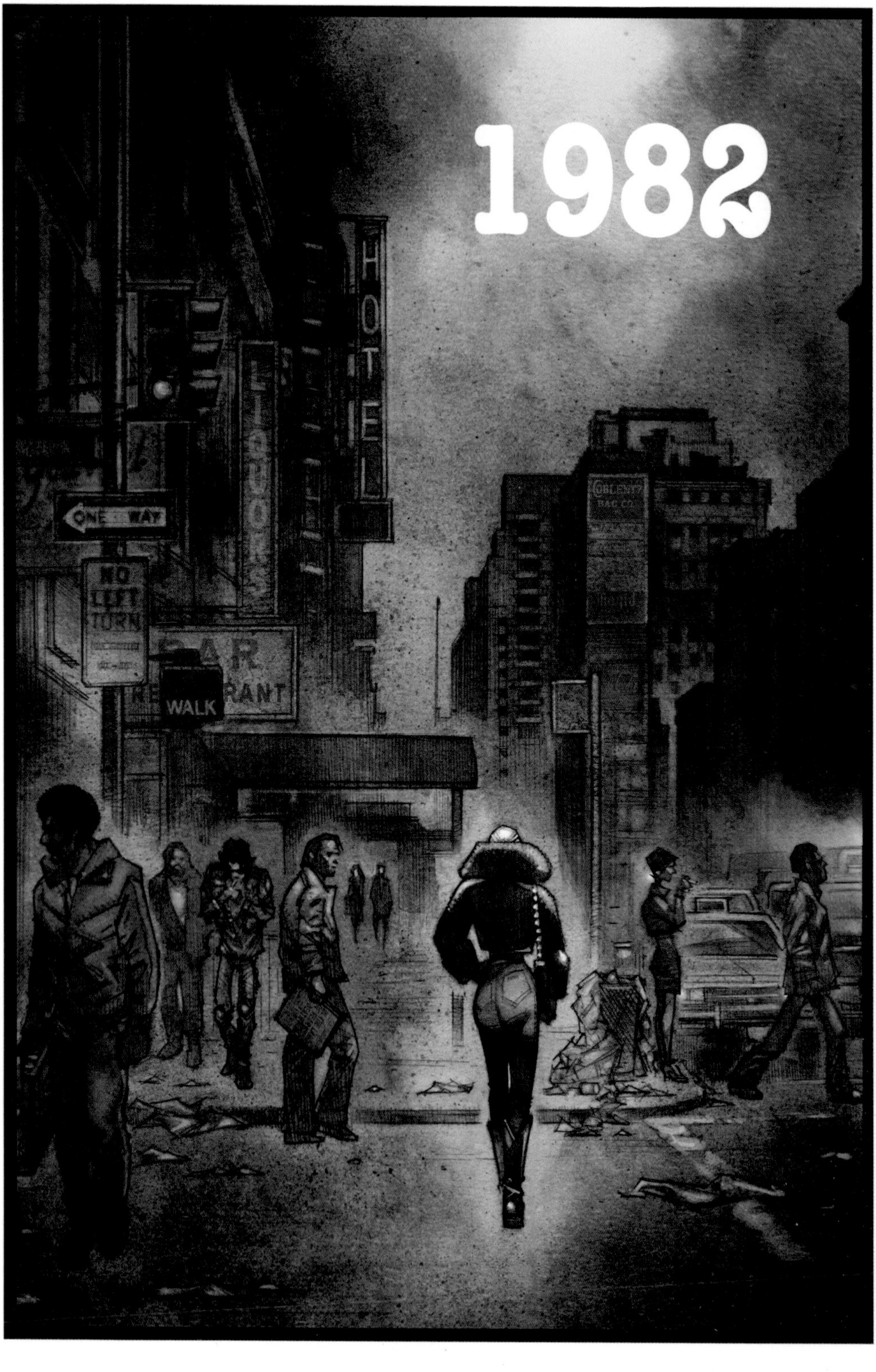
1982
HOTEL
LIQUOR
ONE WAY
NO LEFT TURN
WALK

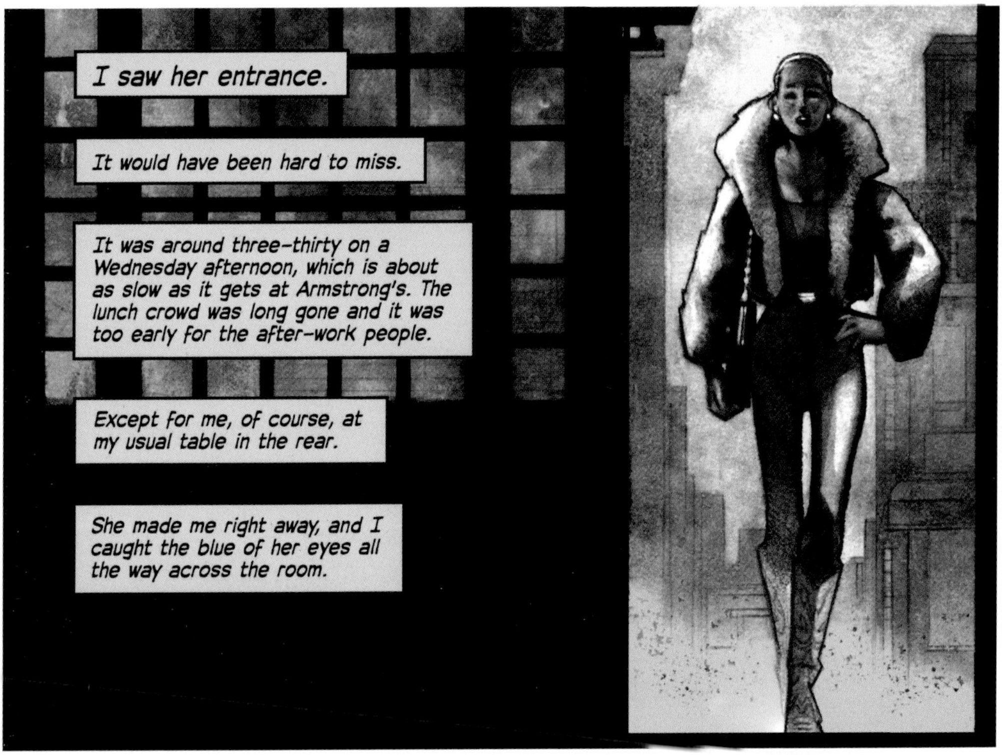
I saw her entrance.
It would have been hard to miss.
It was around three-thirty on a Wednesday afternoon, which is about as slow as it gets at Armstrong's. The lunch crowd was long gone and it was too early for the after-work people.
Except for me, of course, at my usual table in the rear.
She made me right away, and I caught the blue of her eyes all the way across the room.

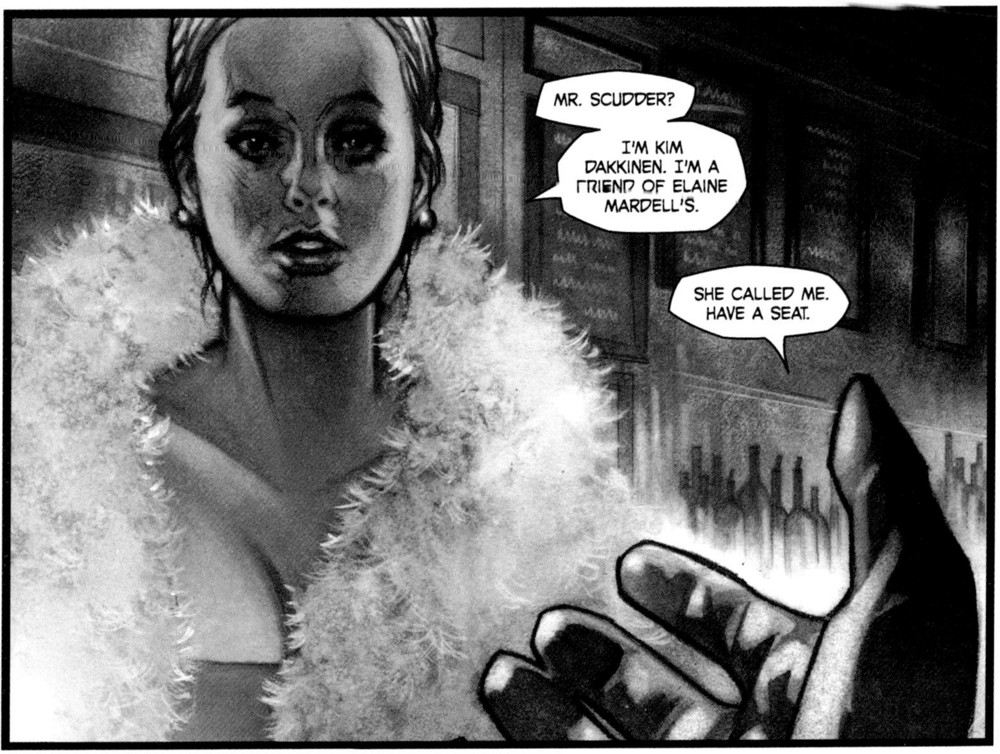
MR. SCUDDER?
I'M KIM DAKKINEN. I'M A FRIEND OF ELAINE MARDELL'S.
SHE CALLED ME. HAVE A SEAT.

When the coffee arrived, she told me she wasn't much of drinker, especially in the day.

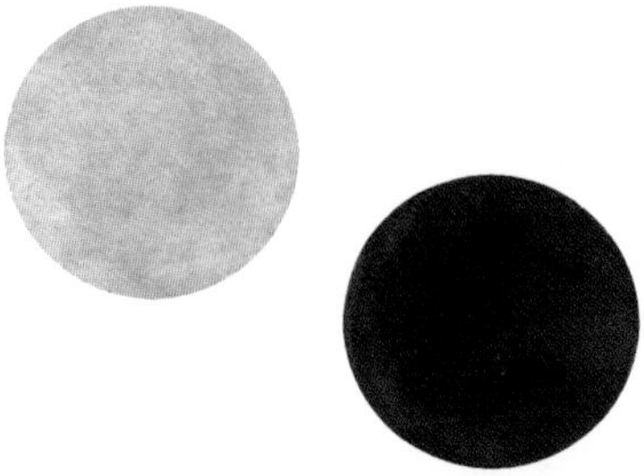

But she couldn't drink it black the way I did, she had to have it sweet, almost like dessert, and she supposed she was just lucky but she'd never had a weight problem, she could eat anything and never gain an ounce.

And wasn't that lucky?

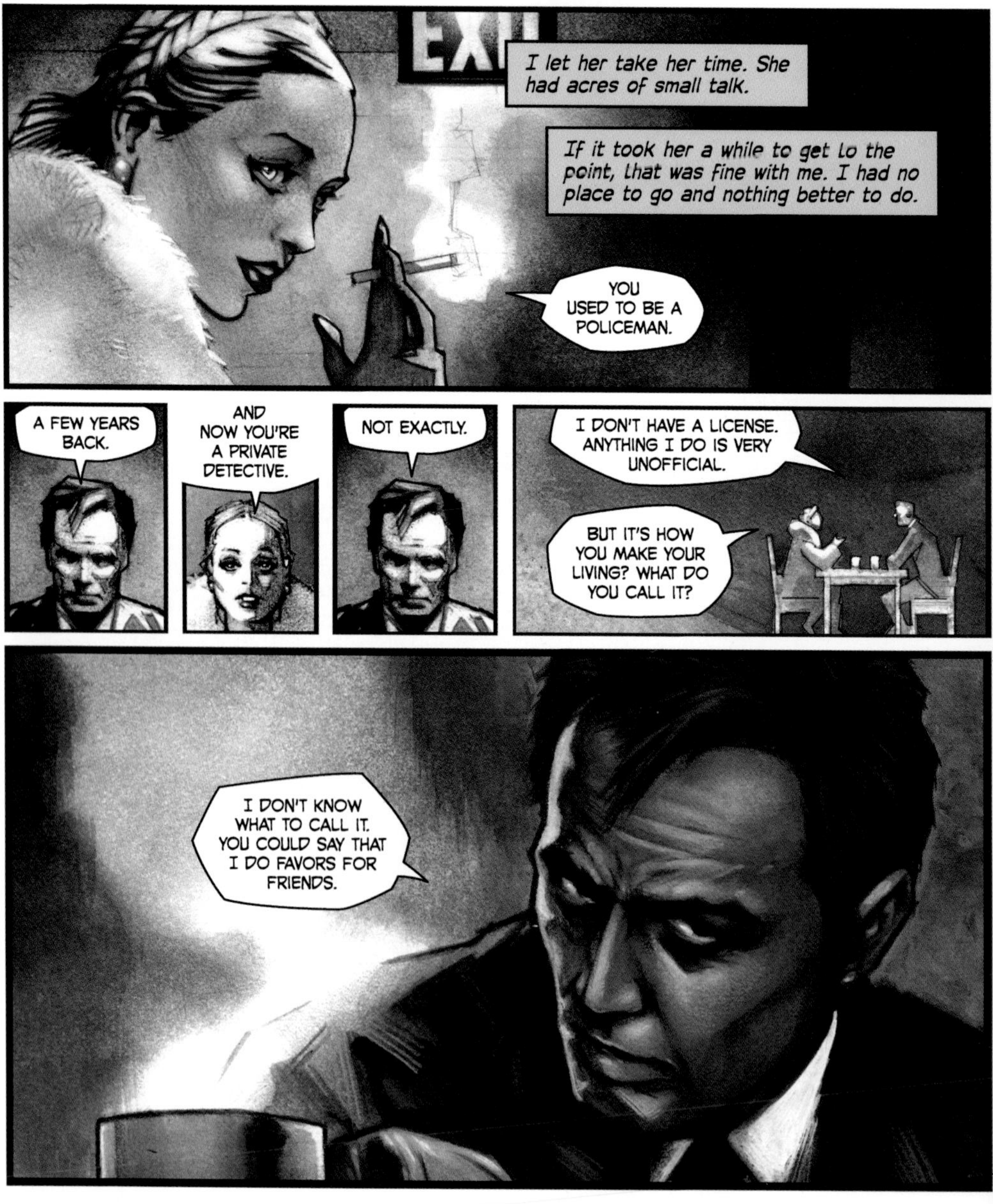

EXIT
I let her take her time. She had acres of small talk.
If it took her a while to get to the point, that was fine with me. I had no place to go and nothing better to do.
YOU USED TO BE A POLICEMAN.
A FEW YEARS BACK.
AND NOW YOU'RE A PRIVATE DETECTIVE.
NOT EXACTLY.
I DON'T HAVE A LICENSE. ANYTHING I DO IS VERY UNOFFICIAL.
BUT IT'S HOW YOU MAKE YOUR LIVING? WHAT DO YOU CALL IT?
I DON'T KNOW WHAT TO CALL IT. YOU COULD SAY THAT I DO FAVORS FOR FRIENDS.

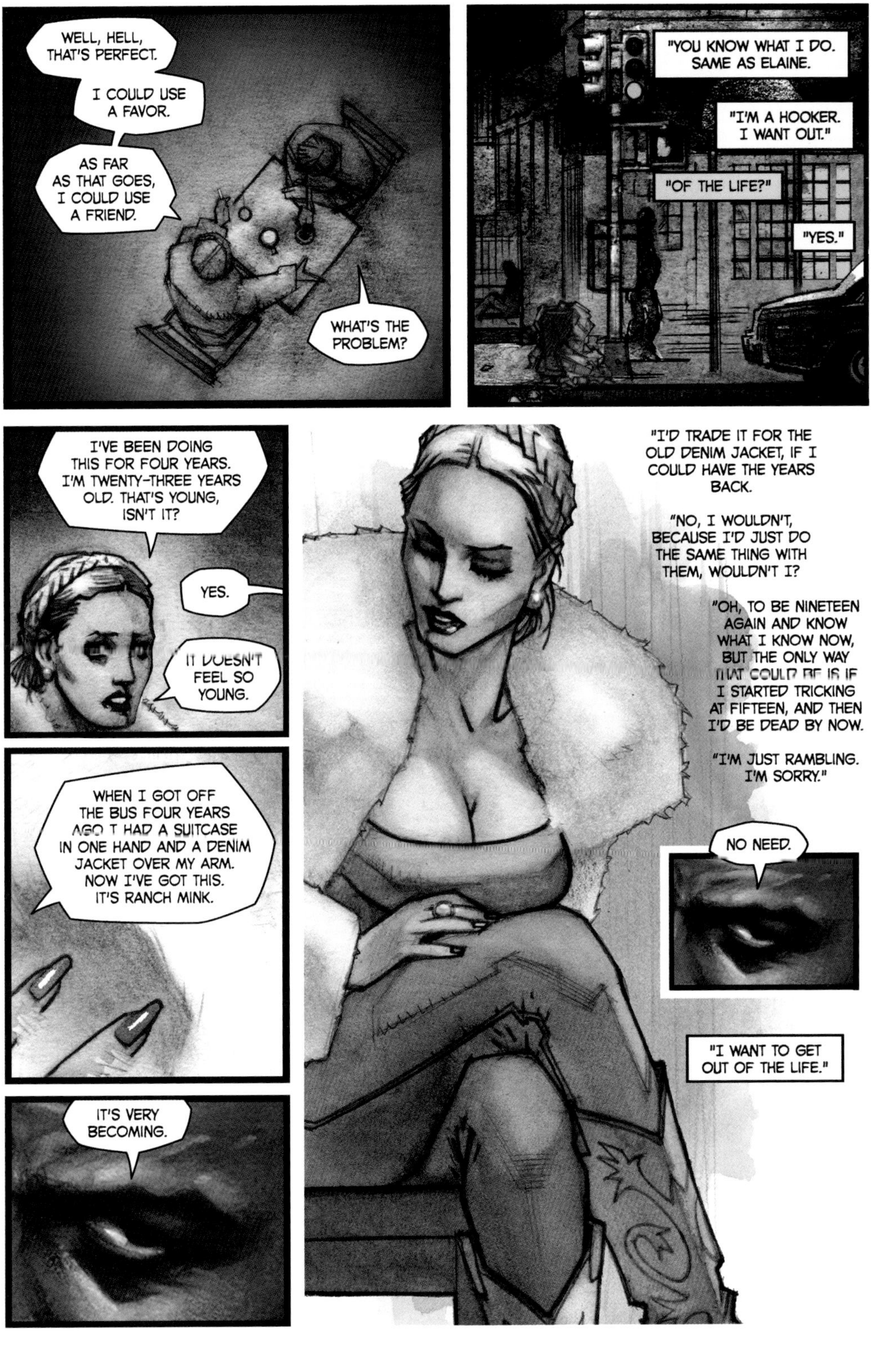
WELL, HELL, THAT'S PERFECT.
I COULD USE A FAVOR.
AS FAR AS THAT GOES, I COULD USE A FRIEND.
WHAT'S THE PROBLEM?
"YOU KNOW WHAT I DO. SAME AS ELAINE.
"I'M A HOOKER. I WANT OUT."
"OF THE LIFE?"
"YES."
I'VE BEEN DOING THIS FOR FOUR YEARS. I'M TWENTY-THREE YEARS OLD. THAT'S YOUNG, ISN'T IT?
YES.
IT DOESN'T FEEL SO YOUNG.
WHEN I GOT OFF THE BUS FOUR YEARS AGO I HAD A SUITCASE IN ONE HAND AND A DENIM JACKET OVER MY ARM. NOW I'VE GOT THIS. IT'S RANCH MINK.
IT'S VERY BECOMING.
"I'D TRADE IT FOR THE OLD DENIM JACKET, IF I COULD HAVE THE YEARS BACK.
"NO, I WOULDN'T, BECAUSE I'D JUST DO THE SAME THING WITH THEM, WOULDN'T I?
"OH, TO BE NINETEEN AGAIN AND KNOW WHAT I KNOW NOW, BUT THE ONLY WAY THAT COULD BE IS IF I STARTED TRICKING AT FIFTEEN, AND THEN I'D BE DEAD BY NOW.
"I'M JUST RAMBLING. I'M SORRY."
NO NEED.
"I WANT TO GET OUT OF THE LIFE."

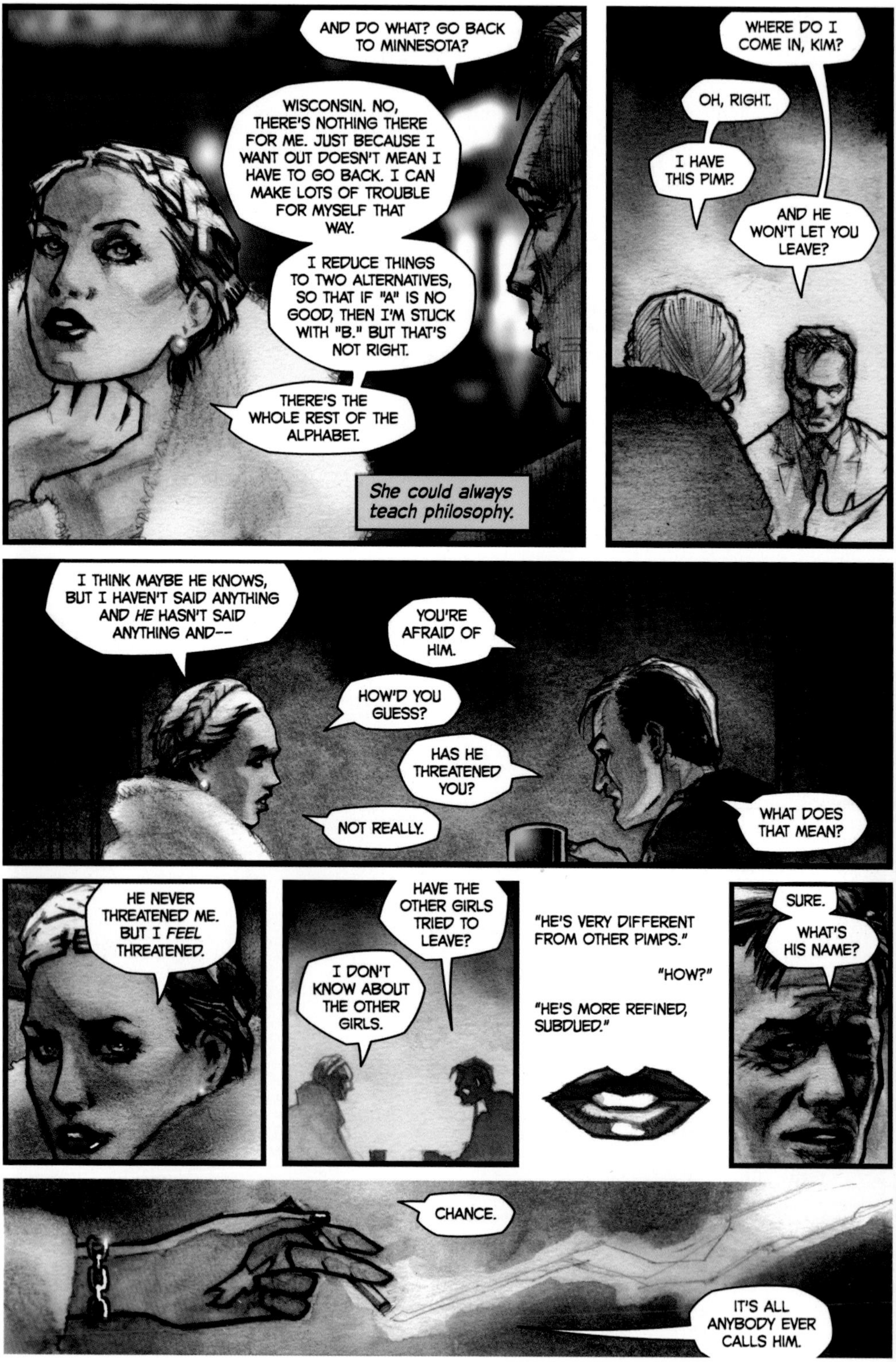
AND DO WHAT? GO BACK TO MINNESOTA?
WISCONSIN. NO, THERE'S NOTHING THERE FOR ME. JUST BECAUSE I WANT OUT DOESN'T MEAN I HAVE TO GO BACK. I CAN MAKE LOTS OF TROUBLE FOR MYSELF THAT WAY.
I REDUCE THINGS TO TWO ALTERNATIVES, SO THAT IF "A" IS NO GOOD, THEN I'M STUCK WITH "B." BUT THAT'S NOT RIGHT.
THERE'S THE WHOLE REST OF THE ALPHABET.
She could always teach philosophy.
WHERE DO I COME IN, KIM?
OH, RIGHT.
I HAVE THIS PIMP.
AND HE WON'T LET YOU LEAVE?
I THINK MAYBE HE KNOWS, BUT I HAVEN'T SAID ANYTHING AND *HE* HASN'T SAID ANYTHING AND--
YOU'RE AFRAID OF HIM.
HOW'D YOU GUESS?
HAS HE THREATENED YOU?
NOT REALLY.
WHAT DOES THAT MEAN?
HE NEVER THREATENED ME. BUT I *FEEL* THREATENED.
HAVE THE OTHER GIRLS TRIED TO LEAVE?
I DON'T KNOW ABOUT THE OTHER GIRLS.
"HE'S VERY DIFFERENT FROM OTHER PIMPS."
"HOW?"
"HE'S MORE REFINED, SUBDUED."
SURE.
WHAT'S HIS NAME?
CHANCE.
IT'S ALL ANYBODY EVER CALLS HIM.

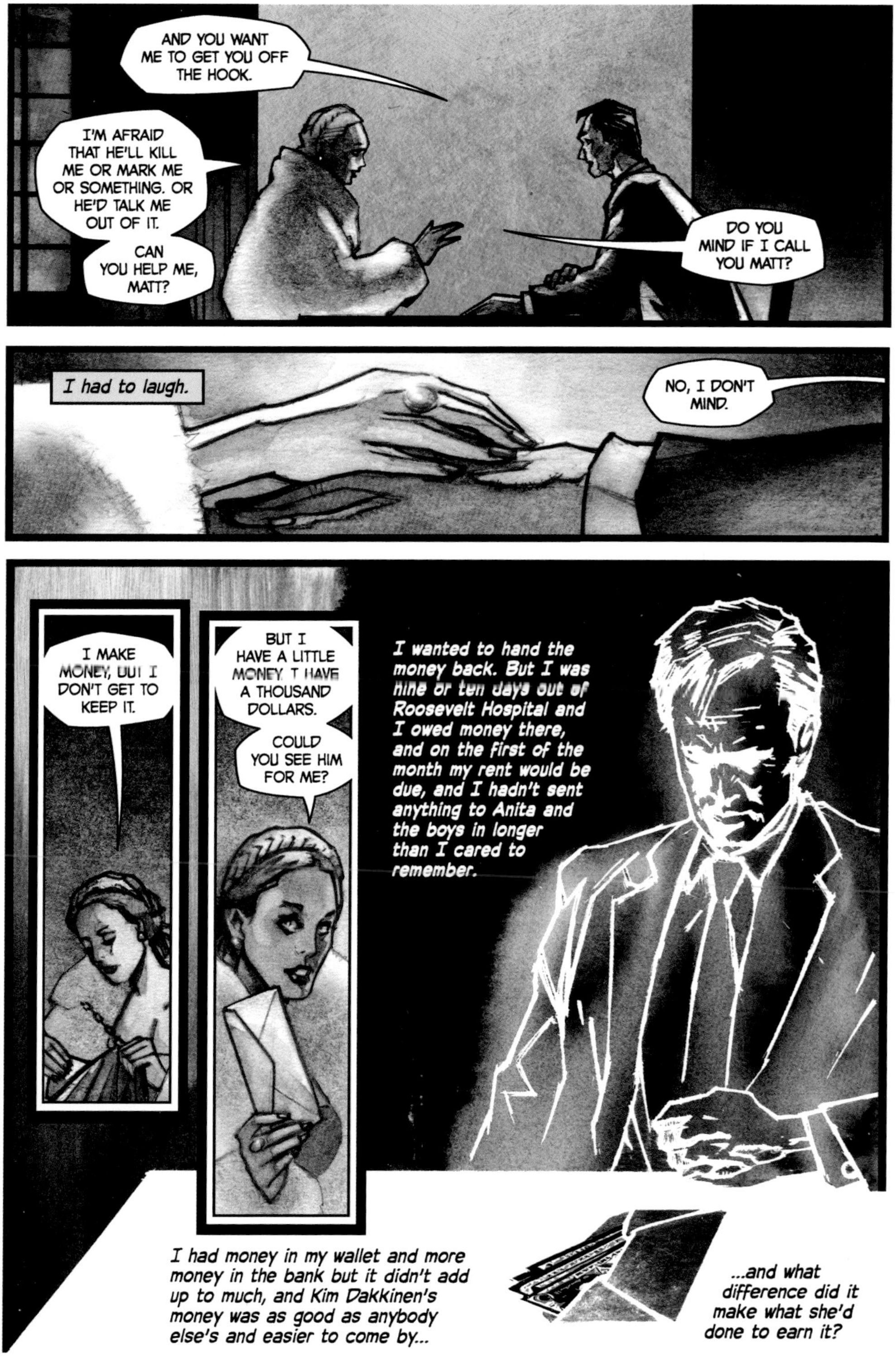
AND YOU WANT ME TO GET YOU OFF THE HOOK.
I'M AFRAID THAT HE'LL KILL ME OR MARK ME OR SOMETHING. OR HE'D TALK ME OUT OF IT.
CAN YOU HELP ME, MATT?
DO YOU MIND IF I CALL YOU MATT?
I had to laugh.
NO, I DON'T MIND.
I MAKE MONEY, BUT I DON'T GET TO KEEP IT.
BUT I HAVE A LITTLE MONEY. I HAVE A THOUSAND DOLLARS.
COULD YOU SEE HIM FOR ME?
I wanted to hand the money back. But I was nine or ten days out of Roosevelt Hospital and I owed money there, and on the first of the month my rent would be due, and I hadn't sent anything to Anita and the boys in longer than I cared to remember.
I had money in my wallet and more money in the bank but it didn't add up to much, and Kim Dakkinen's money was as good as anybody else's and easier to come by...
...and what difference did it make what she'd done to earn it?

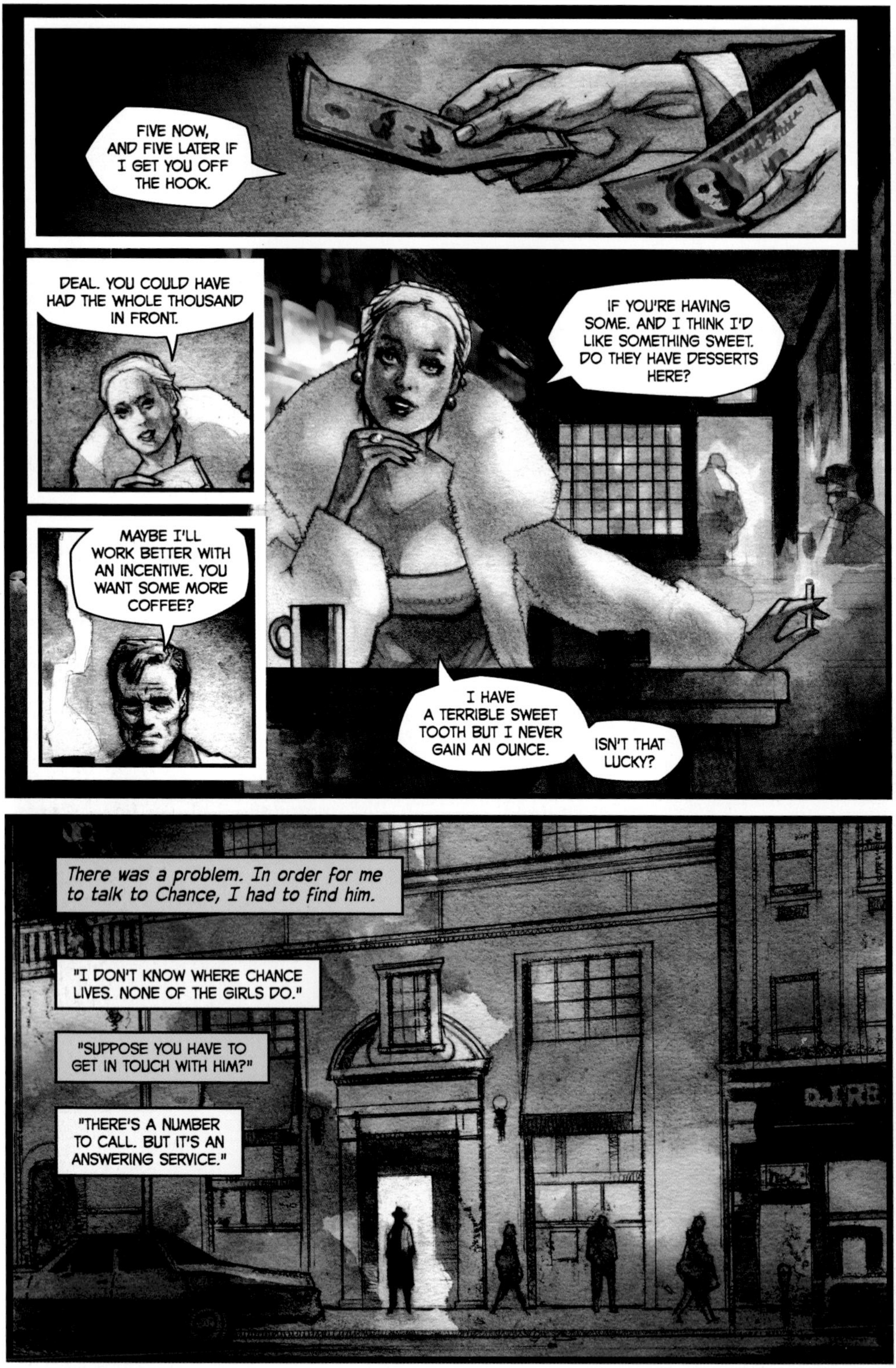

FIVE NOW, AND FIVE LATER IF I GET YOU OFF THE HOOK.
DEAL. YOU COULD HAVE HAD THE WHOLE THOUSAND IN FRONT.
MAYBE I'LL WORK BETTER WITH AN INCENTIVE. YOU WANT SOME MORE COFFEE?
IF YOU'RE HAVING SOME. AND I THINK I'D LIKE SOMETHING SWEET. DO THEY HAVE DESSERTS HERE?
I HAVE A TERRIBLE SWEET TOOTH BUT I NEVER GAIN AN OUNCE.
ISN'T THAT LUCKY?
There was a problem. In order for me to talk to Chance, I had to find him.
"I DON'T KNOW WHERE CHANCE LIVES. NONE OF THE GIRLS DO."
"SUPPOSE YOU HAVE TO GET IN TOUCH WITH HIM?"
"THERE'S A NUMBER TO CALL. BUT IT'S AN ANSWERING SERVICE."

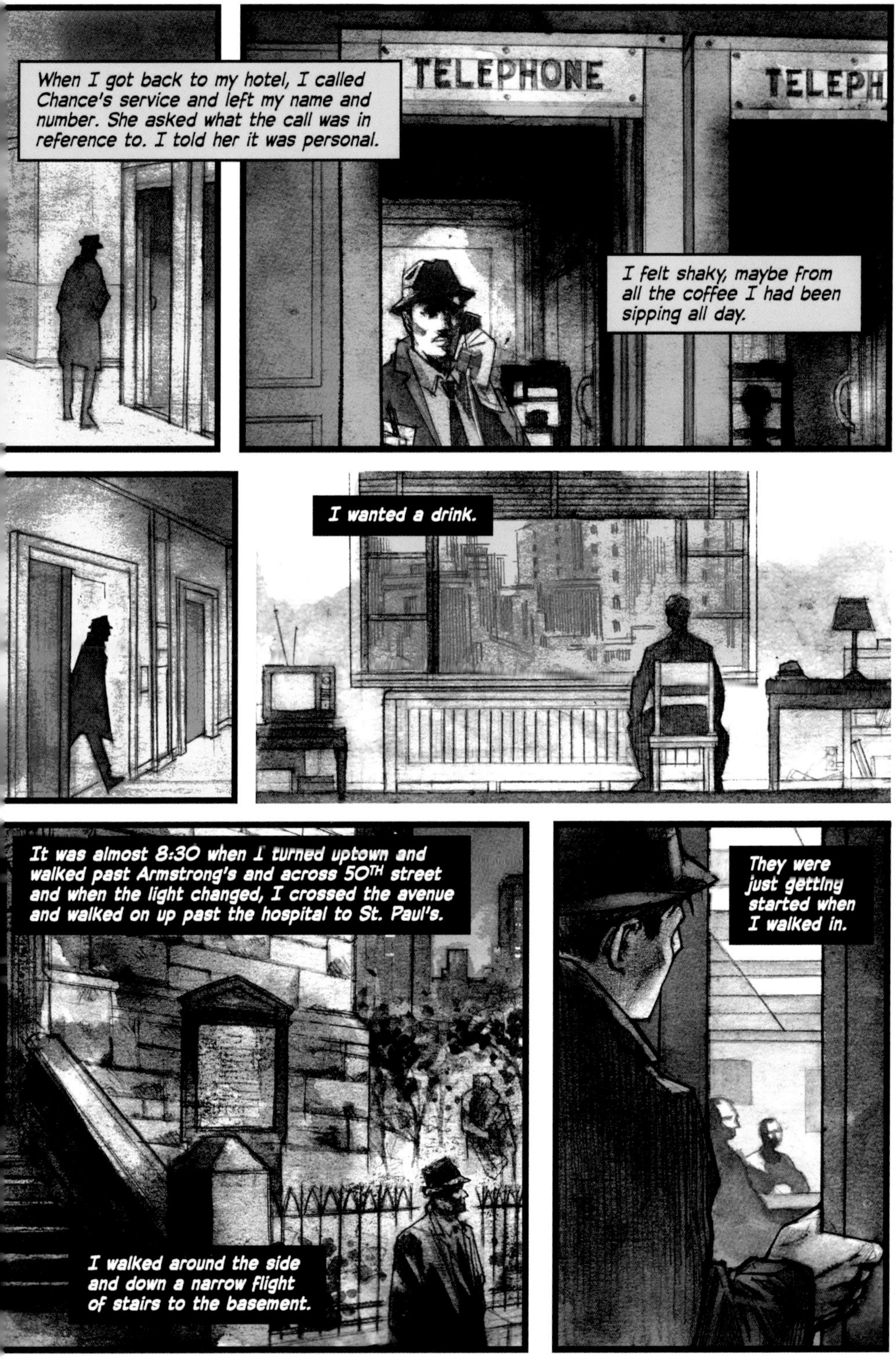
When I got back to my hotel, I called Chance's service and left my name and number. She asked what the call was in reference to. I told her it was personal.
TELEPHONE
TELEPH
I felt shaky, maybe from all the coffee I had been sipping all day.
I wanted a drink.
It was almost 8:30 when I turned uptown and walked past Armstrong's and across 50TH street and when the light changed, I crossed the avenue and walked on up past the hospital to St. Paul's.
I walked around the side and down a narrow flight of stairs to the basement.
They were just getting started when I walked in.

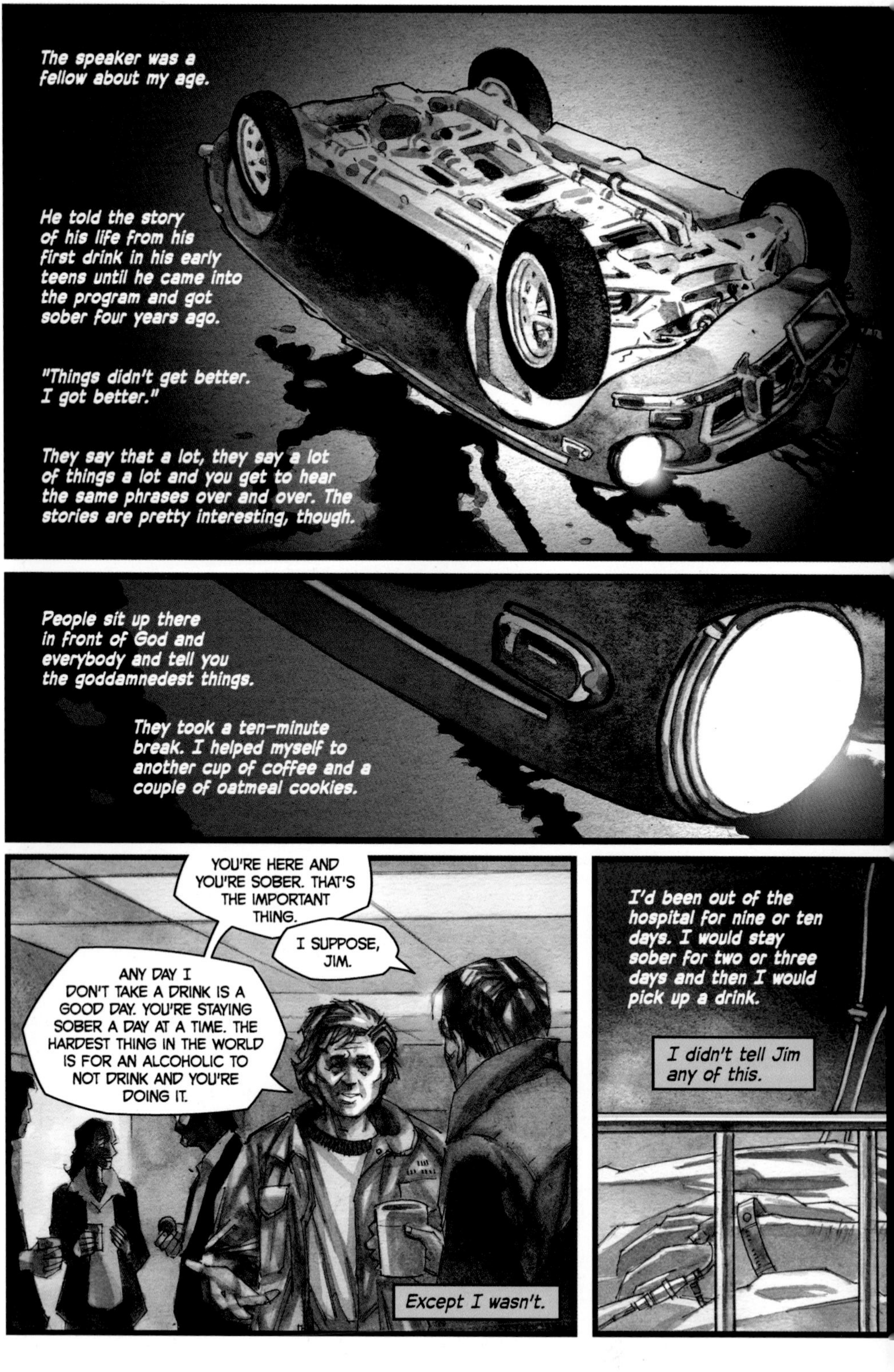
The speaker was a fellow about my age.
He told the story of his life from his first drink in his early teens until he came into the program and got sober four years ago.
"Things didn't get better. I got better."
They say that a lot, they say a lot of things a lot and you get to hear the same phrases over and over. The stories are pretty interesting, though.
People sit up there in front of God and everybody and tell you the goddamnedest things.
They took a ten-minute break. I helped myself to another cup of coffee and a couple of oatmeal cookies.
ANY DAY I DON'T TAKE A DRINK IS A GOOD DAY. YOU'RE STAYING SOBER A DAY AT A TIME. THE HARDEST THING IN THE WORLD IS FOR AN ALCOHOLIC TO NOT DRINK AND YOU'RE DOING IT.
YOU'RE HERE AND YOU'RE SOBER. THAT'S THE IMPORTANT THING.
I SUPPOSE, JIM.
Except I wasn't.
I'd been out of the hospital for nine or ten days. I would stay sober for two or three days and then I would pick up a drink.
I didn't tell Jim any of this.

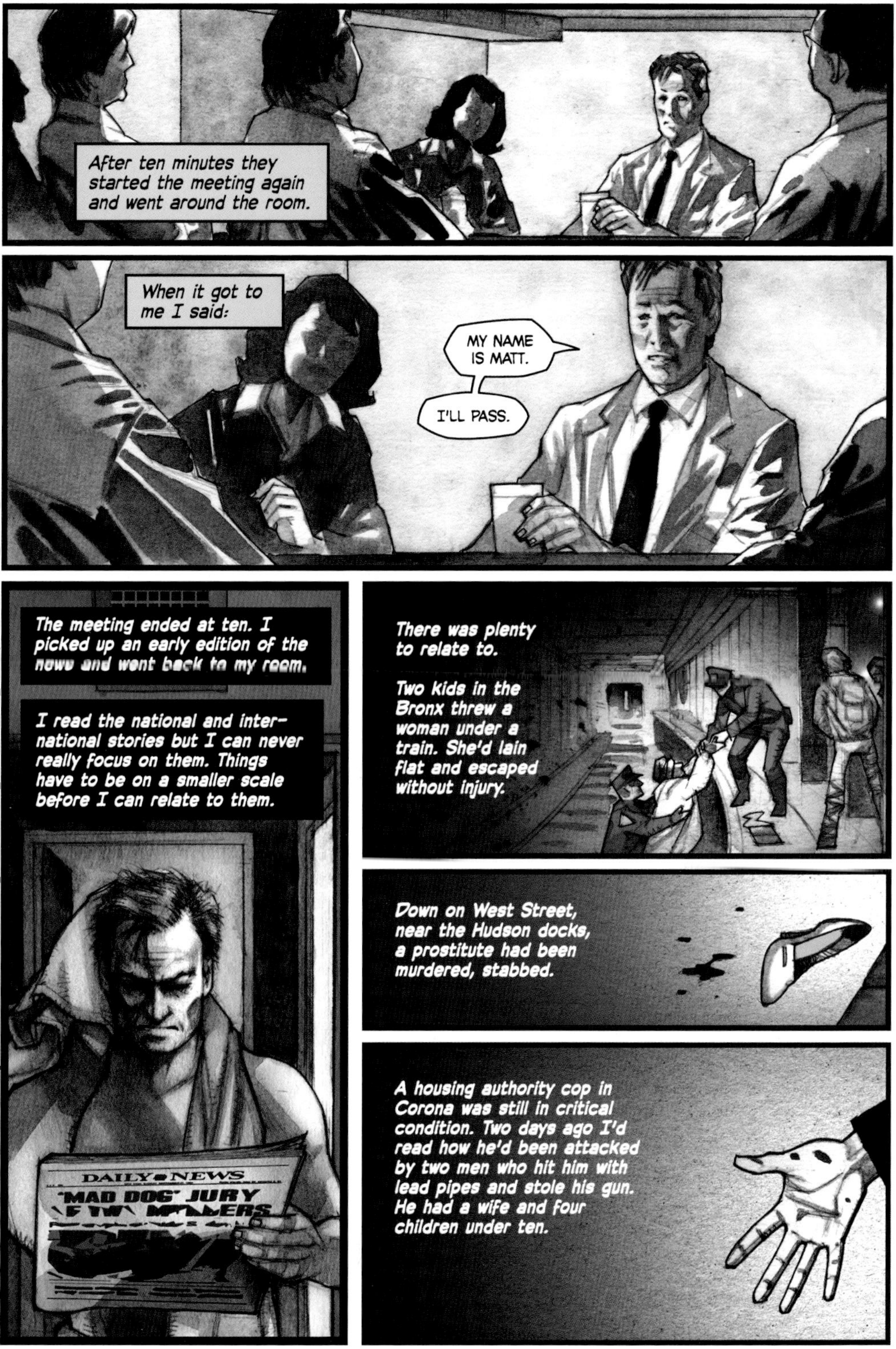
After ten minutes they started the meeting again and went around the room.
When it got to me I said:
MY NAME IS MATT.
I'LL PASS.
The meeting ended at ten. I picked up an early edition of the news and went back to my room.
I read the national and international stories but I can never really focus on them. Things have to be on a smaller scale before I can relate to them.
DAILY NEWS
"MAD DOG" JURY
There was plenty to relate to.
Two kids in the Bronx threw a woman under a train. She'd lain flat and escaped without injury.
Down on West Street, near the Hudson docks, a prostitute had been murdered, stabbed.
A housing authority cop in Corona was still in critical condition. Two days ago I'd read how he'd been attacked by two men who hit him with lead pipes and stole his gun. He had a wife and four children under ten.

The telephone didn't ring.
I didn't really expect it to.

So I'd have to find Chance.

That was just as well. It would
give me something to do.

IT'S MATT SCUDDER, KIM. I JUST WONDERED IF YOU HAPPENED TO SPEAK TO YOUR FRIEND SINCE I SAW YOU.

NO. I HAVEN'T. WHY?

YOU HAVEN'T SAID ANYTHING TO HIM ABOUT WANTING OUT?

NOT A WORD.

GOOD.

I calmed her down after
having alarmed her with
the call in the first place.

At least I knew she
hadn't died on West
Street. At least I
could sleep easy.

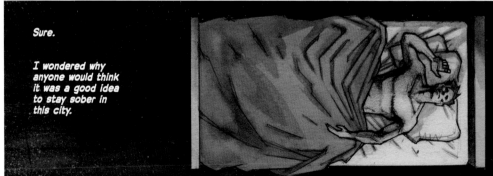

Sure.

I wondered why
anyone would think
it was a good idea
to stay sober in
this city.

I got up around 10:30 and went over to St. Paul's. Not to the basement this time, but the church proper.

I lit a couple of candles and put fifty dollars into the poor box.

I bought a money order to mail to my ex-wife in Syosset. I tried to write a note--the money was too little and too late, but she would know that without my having to tell her.

After I paid half of the coming month's rent, I had only one of the hundreds intact and I cracked that into tens and twenties while I was at it.

Why hadn't I taken the full thousand up front? I remembered what I had said about an incentive. Well, I had one.

EATH OVER
E WORLD
LA
E VIOLENCE
NY TIMES

No message from Chance. Not that I had expected one. I called his service and left another message for the hell of it.

I stayed out all afternoon.

By 8:30, I'd managed to get out the door at Armstrong's and down the stairs at St. Paul's to the meeting.

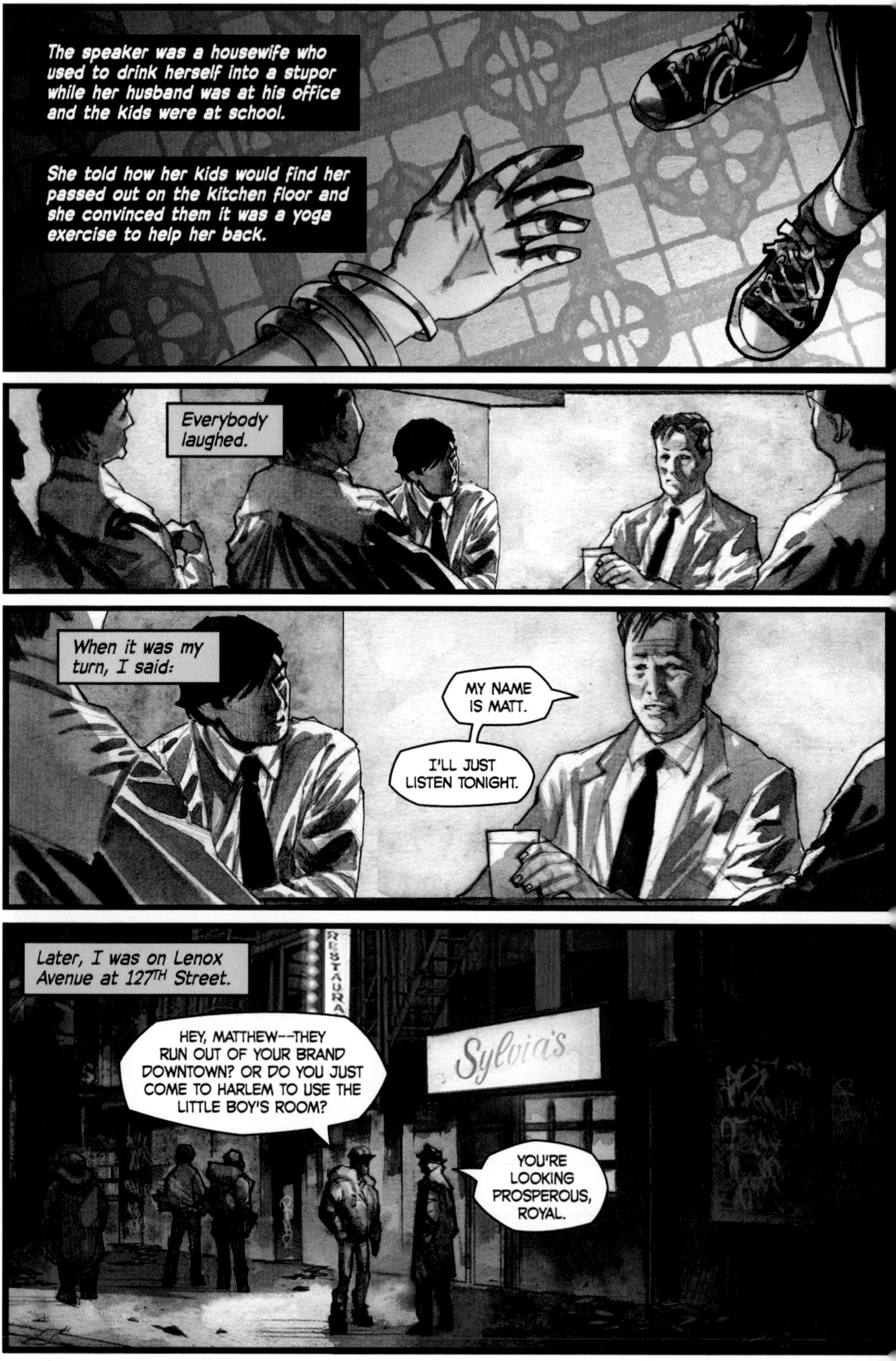
The speaker was a housewife who used to drink herself into a stupor while her husband was at his office and the kids were at school.
She told how her kids would find her passed out on the kitchen floor and she convinced them it was a yoga exercise to help her back.
Everybody laughed.
When it was my turn, I said:
MY NAME IS MATT.
I'LL JUST LISTEN TONIGHT.
Later, I was on Lenox Avenue at 127TH Street.
RESTAURA
HEY, MATTHEW--THEY RUN OUT OF YOUR BRAND DOWNTOWN? OR DO YOU JUST COME TO HARLEM TO USE THE LITTLE BOY'S ROOM?
Sylvia's
YOU'RE LOOKING PROSPEROUS, ROYAL.

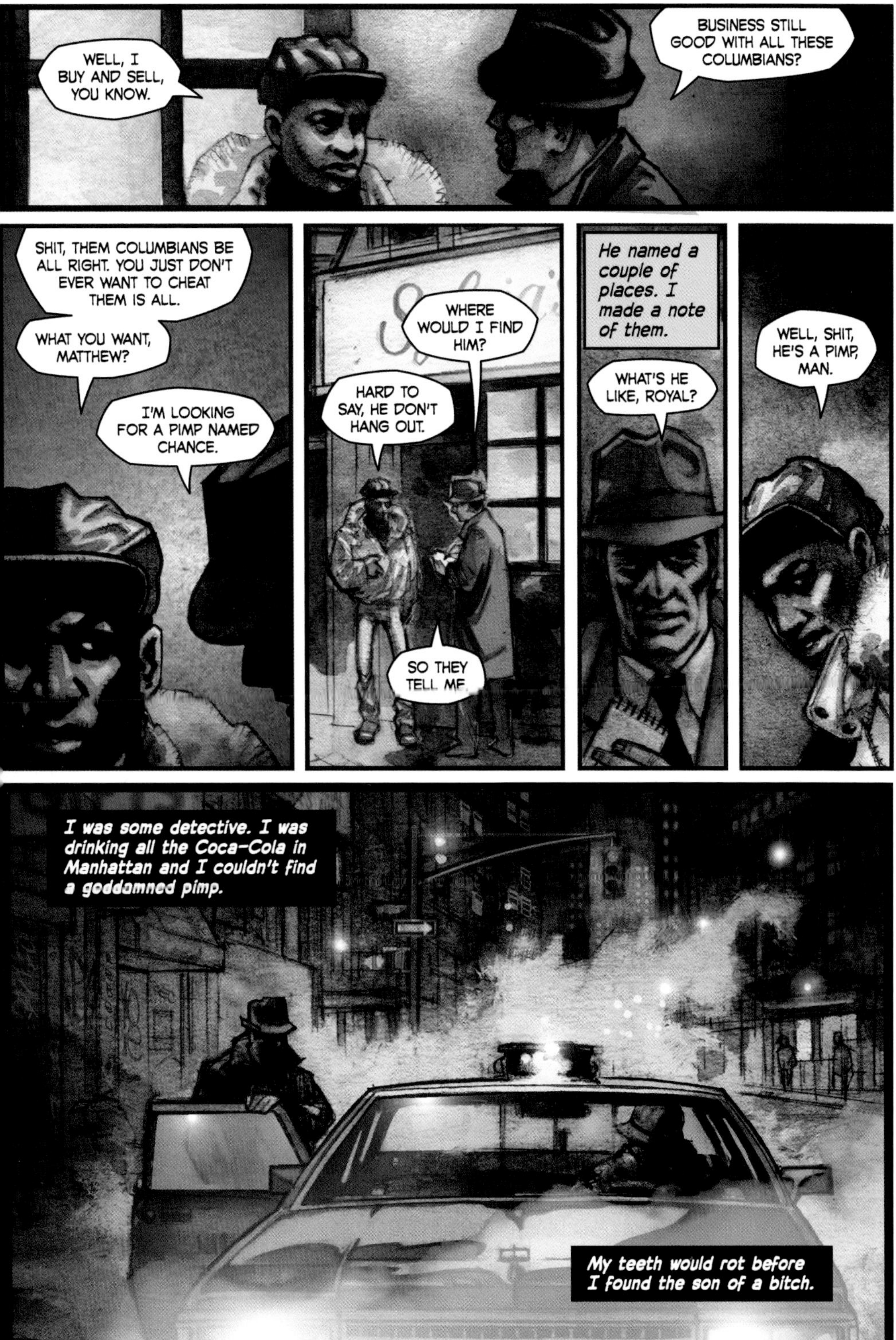
WELL, I BUY AND SELL, YOU KNOW.
BUSINESS STILL GOOD WITH ALL THESE COLUMBIANS?
SHIT, THEM COLUMBIANS BE ALL RIGHT. YOU JUST DON'T EVER WANT TO CHEAT THEM IS ALL.
WHAT YOU WANT, MATTHEW?
I'M LOOKING FOR A PIMP NAMED CHANCE.
WHERE WOULD I FIND HIM?
HARD TO SAY, HE DON'T HANG OUT.
SO THEY TELL ME.
He named a couple of places. I made a note of them.
WHAT'S HE LIKE, ROYAL?
WELL, SHIT, HE'S A PIMP, MAN.
I was some detective. I was drinking all the Coca-Cola in Manhattan and I couldn't find a goddamned pimp.
My teeth would rot before I found the son of a bitch.

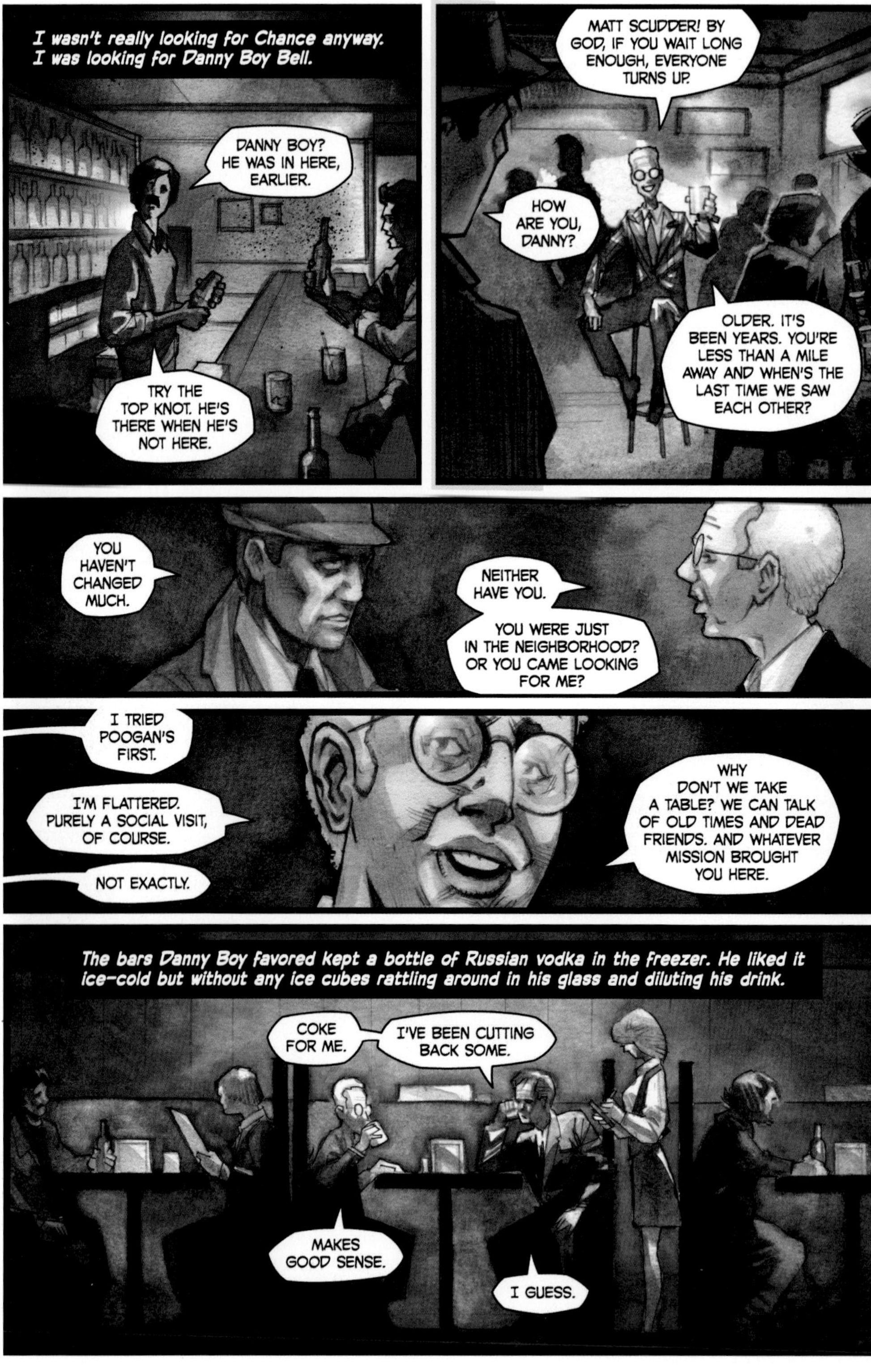
I wasn't really looking for Chance anyway.
I was looking for Danny Boy Bell.
DANNY BOY? HE WAS IN HERE, EARLIER.
TRY THE TOP KNOT. HE'S THERE WHEN HE'S NOT HERE.
MATT SCUDDER! BY GOD, IF YOU WAIT LONG ENOUGH, EVERYONE TURNS UP.
HOW ARE YOU, DANNY?
OLDER. IT'S BEEN YEARS. YOU'RE LESS THAN A MILE AWAY AND WHEN'S THE LAST TIME WE SAW EACH OTHER?
YOU HAVEN'T CHANGED MUCH.
NEITHER HAVE YOU.
YOU WERE JUST IN THE NEIGHBORHOOD? OR YOU CAME LOOKING FOR ME?
I TRIED POOGAN'S FIRST.
I'M FLATTERED. PURELY A SOCIAL VISIT, OF COURSE.
NOT EXACTLY.
WHY DON'T WE TAKE A TABLE? WE CAN TALK OF OLD TIMES AND DEAD FRIENDS. AND WHATEVER MISSION BROUGHT YOU HERE.
The bars Danny Boy favored kept a bottle of Russian vodka in the freezer. He liked it ice-cold but without any ice cubes rattling around in his glass and diluting his drink.
COKE FOR ME.
I'VE BEEN CUTTING BACK SOME.
MAKES GOOD SENSE.
I GUESS.

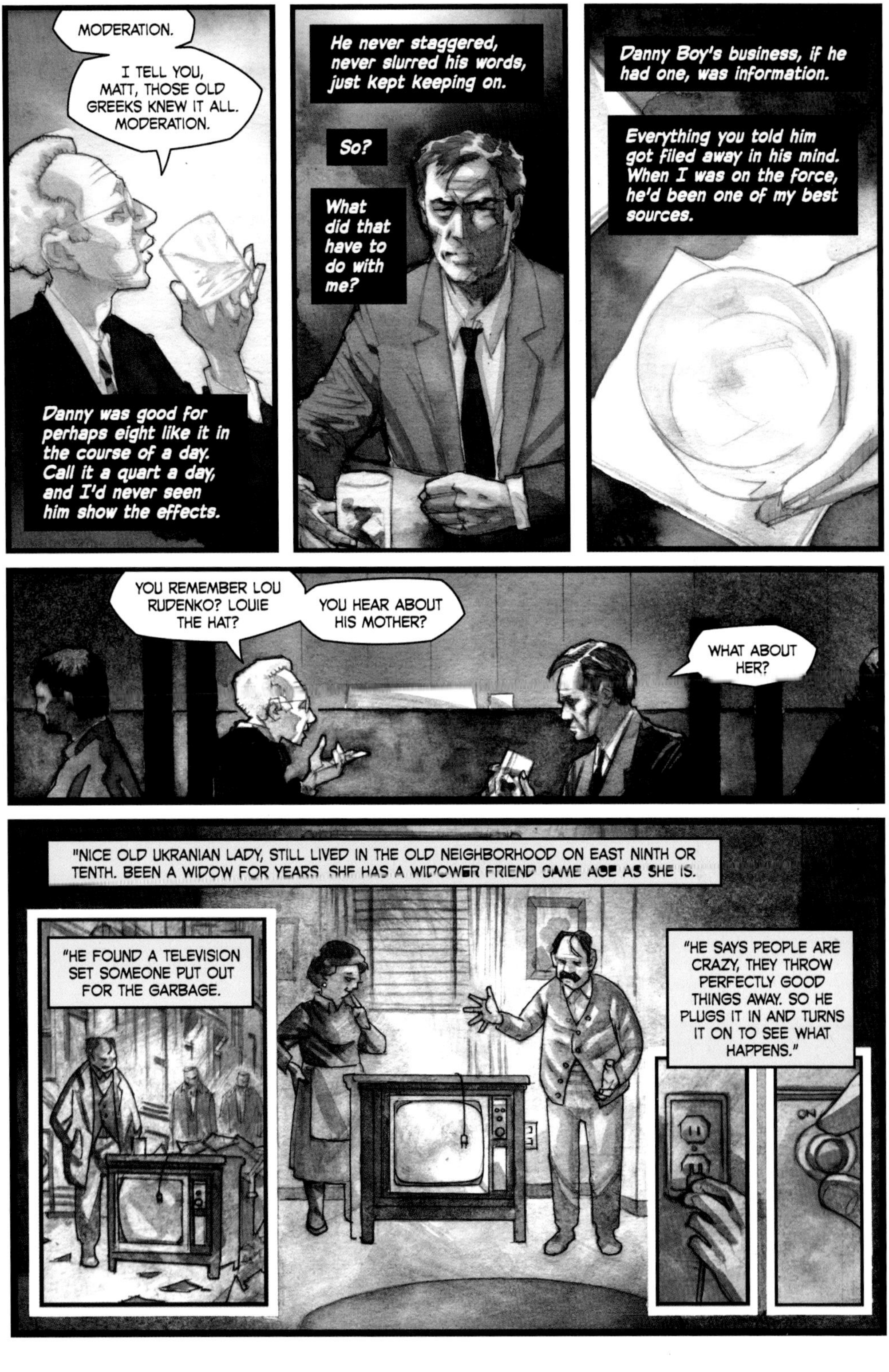
MODERATION.
I TELL YOU, MATT, THOSE OLD GREEKS KNEW IT ALL. MODERATION.
Danny was good for perhaps eight like it in the course of a day. Call it a quart a day, and I'd never seen him show the effects.
He never staggered, never slurred his words, just kept keeping on.
So?
What did that have to do with me?
Danny Boy's business, if he had one, was information.
Everything you told him got filed away in his mind. When I was on the force, he'd been one of my best sources.
YOU REMEMBER LOU RUDENKO? LOUIE THE HAT?
YOU HEAR ABOUT HIS MOTHER?
WHAT ABOUT HER?
"NICE OLD UKRANIAN LADY, STILL LIVED IN THE OLD NEIGHBORHOOD ON EAST NINTH OR TENTH. BEEN A WIDOW FOR YEARS. SHE HAS A WIDOWER FRIEND SAME AGE AS SHE IS.
"HE FOUND A TELEVISION SET SOMEONE PUT OUT FOR THE GARBAGE.
"HE SAYS PEOPLE ARE CRAZY, THEY THROW PERFECTLY GOOD THINGS AWAY. SO HE PLUGS IT IN AND TURNS IT ON TO SEE WHAT HAPPENS."
ON

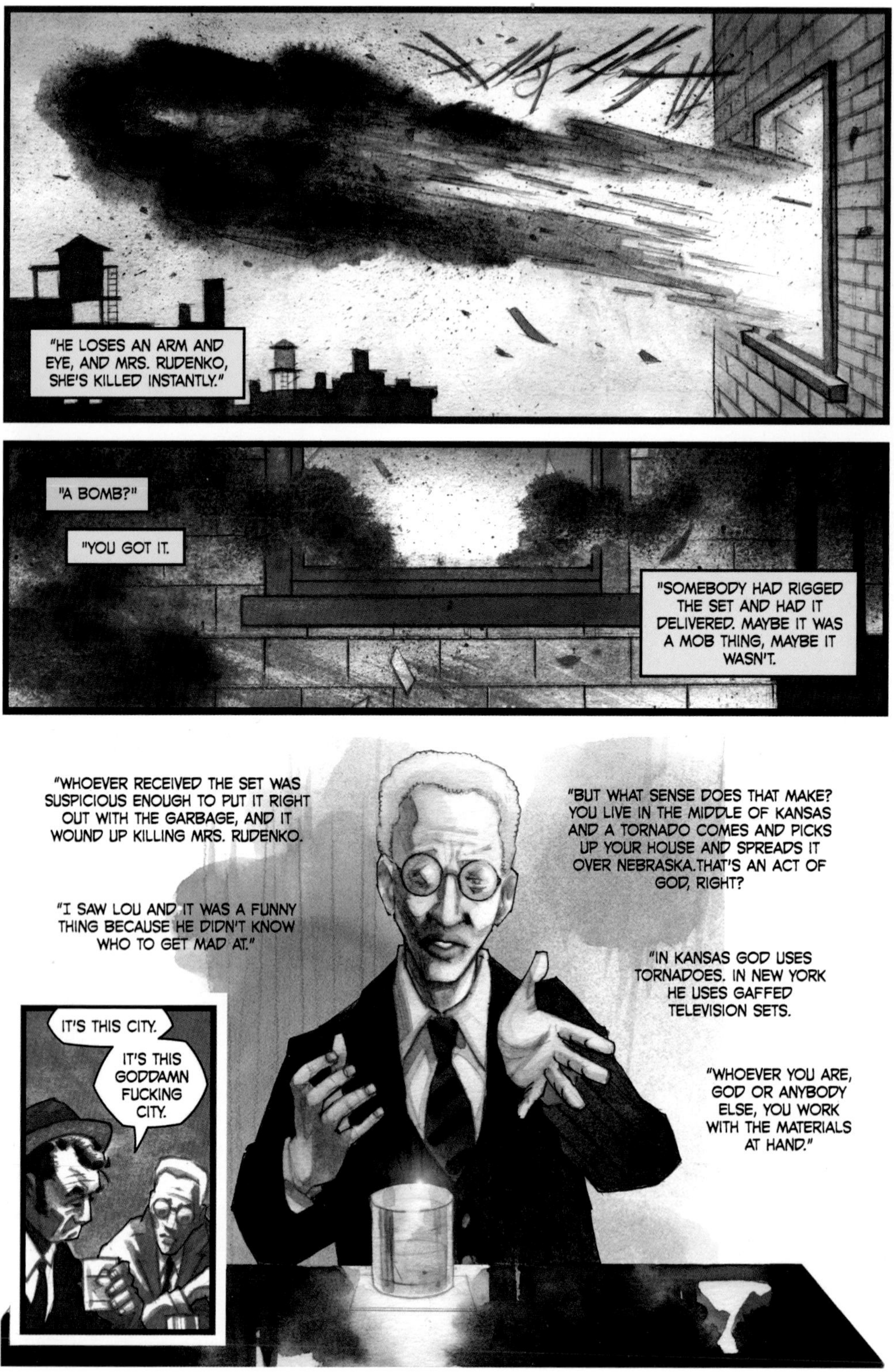
"HE LOSES AN ARM AND EYE, AND MRS. RUDENKO, SHE'S KILLED INSTANTLY."
"A BOMB?"
"YOU GOT IT.
"SOMEBODY HAD RIGGED THE SET AND HAD IT DELIVERED. MAYBE IT WAS A MOB THING, MAYBE IT WASN'T.
"WHOEVER RECEIVED THE SET WAS SUSPICIOUS ENOUGH TO PUT IT RIGHT OUT WITH THE GARBAGE, AND IT WOUND UP KILLING MRS. RUDENKO.
"I SAW LOU AND IT WAS A FUNNY THING BECAUSE HE DIDN'T KNOW WHO TO GET MAD AT."
IT'S THIS CITY.
IT'S THIS GODDAMN FUCKING CITY.
"BUT WHAT SENSE DOES THAT MAKE? YOU LIVE IN THE MIDDLE OF KANSAS AND A TORNADO COMES AND PICKS UP YOUR HOUSE AND SPREADS IT OVER NEBRASKA.THAT'S AN ACT OF GOD, RIGHT?
"IN KANSAS GOD USES TORNADOES. IN NEW YORK HE USES GAFFED TELEVISION SETS.
"WHOEVER YOU ARE, GOD OR ANYBODY ELSE, YOU WORK WITH THE MATERIALS AT HAND."

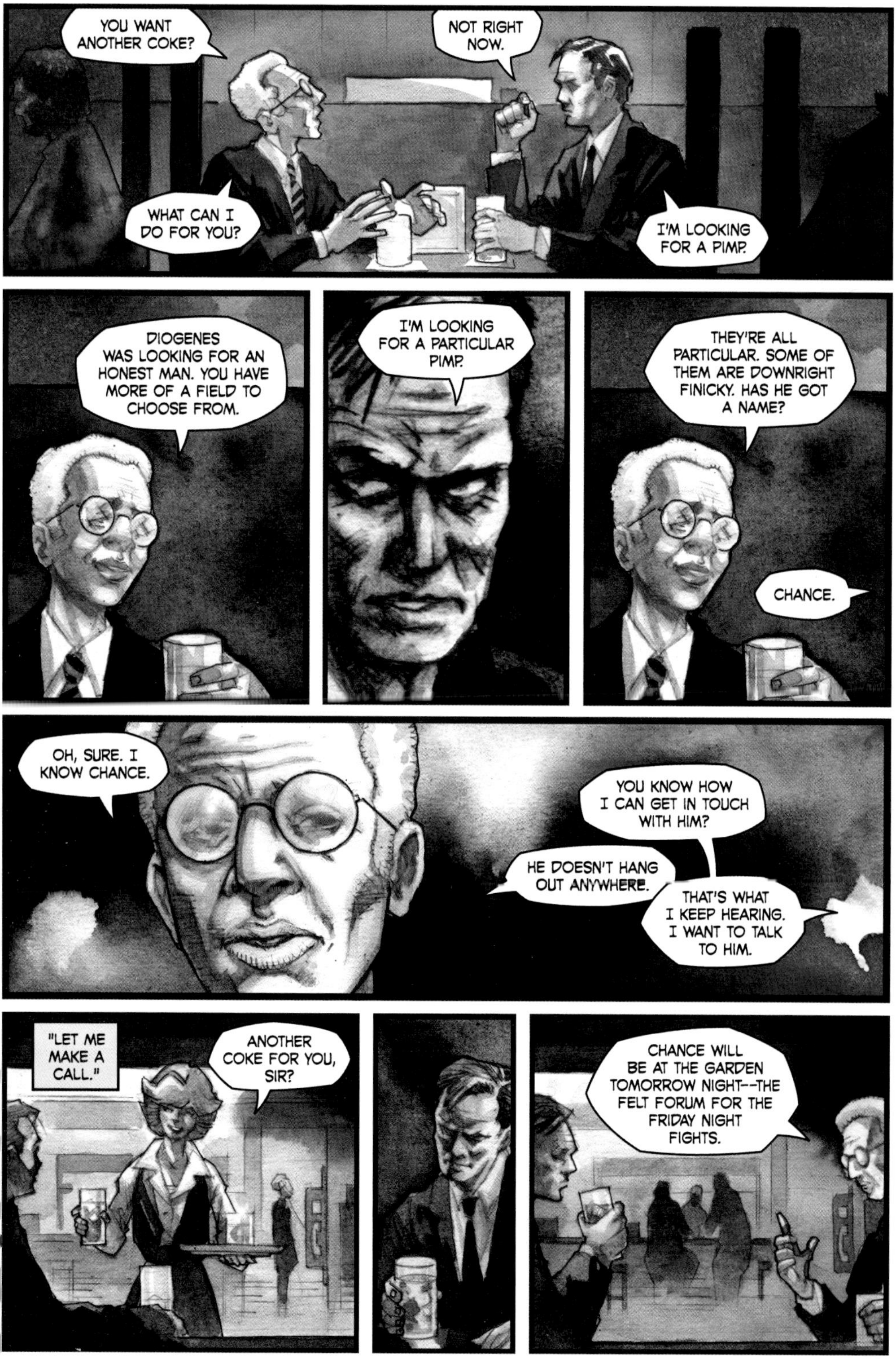
YOU WANT ANOTHER COKE?
NOT RIGHT NOW.
WHAT CAN I DO FOR YOU?
I'M LOOKING FOR A PIMP.
DIOGENES WAS LOOKING FOR AN HONEST MAN. YOU HAVE MORE OF A FIELD TO CHOOSE FROM.
I'M LOOKING FOR A PARTICULAR PIMP.
THEY'RE ALL PARTICULAR. SOME OF THEM ARE DOWNRIGHT FINICKY. HAS HE GOT A NAME?
CHANCE.
OH, SURE. I KNOW CHANCE.
YOU KNOW HOW I CAN GET IN TOUCH WITH HIM?
HE DOESN'T HANG OUT ANYWHERE.
THAT'S WHAT I KEEP HEARING. I WANT TO TALK TO HIM.
"LET ME MAKE A CALL."
ANOTHER COKE FOR YOU, SIR?
CHANCE WILL BE AT THE GARDEN TOMORROW NIGHT--THE FELT FORUM FOR THE FRIDAY NIGHT FIGHTS.

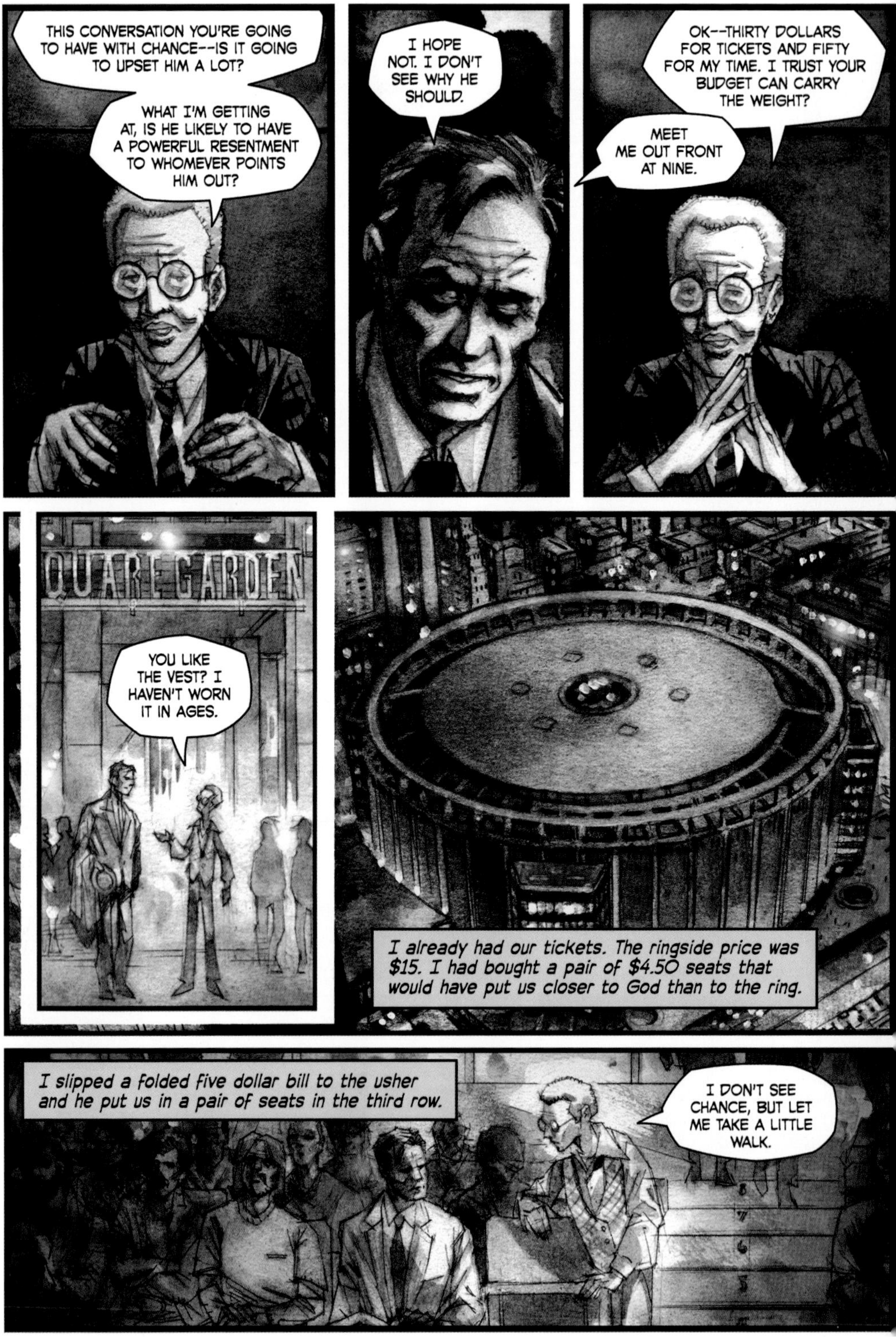
THIS CONVERSATION YOU'RE GOING TO HAVE WITH CHANCE--IS IT GOING TO UPSET HIM A LOT?
WHAT I'M GETTING AT, IS HE LIKELY TO HAVE A POWERFUL RESENTMENT TO WHOMEVER POINTS HIM OUT?
I HOPE NOT. I DON'T SEE WHY HE SHOULD.
OK--THIRTY DOLLARS FOR TICKETS AND FIFTY FOR MY TIME. I TRUST YOUR BUDGET CAN CARRY THE WEIGHT?
MEET ME OUT FRONT AT NINE.
QUARE GARDEN
YOU LIKE THE VEST? I HAVEN'T WORN IT IN AGES.
I already had our tickets. The ringside price was $15. I had bought a pair of $4.50 seats that would have put us closer to God than to the ring.
I slipped a folded five dollar bill to the usher and he put us in a pair of seats in the third row.
I DON'T SEE CHANCE, BUT LET ME TAKE A LITTLE WALK.

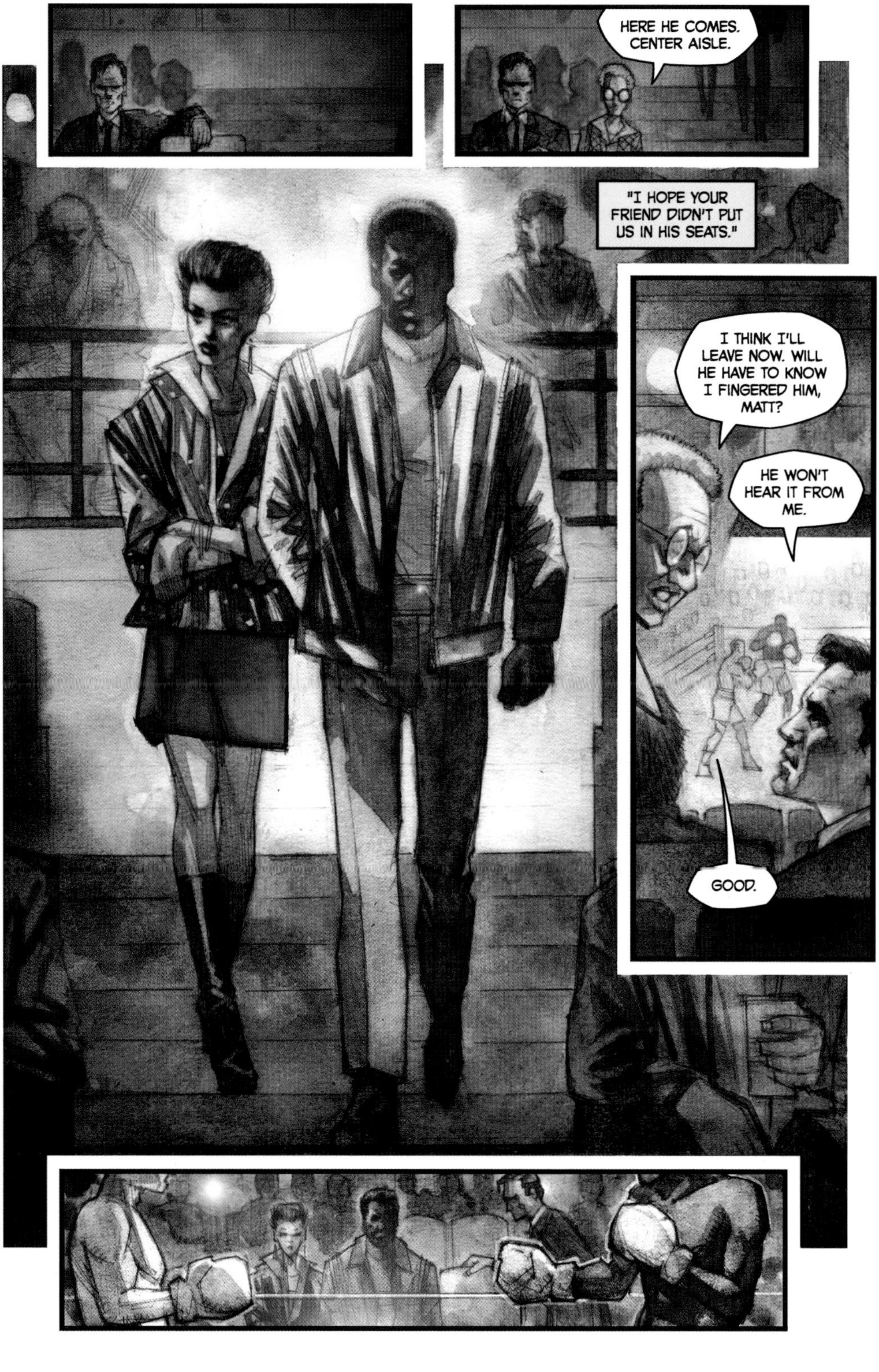
HERE HE COMES. CENTER AISLE.
"I HOPE YOUR FRIEND DIDN'T PUT US IN HIS SEATS."
I THINK I'LL LEAVE NOW. WILL HE HAVE TO KNOW I FINGERED HIM, MATT?
HE WON'T HEAR IT FROM ME.
GOOD.

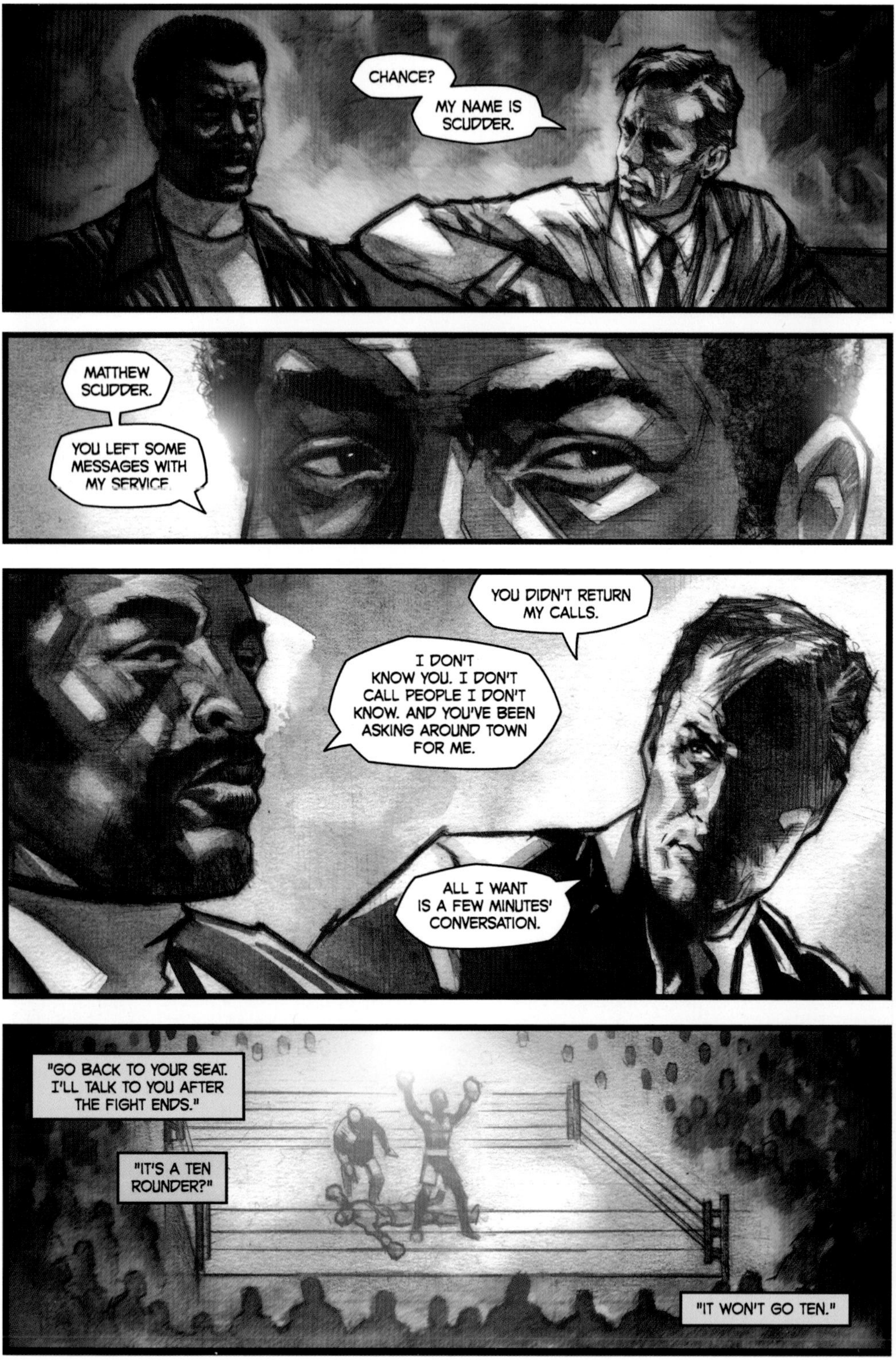
CHANCE?
MY NAME IS SCUDDER.
MATTHEW SCUDDER.
YOU LEFT SOME MESSAGES WITH MY SERVICE.
YOU DIDN'T RETURN MY CALLS.
I DON'T KNOW YOU. I DON'T CALL PEOPLE I DON'T KNOW. AND YOU'VE BEEN ASKING AROUND TOWN FOR ME.
ALL I WANT IS A FEW MINUTES' CONVERSATION.
"GO BACK TO YOUR SEAT. I'LL TALK TO YOU AFTER THE FIGHT ENDS."
"IT'S A TEN ROUNDER?"
"IT WON'T GO TEN."

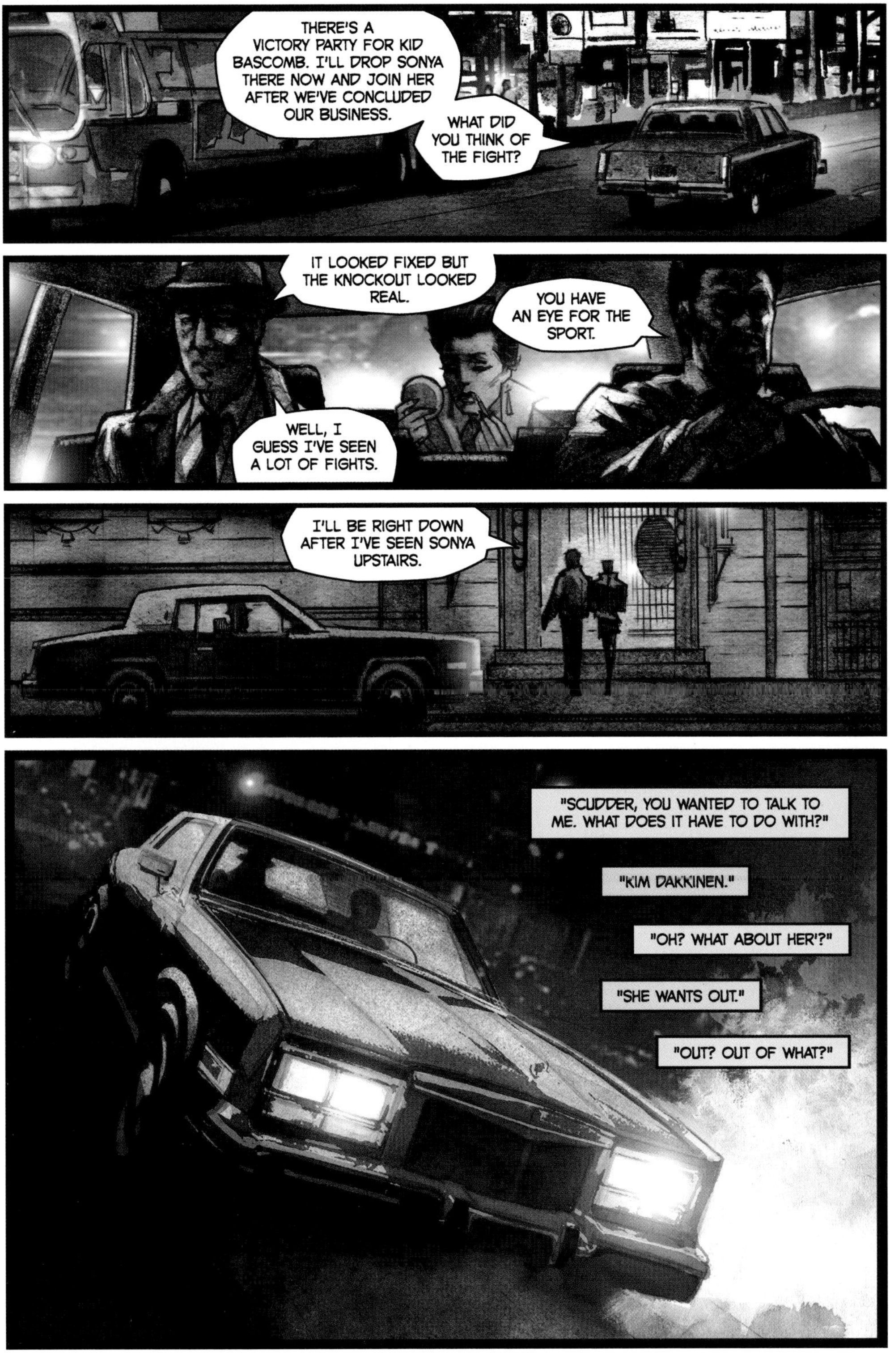
THERE'S A VICTORY PARTY FOR KID BASCOMB. I'LL DROP SONYA THERE NOW AND JOIN HER AFTER WE'VE CONCLUDED OUR BUSINESS.
WHAT DID YOU THINK OF THE FIGHT?
IT LOOKED FIXED BUT THE KNOCKOUT LOOKED REAL.
YOU HAVE AN EYE FOR THE SPORT.
WELL, I GUESS I'VE SEEN A LOT OF FIGHTS.
I'LL BE RIGHT DOWN AFTER I'VE SEEN SONYA UPSTAIRS.
"SCUDDER, YOU WANTED TO TALK TO ME. WHAT DOES IT HAVE TO DO WITH?"
"KIM DAKKINEN."
"OH? WHAT ABOUT HER'?"
"SHE WANTS OUT."
"OUT? OUT OF WHAT?"

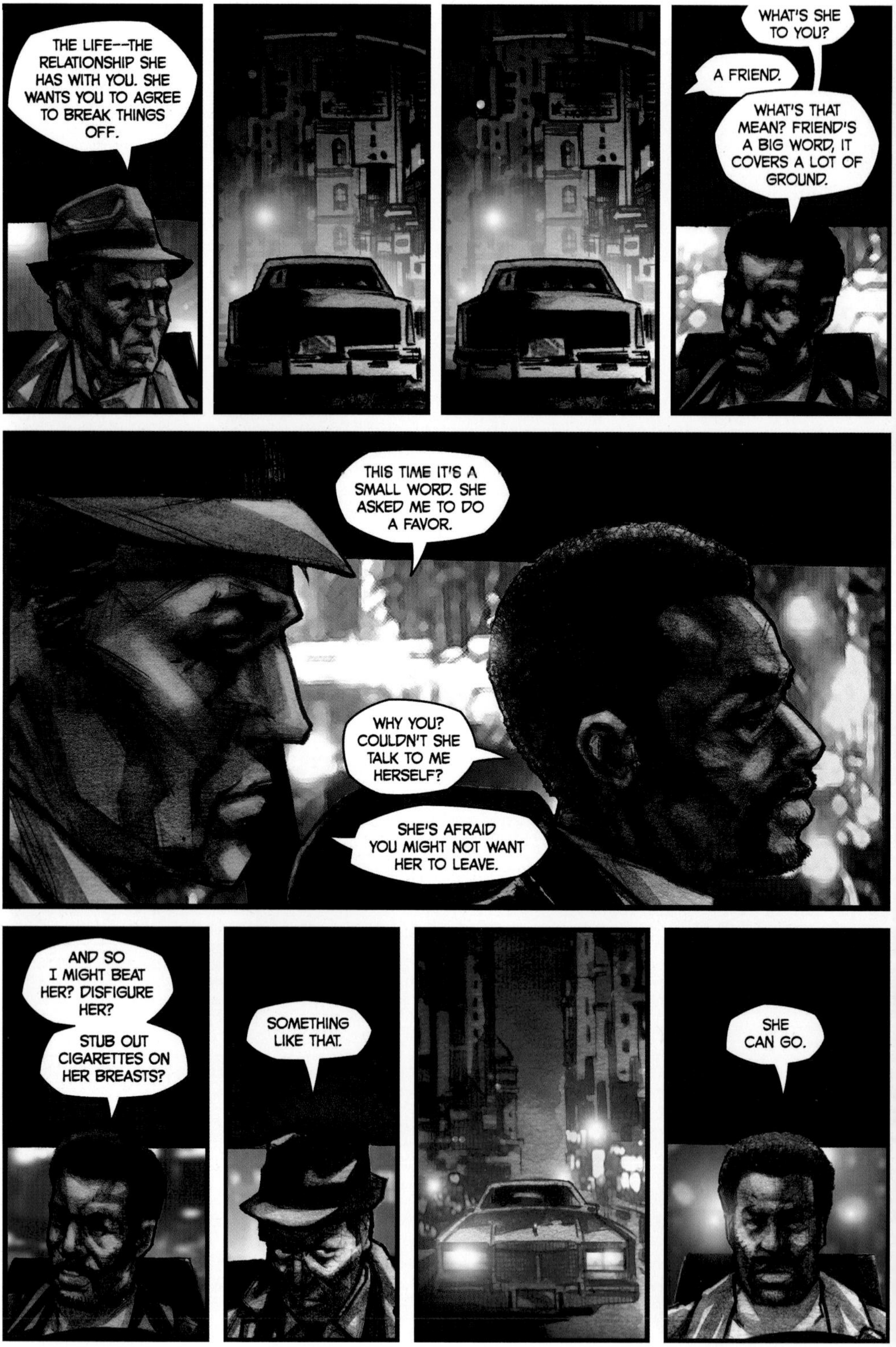
THE LIFE--THE RELATIONSHIP SHE HAS WITH YOU. SHE WANTS YOU TO AGREE TO BREAK THINGS OFF.
WHAT'S SHE TO YOU?
A FRIEND.
WHAT'S THAT MEAN? FRIEND'S A BIG WORD, IT COVERS A LOT OF GROUND.
THIS TIME IT'S A SMALL WORD. SHE ASKED ME TO DO A FAVOR.
WHY YOU? COULDN'T SHE TALK TO ME HERSELF?
SHE'S AFRAID YOU MIGHT NOT WANT HER TO LEAVE.
AND SO I MIGHT BEAT HER? DISFIGURE HER?
STUB OUT CIGARETTES ON HER BREASTS?
SOMETHING LIKE THAT.
SHE CAN GO.

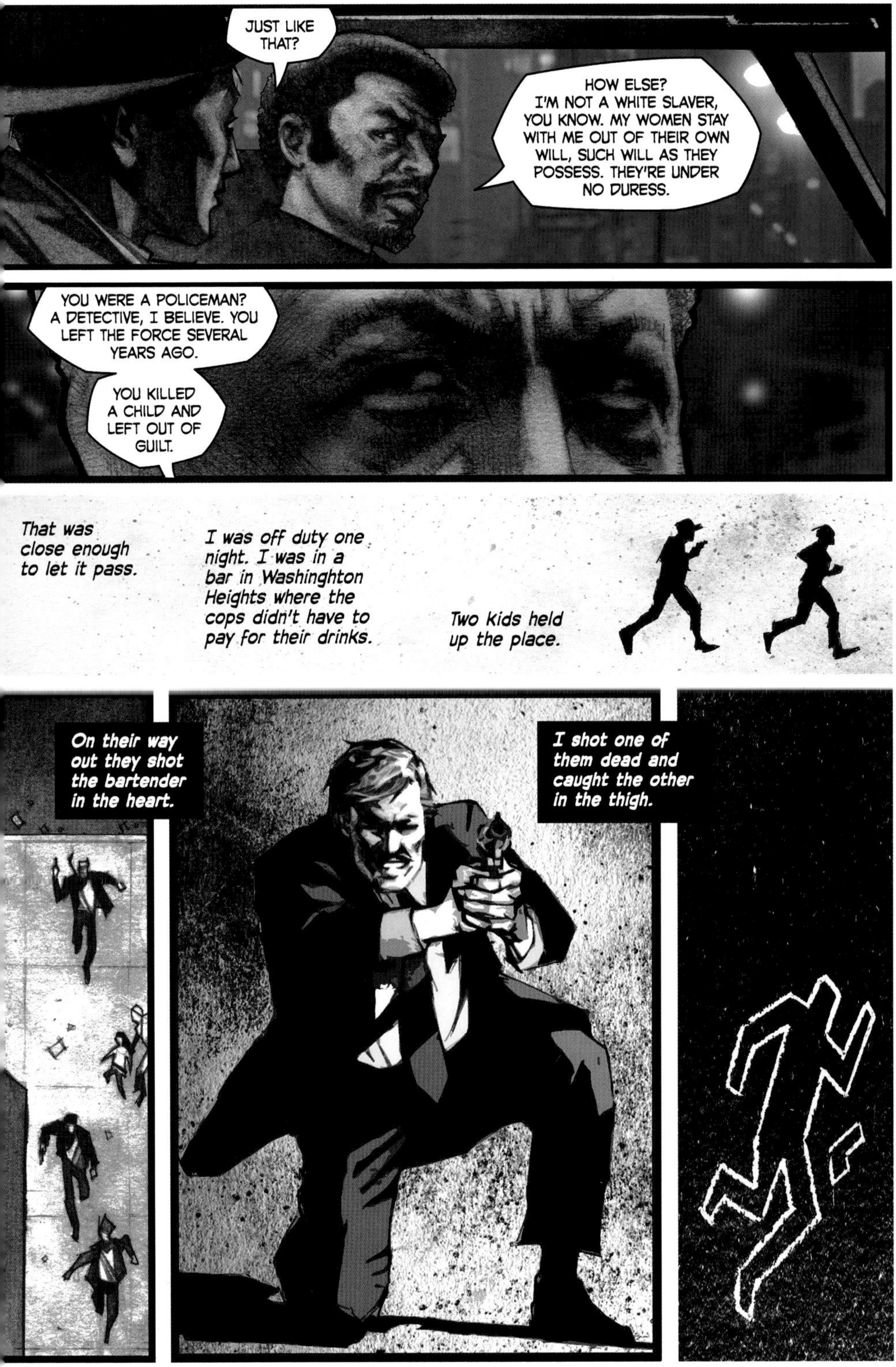
JUST LIKE THAT?
HOW ELSE? I'M NOT A WHITE SLAVER, YOU KNOW. MY WOMEN STAY WITH ME OUT OF THEIR OWN WILL, SUCH WILL AS THEY POSSESS. THEY'RE UNDER NO DURESS.
YOU WERE A POLICEMAN? A DETECTIVE, I BELIEVE. YOU LEFT THE FORCE SEVERAL YEARS AGO.
YOU KILLED A CHILD AND LEFT OUT OF GUILT.
That was close enough to let it pass.
I was off duty one night. I was in a bar in Washington Heights where the cops didn't have to pay for their drinks.
Two kids held up the place.
On their way out they shot the bartender in the heart.
I shot one of them dead and caught the other in the thigh.

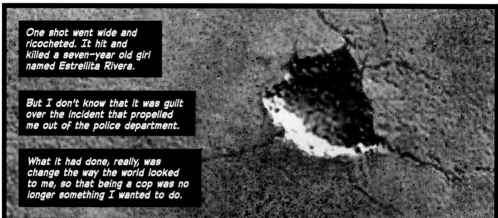

One shot went wide and ricocheted. It hit and killed a seven-year old girl named Estrellita Rivera.

But I don't know that it was guilt over the incident that propelled me out of the police department.

What it had done, really, was change the way the world looked to me, so that being a cop was no longer something I wanted to do.

Neither was being a husband and a father and living on Long Island, and in due course I was out of work and out of the marriage and living on Fifty-Seventh Street and putting in the hours at Armstrong's.

The shooting unquestionably set those currents in motion.

But I think I was pointed in those directions and would've got there sooner or later.

NOW YOU'RE A SORT OF HALF-ASSED DETECTIVE.

SHE HIRE YOU?

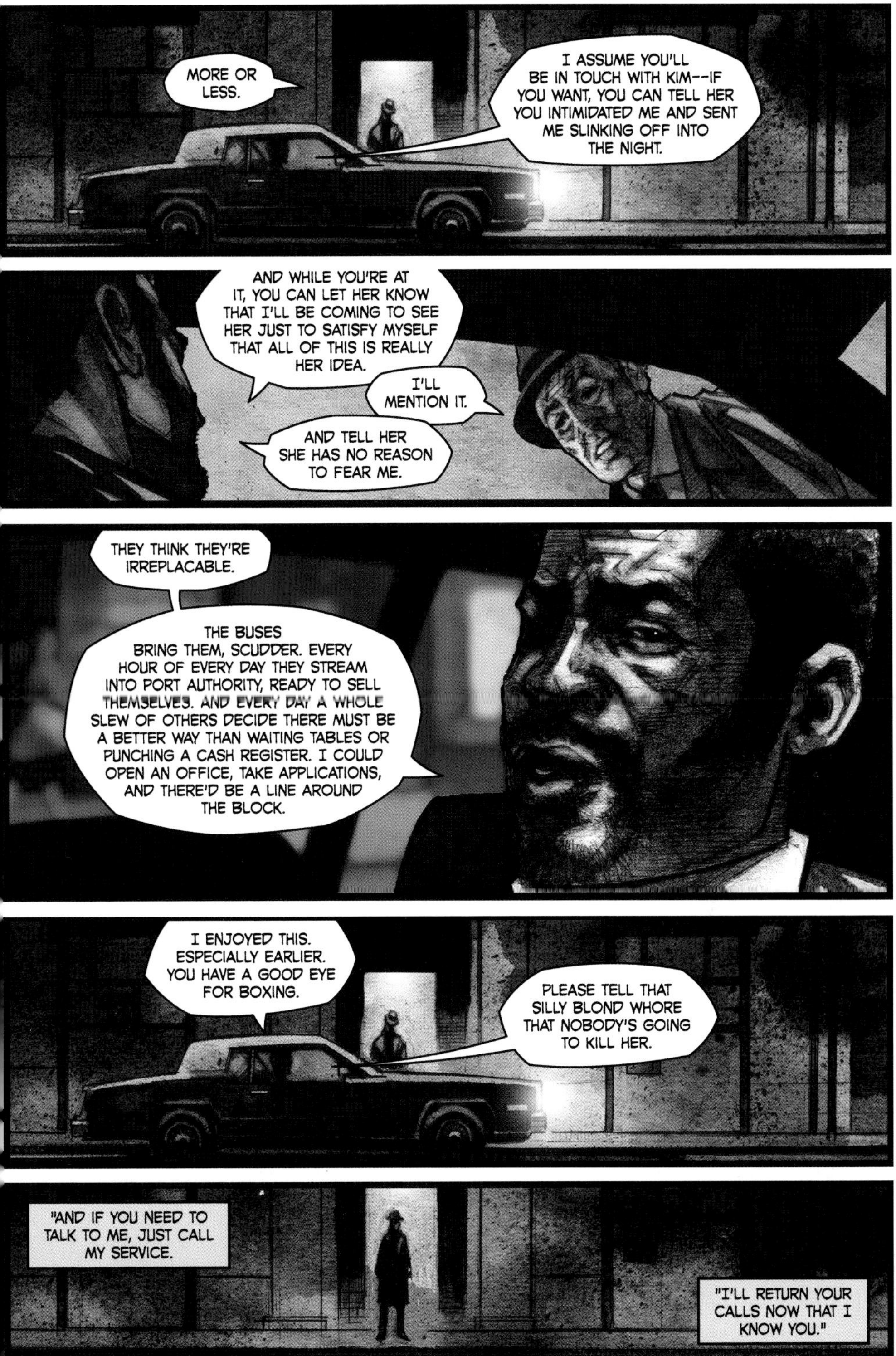
MORE OR LESS.
I ASSUME YOU'LL BE IN TOUCH WITH KIM--IF YOU WANT, YOU CAN TELL HER YOU INTIMIDATED ME AND SENT ME SLINKING OFF INTO THE NIGHT.
AND WHILE YOU'RE AT IT, YOU CAN LET HER KNOW THAT I'LL BE COMING TO SEE HER JUST TO SATISFY MYSELF THAT ALL OF THIS IS REALLY HER IDEA.
I'LL MENTION IT.
AND TELL HER SHE HAS NO REASON TO FEAR ME.
THEY THINK THEY'RE IRREPLACABLE.
THE BUSES BRING THEM, SCUDDER. EVERY HOUR OF EVERY DAY THEY STREAM INTO PORT AUTHORITY, READY TO SELL THEMSELVES. AND EVERY DAY A WHOLE SLEW OF OTHERS DECIDE THERE MUST BE A BETTER WAY THAN WAITING TABLES OR PUNCHING A CASH REGISTER. I COULD OPEN AN OFFICE, TAKE APPLICATIONS, AND THERE'D BE A LINE AROUND THE BLOCK.
I ENJOYED THIS. ESPECIALLY EARLIER. YOU HAVE A GOOD EYE FOR BOXING.
PLEASE TELL THAT SILLY BLOND WHORE THAT NOBODY'S GOING TO KILL HER.
"AND IF YOU NEED TO TALK TO ME, JUST CALL MY SERVICE.
"I'LL RETURN YOUR CALLS NOW THAT I KNOW YOU."

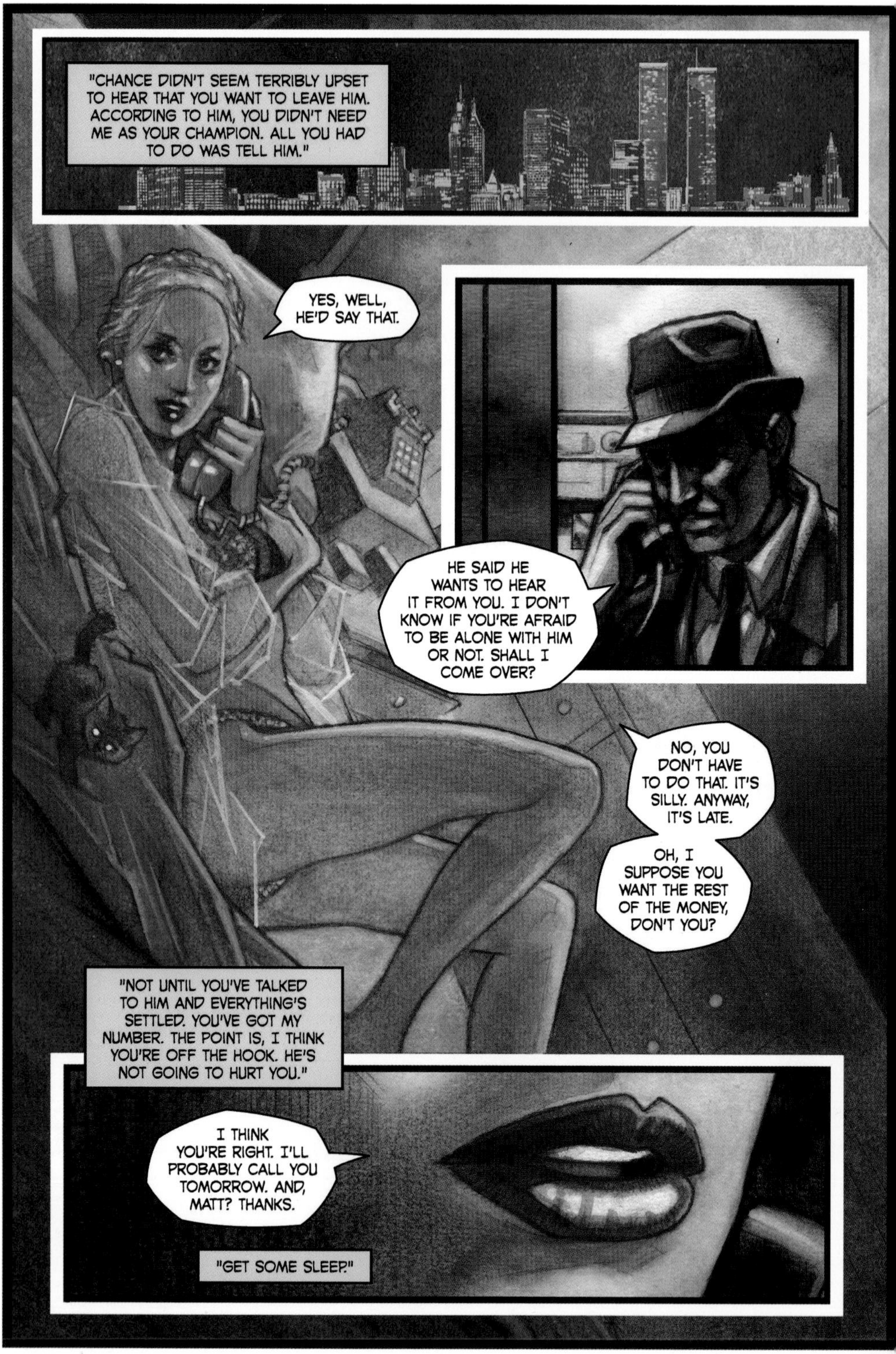

"CHANCE DIDN'T SEEM TERRIBLY UPSET TO HEAR THAT YOU WANT TO LEAVE HIM. ACCORDING TO HIM, YOU DIDN'T NEED ME AS YOUR CHAMPION. ALL YOU HAD TO DO WAS TELL HIM."
YES, WELL, HE'D SAY THAT.
HE SAID HE WANTS TO HEAR IT FROM YOU. I DON'T KNOW IF YOU'RE AFRAID TO BE ALONE WITH HIM OR NOT. SHALL I COME OVER?
NO, YOU DON'T HAVE TO DO THAT. IT'S SILLY. ANYWAY, IT'S LATE.
OH, I SUPPOSE YOU WANT THE REST OF THE MONEY, DON'T YOU?
"NOT UNTIL YOU'VE TALKED TO HIM AND EVERYTHING'S SETTLED. YOU'VE GOT MY NUMBER. THE POINT IS, I THINK YOU'RE OFF THE HOOK. HE'S NOT GOING TO HURT YOU."
I THINK YOU'RE RIGHT. I'LL PROBABLY CALL YOU TOMORROW. AND, MATT? THANKS.
"GET SOME SLEEP."

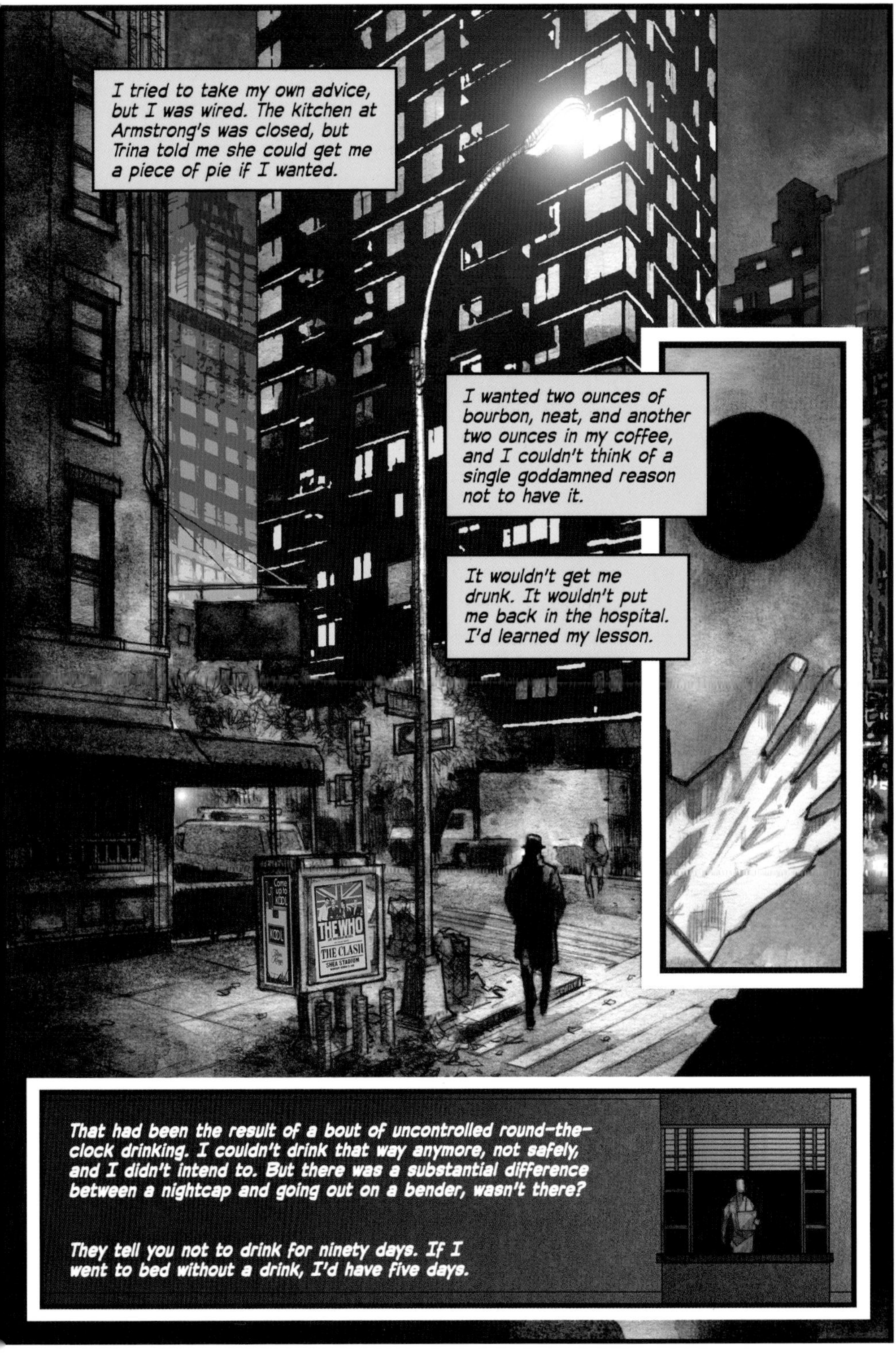
I tried to take my own advice, but I was wired. The kitchen at Armstrong's was closed, but Trina told me she could get me a piece of pie if I wanted.
I wanted two ounces of bourbon, neat, and another two ounces in my coffee, and I couldn't think of a single goddamned reason not to have it.
It wouldn't get me drunk. It wouldn't put me back in the hospital. I'd learned my lesson.
Come up to KOOL
THE WHO
THE CLASH
SHEA STADIUM
That had been the result of a bout of uncontrolled round-the-clock drinking. I couldn't drink that way anymore, not safely, and I didn't intend to. But there was a substantial difference between a nightcap and going out on a bender, wasn't there?
They tell you not to drink for ninety days. If I went to bed without a drink, I'd have five days.

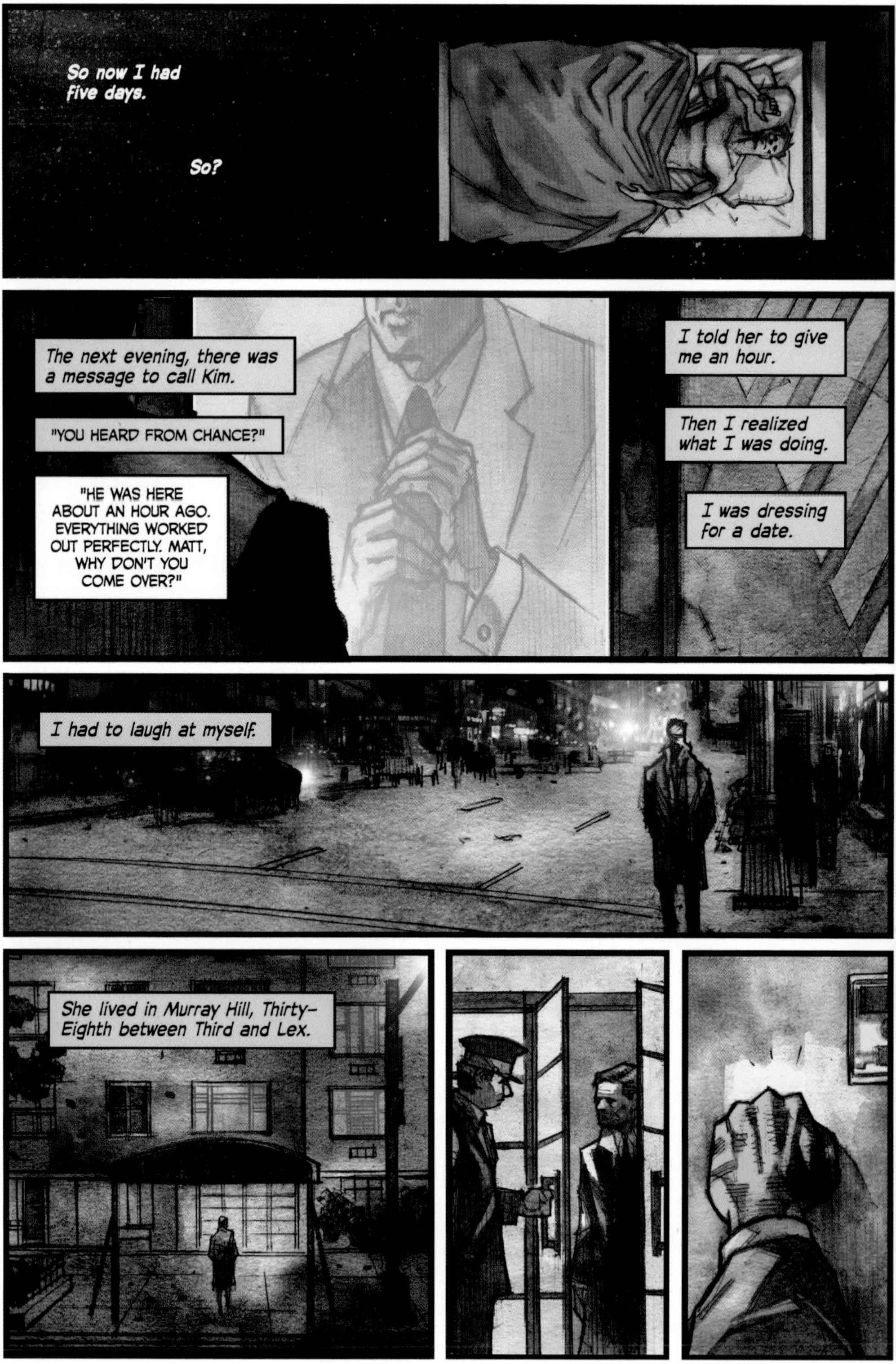
So now I had five days.
So?
The next evening, there was a message to call Kim.
"YOU HEARD FROM CHANCE?"
"HE WAS HERE ABOUT AN HOUR AGO. EVERYTHING WORKED OUT PERFECTLY. MATT, WHY DON'T YOU COME OVER?"
I told her to give me an hour.
Then I realized what I was doing.
I was dressing for a date.
I had to laugh at myself.
She lived in Murray Hill, Thirty-Eighth between Third and Lex.

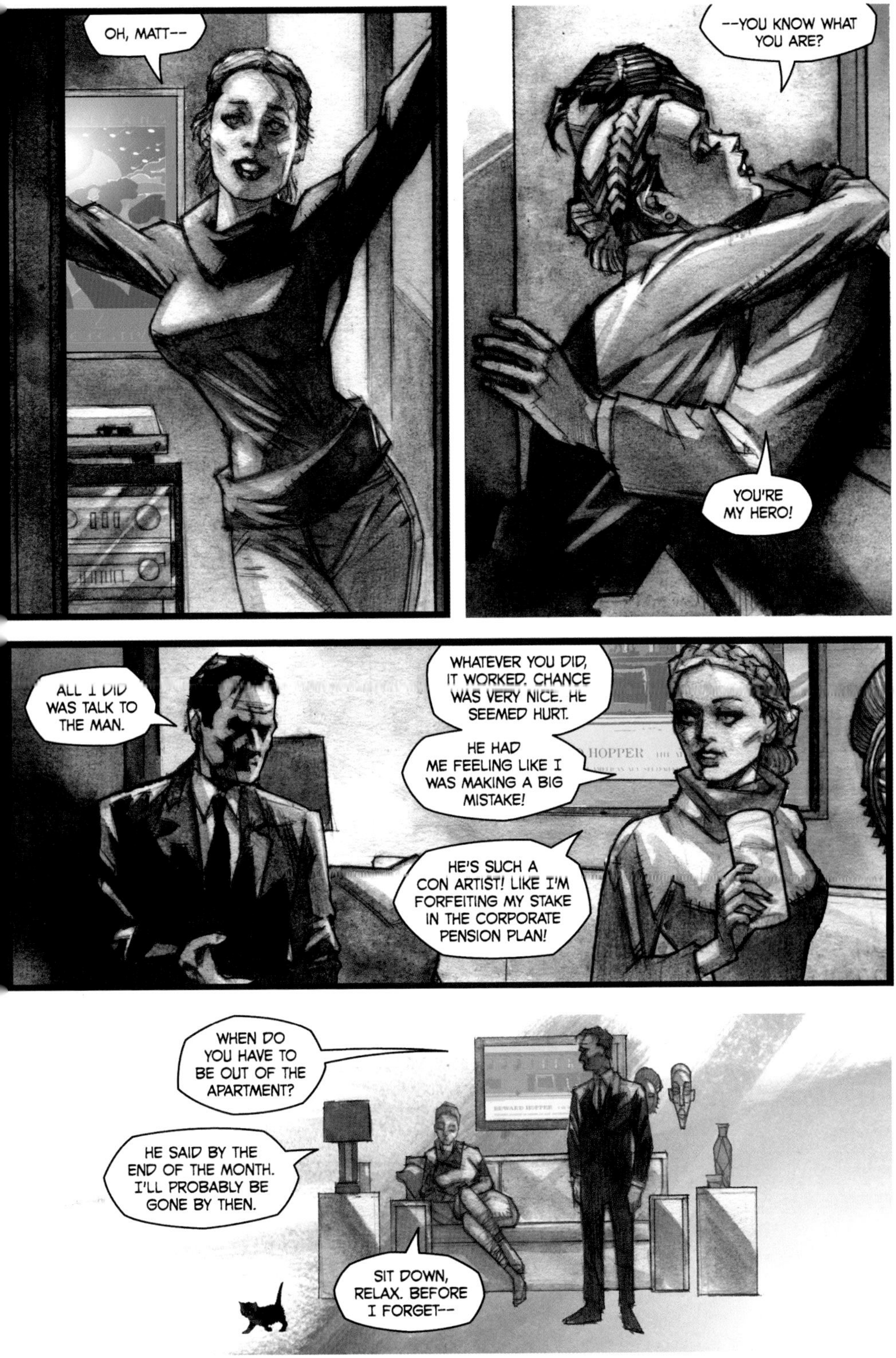
OH, MATT--
--YOU KNOW WHAT YOU ARE?
YOU'RE MY HERO!
ALL I DID WAS TALK TO THE MAN.
WHATEVER YOU DID, IT WORKED. CHANCE WAS VERY NICE. HE SEEMED HURT.
HE HAD ME FEELING LIKE I WAS MAKING A BIG MISTAKE!
HOPPER
HE'S SUCH A CON ARTIST! LIKE I'M FORFEITING MY STAKE IN THE CORPORATE PENSION PLAN!
WHEN DO YOU HAVE TO BE OUT OF THE APARTMENT?
HE SAID BY THE END OF THE MONTH. I'LL PROBABLY BE GONE BY THEN.
SIT DOWN, RELAX. BEFORE I FORGET--

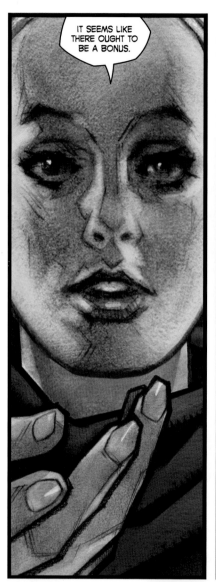

IT SEEMS LIKE THERE OUGHT TO BE A BONUS.

WELL, NOW--

THAT WAS NICE, MATT.

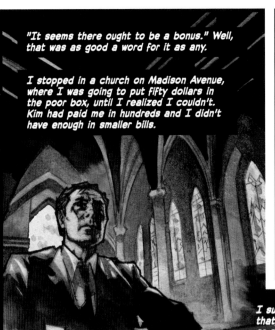

"It seems there ought to be a bonus." Well, that was as good a word for it as any.

I stopped in a church on Madison Avenue, where I was going to put fifty dollars in the poor box, until I realized I couldn't. Kim had paid me in hundreds and I didn't have enough in smaller bills.

I don't know why I tithe, or how I got in the habit in the first place. It was one of the things I began doing after I left Anita and the boys.

I suppose it's superstition. I suppose I think that, having started this, I have to keep it up or something terrible will happen.

God knows it doesn't make any sense. Terrible things will happen anyway, and will go on happening whether I give all or none of my income to churches.

This particular tithe would have to wait.

During the meeting that night, a kid told how he'd reached his ninety days, and he got a round of applause. The speaker said, "You know what comes after your ninetieth day?"

"Your ninety-first day."

Around three the next day, I thought of Kim. I reached for the phone to call her and had to stop myself. Whatever business we'd had with each other was finished.

I remembered her hair and thought of a sculptor I knew in Tribeca. Jan Keane had done a head of Medusa with the same broad brow and high cheekbones as Kim's.

I could call Jan. I could tell her I was halfway through my seventh sober day. I hadn't had any contact with her since she started going to meetings.

We'd had a couple of evenings when we had a good time drinking together. Maybe we could have the same kind of enjoyment sober. Or maybe it would be like sitting in Armstrong's without bourbon in the coffee.

I got as far as looking up her number but never made the call.

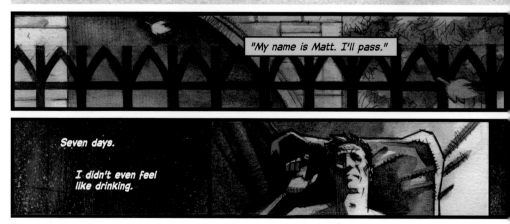

"My name is Matt. I'll pass."

Seven days.

I didn't even feel like drinking.

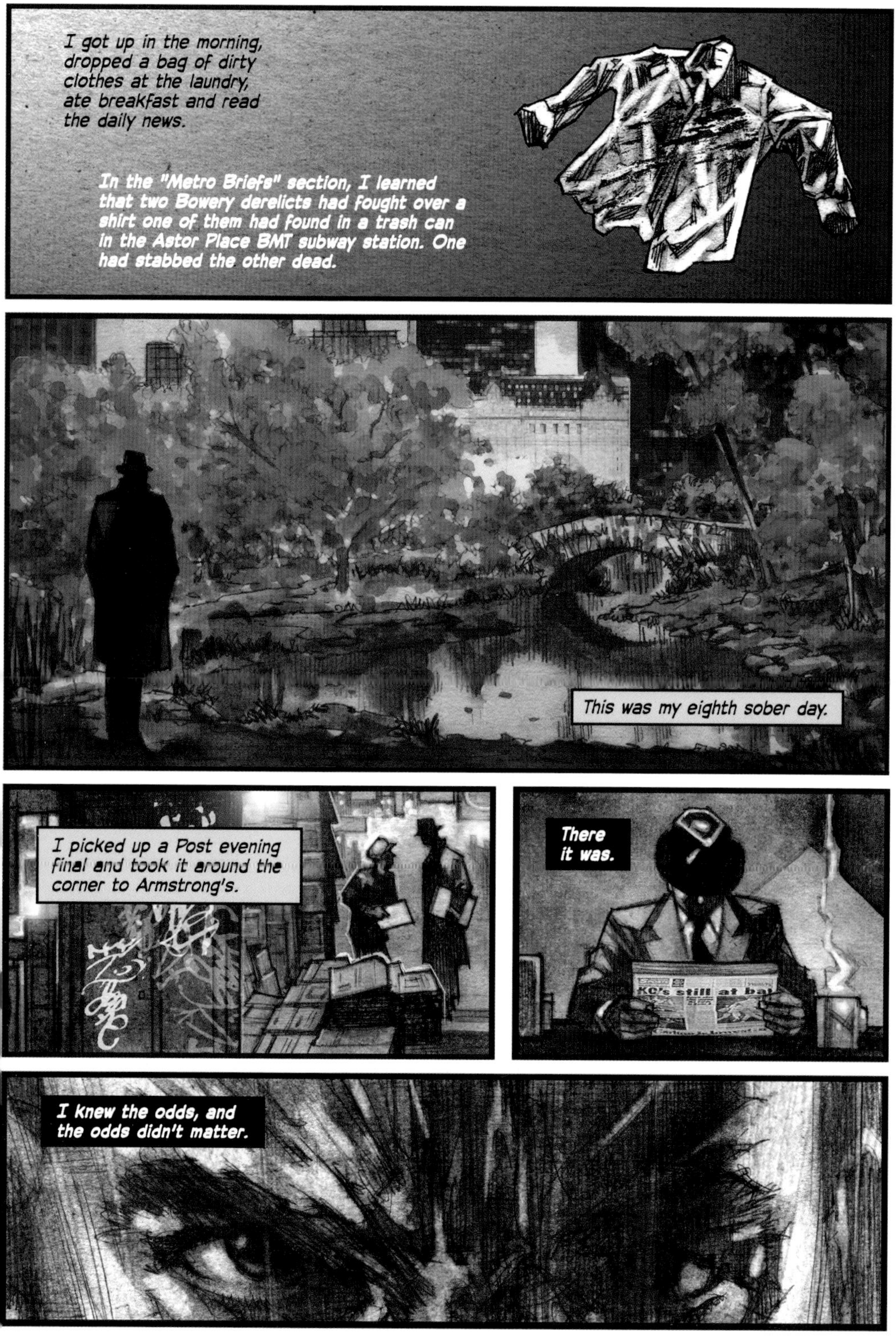

I got up in the morning, dropped a bag of dirty clothes at the laundry, ate breakfast and read the daily news.
In the "Metro Briefs" section, I learned that two Bowery derelicts had fought over a shirt one of them had found in a trash can in the Astor Place BMT subway station. One had stabbed the other dead.
This was my eighth sober day.
I picked up a Post evening final and took it around the corner to Armstrong's.
There it was.
I knew the odds, and the odds didn't matter.

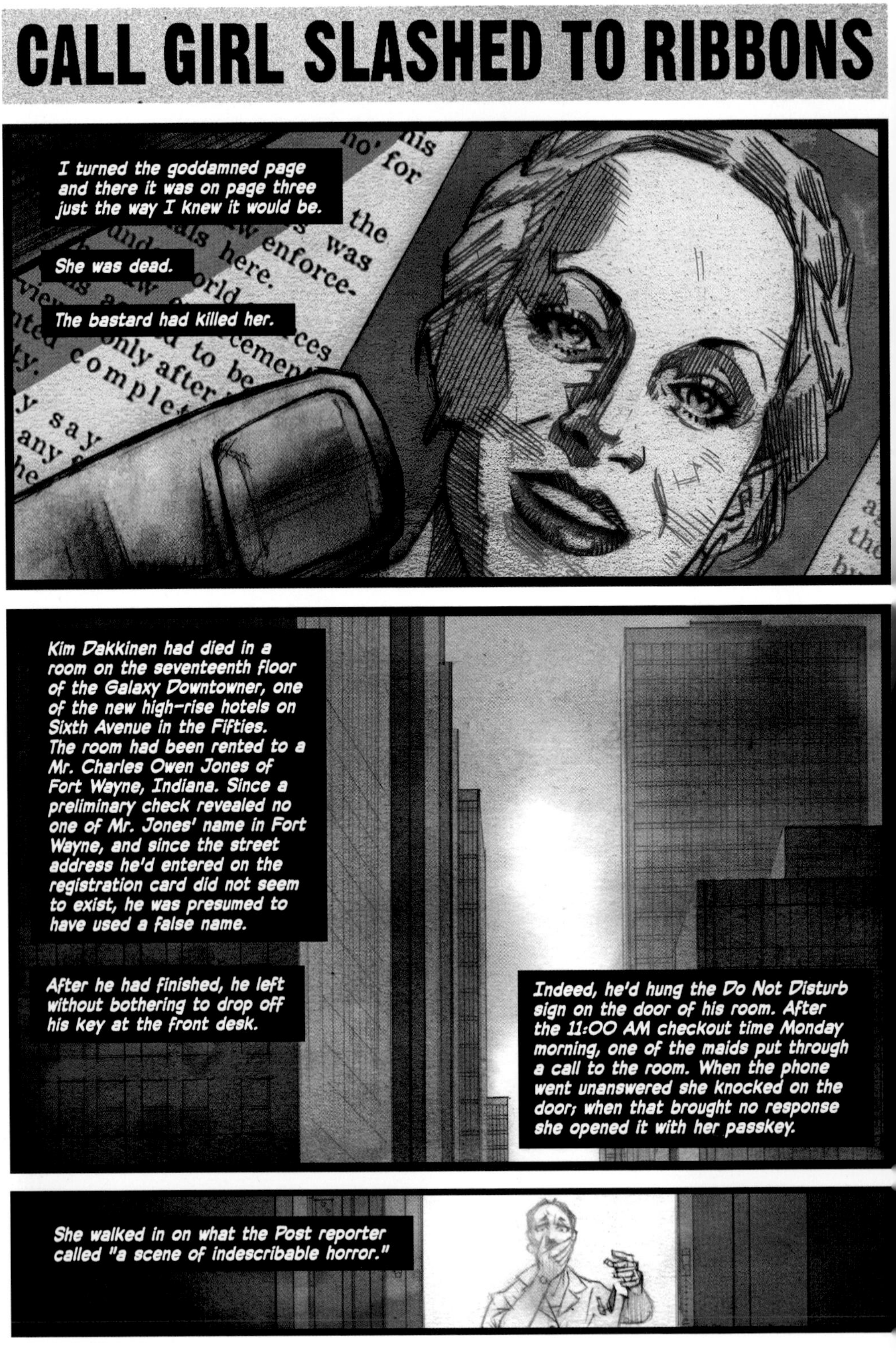
CALL GIRL SLASHED TO RIBBONS
I turned the goddamned page and there it was on page three just the way I knew it would be.
She was dead.
The bastard had killed her.
Kim Dakkinen had died in a room on the seventeenth floor of the Galaxy Downtowner, one of the new high-rise hotels on Sixth Avenue in the Fifties. The room had been rented to a Mr. Charles Owen Jones of Fort Wayne, Indiana. Since a preliminary check revealed no one of Mr. Jones' name in Fort Wayne, and since the street address he'd entered on the registration card did not seem to exist, he was presumed to have used a false name.
After he had finished, he left without bothering to drop off his key at the front desk.
Indeed, he'd hung the Do Not Disturb sign on the door of his room. After the 11:00 AM checkout time Monday morning, one of the maids put through a call to the room. When the phone went unanswered she knocked on the door; when that brought no response she opened it with her passkey.
She walked in on what the Post reporter called "a scene of indescribable horror."

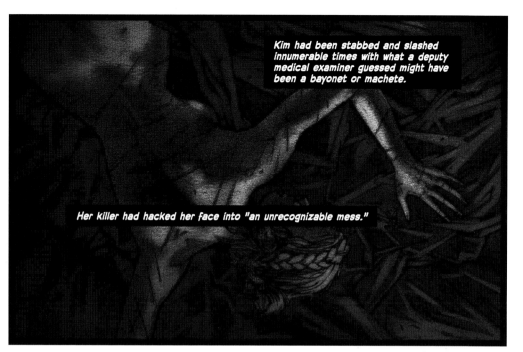

Kim had been stabbed and slashed innumerable times with what a deputy medical examiner guessed might have been a bayonet or machete.

Her killer had hacked her face into "an unrecognizable mess."

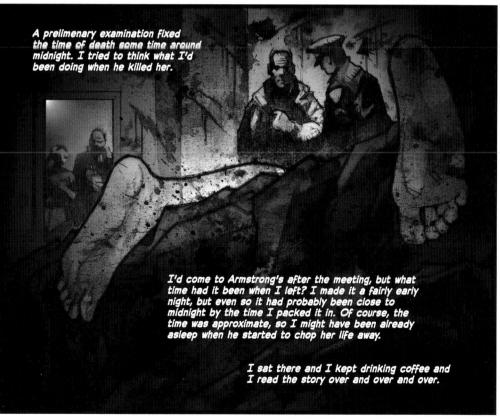

A prelimenary examination fixed the time of death some time around midnight. I tried to think what I'd been doing when he killed her.

I'd come to Armstrong's after the meeting, but what time had it been when I left? I made it a fairly early night, but even so it had probably been close to midnight by the time I packed it in. Of course, the time was approximate, so I might have been already asleep when he started to chop her life away.

I sat there and I kept drinking coffee and I read the story over and over and over.

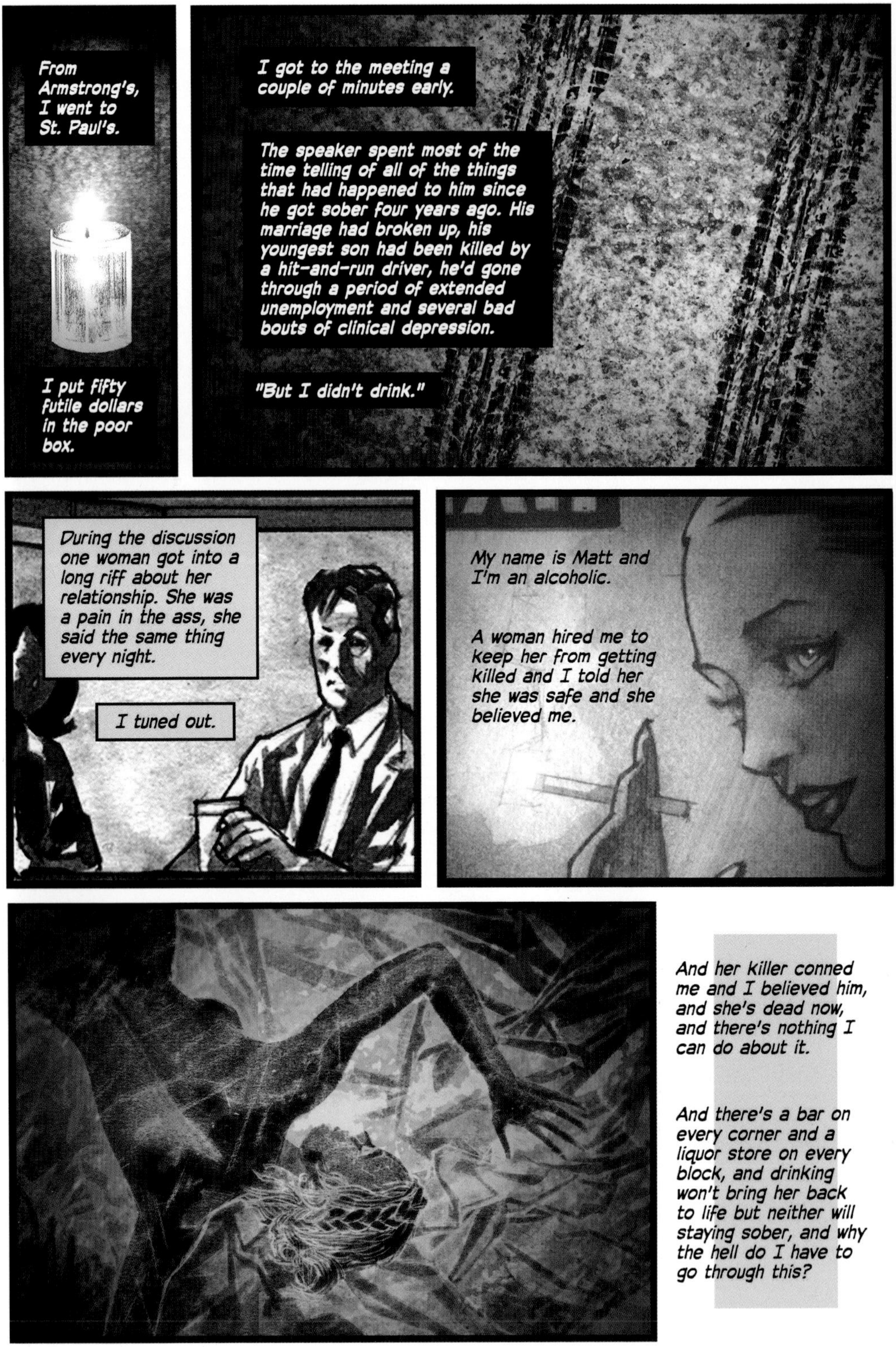

From Armstrong's, I went to St. Paul's.
I put fifty futile dollars in the poor box.
I got to the meeting a couple of minutes early.
The speaker spent most of the time telling of all of the things that had happened to him since he got sober four years ago. His marriage had broken up, his youngest son had been killed by a hit-and-run driver, he'd gone through a period of extended unemployment and several bad bouts of clinical depression.
"But I didn't drink."
During the discussion one woman got into a long riff about her relationship. She was a pain in the ass, she said the same thing every night.
I tuned out.
My name is Matt and I'm an alcoholic.
A woman hired me to keep her from getting killed and I told her she was safe and she believed me.
And her killer conned me and I believed him, and she's dead now, and there's nothing I can do about it.
And there's a bar on every corner and a liquor store on every block, and drinking won't bring her back to life but neither will staying sober, and why the hell do I have to go through this?

My name is Matt and I'm an alcoholic and we sit around in these goddamned rooms and say the same damned things all the time and meanwhile out there all the animals are killing each other. We say Don't drink and go to meetings and we say the important thing is you're sober and we say Easy does it and we say One day at a time and while we natter on like brainwashed zombies the world is coming to an end.

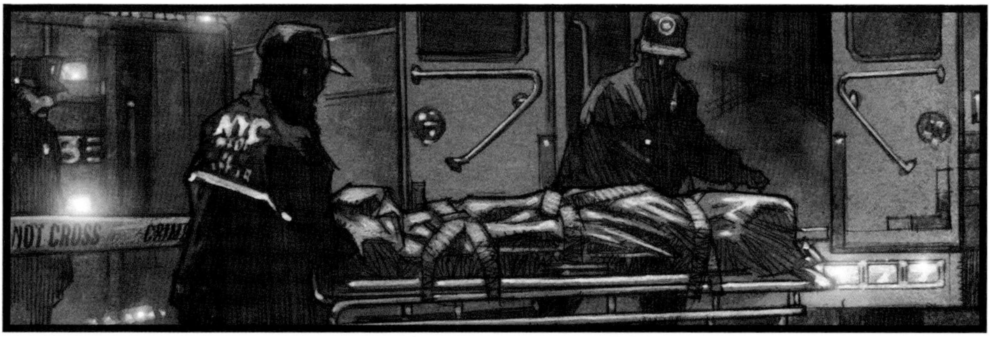

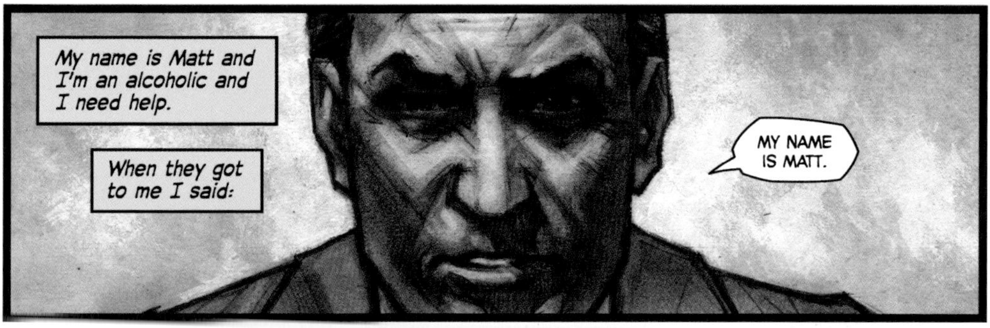
My name is Matt and I'm an alcoholic and I need help.
When they got to me I said:
MY NAME IS MATT.

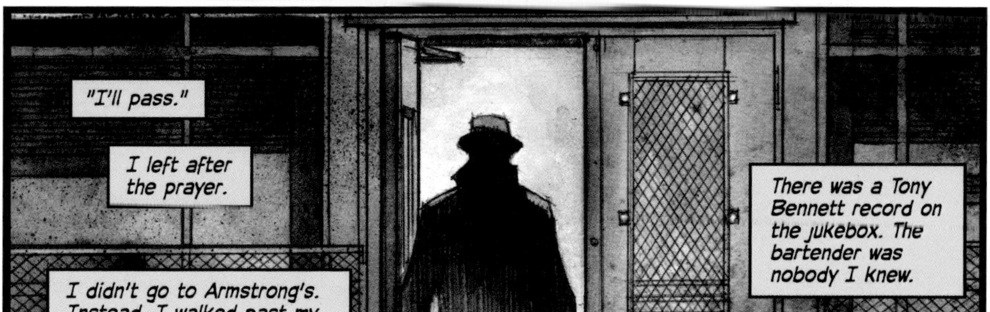
"I'll pass."
I left after the prayer.
I didn't go to Armstrong's. Instead, I walked past my hotel to Fifty-Eighth Street.
There was a Tony Bennett record on the jukebox. The bartender was nobody I knew.
I ordered the first bourbon that caught my eye.

I wondered what I expected to see.

I drank it down. It was no big deal.

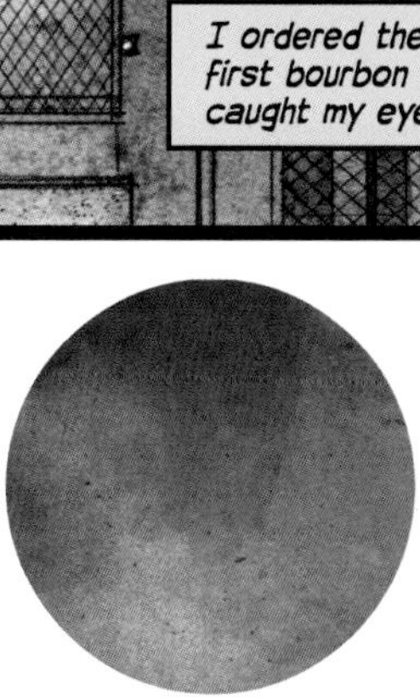

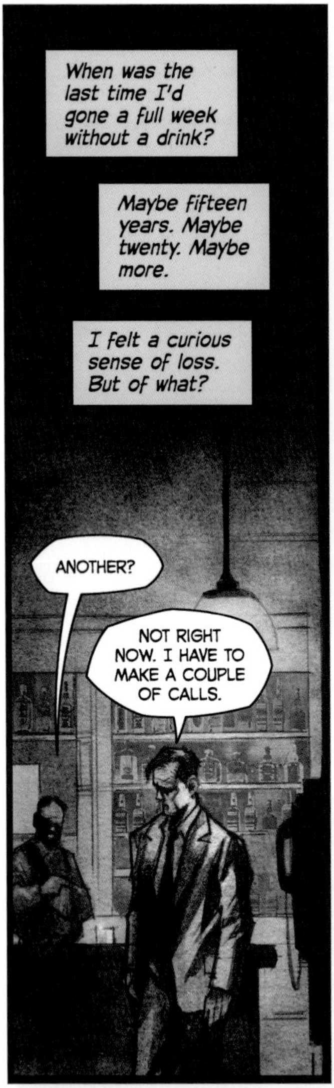
When was the last time I'd gone a full week without a drink?
Maybe fifteen years. Maybe twenty. Maybe more.
I felt a curious sense of loss. But of what?
ANOTHER?
NOT RIGHT NOW. I HAVE TO MAKE A COUPLE OF CALLS.

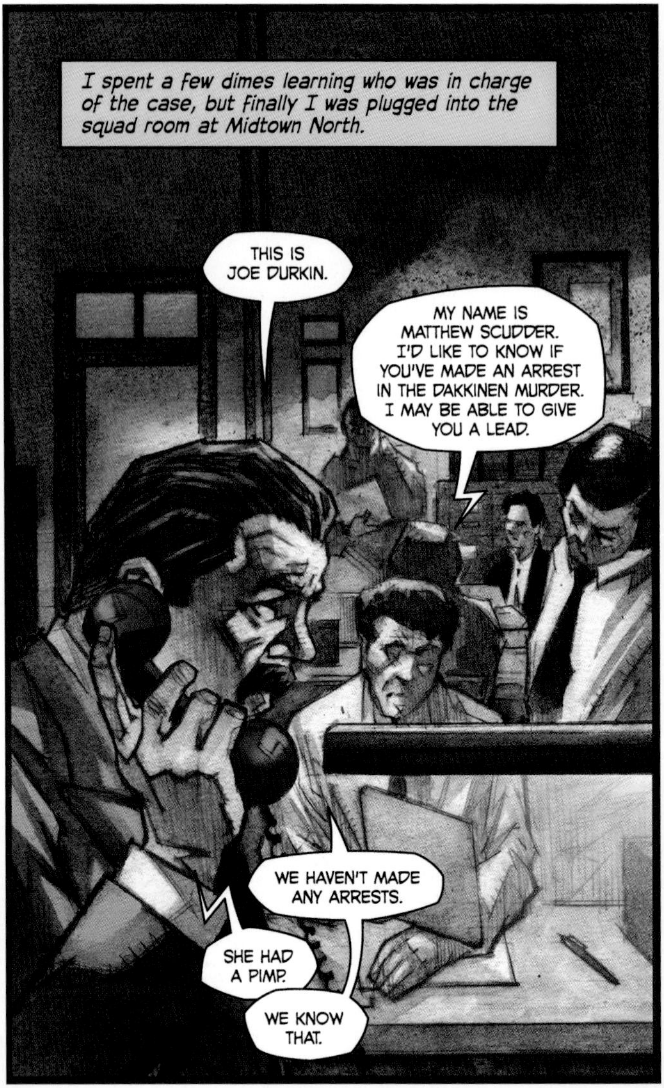
I spent a few dimes learning who was in charge of the case, but finally I was plugged into the squad room at Midtown North.
THIS IS JOE DURKIN.
MY NAME IS MATTHEW SCUDDER. I'D LIKE TO KNOW IF YOU'VE MADE AN ARREST IN THE DAKKINEN MURDER. I MAY BE ABLE TO GIVE YOU A LEAD.
WE HAVEN'T MADE ANY ARRESTS.
SHE HAD A PIMP.
WE KNOW THAT.

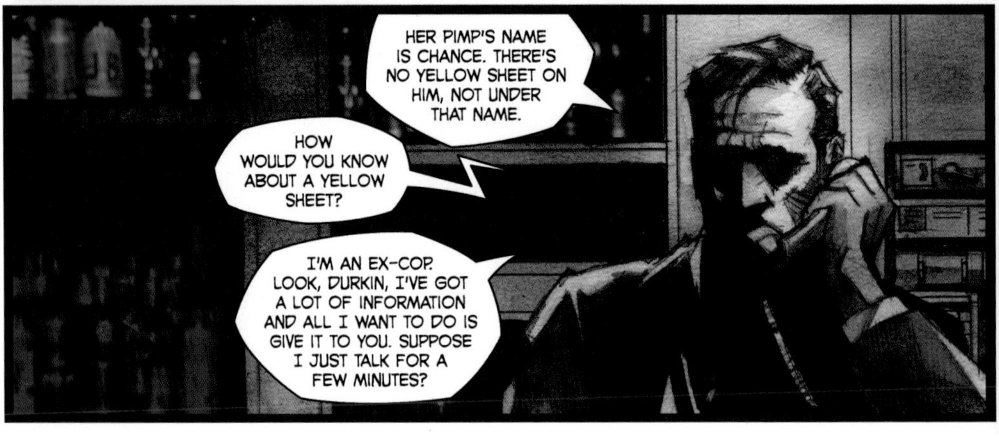
HER PIMP'S NAME IS CHANCE. THERE'S NO YELLOW SHEET ON HIM, NOT UNDER THAT NAME.
HOW WOULD YOU KNOW ABOUT A YELLOW SHEET?
I'M AN EX-COP. LOOK, DURKIN, I'VE GOT A LOT OF INFORMATION AND ALL I WANT TO DO IS GIVE IT TO YOU. SUPPOSE I JUST TALK FOR A FEW MINUTES?

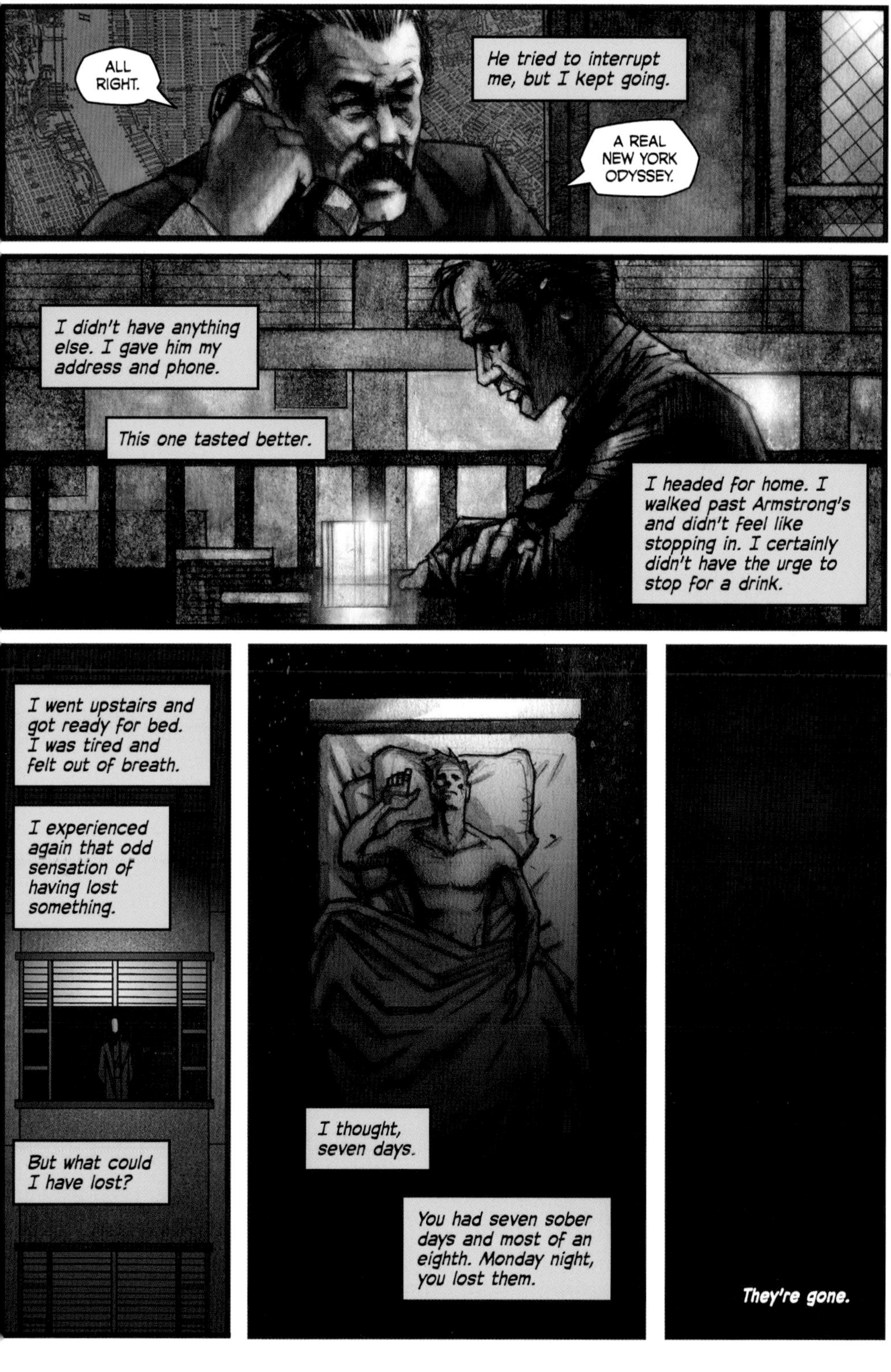
ALL RIGHT.
He tried to interrupt me, but I kept going.
A REAL NEW YORK ODYSSEY.
I didn't have anything else. I gave him my address and phone.
This one tasted better.
I headed for home. I walked past Armstrong's and didn't feel like stopping in. I certainly didn't have the urge to stop for a drink.
I went upstairs and got ready for bed. I was tired and felt out of breath.
I experienced again that odd sensation of having lost something.
But what could I have lost?
I thought, seven days.
You had seven sober days and most of an eighth. Monday night, you lost them.
They're gone.

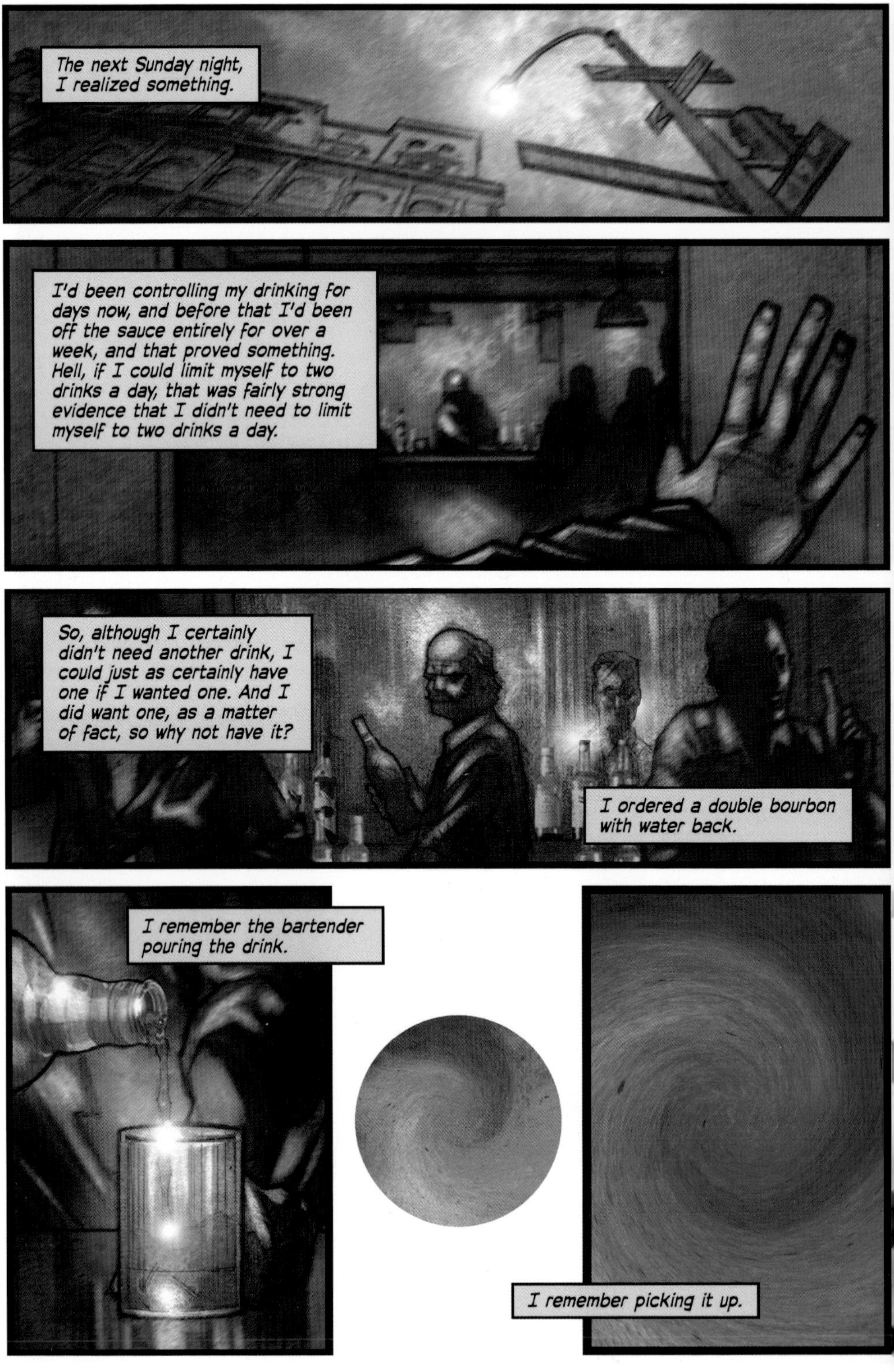
The next Sunday night, I realized something.
I'd been controlling my drinking for days now, and before that I'd been off the sauce entirely for over a week, and that proved something. Hell, if I could limit myself to two drinks a day, that was fairly strong evidence that I didn't need to limit myself to two drinks a day.
So, although I certainly didn't need another drink, I could just as certainly have one if I wanted one. And I did want one, as a matter of fact, so why not have it?
I ordered a double bourbon with water back.
I remember the bartender pouring the drink.
I remember picking it up.

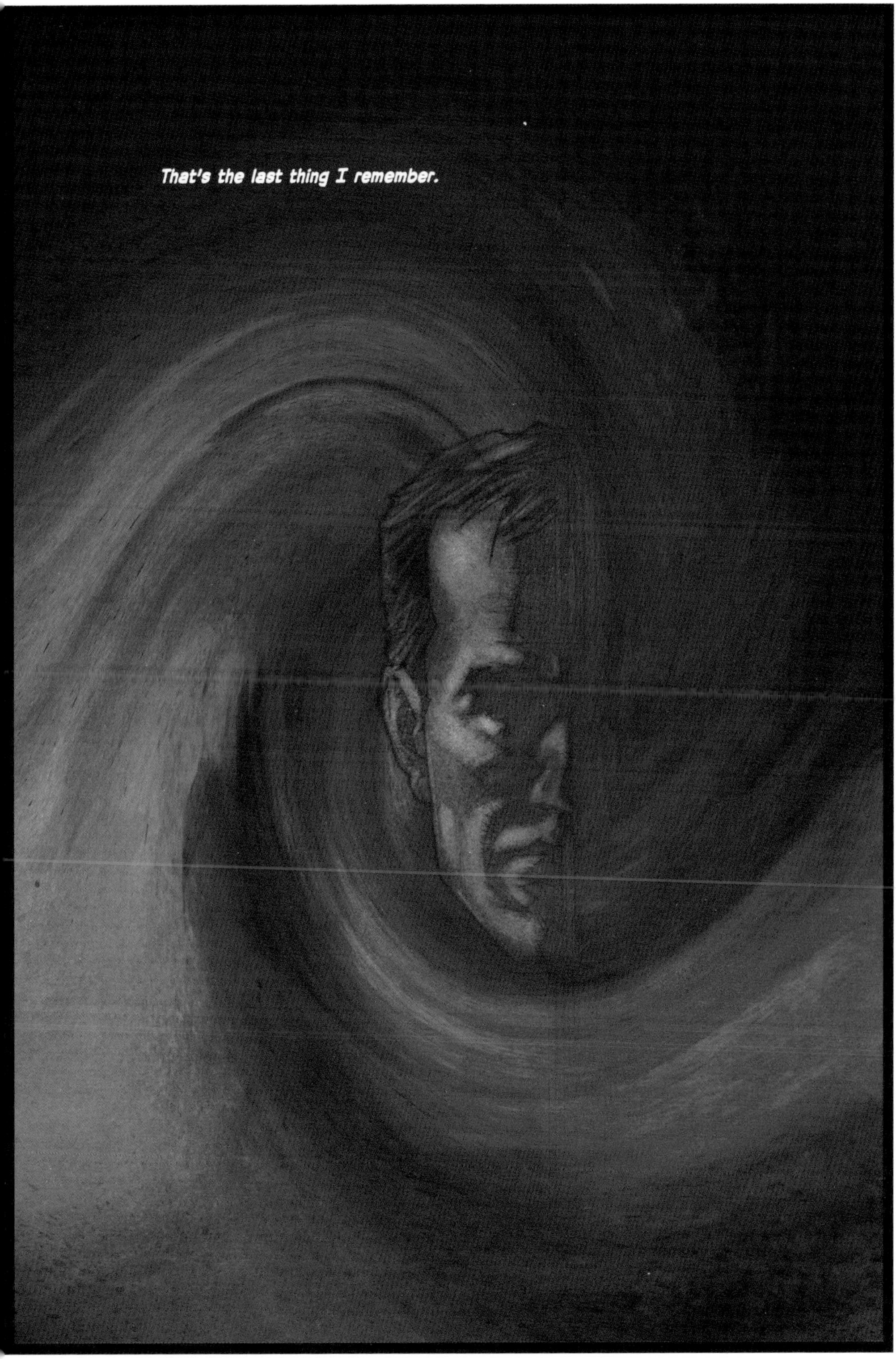
That's the last thing I remember.

I woke up suddenly, consciousness coming on abruptly and at top volume.

It was Wednesday.

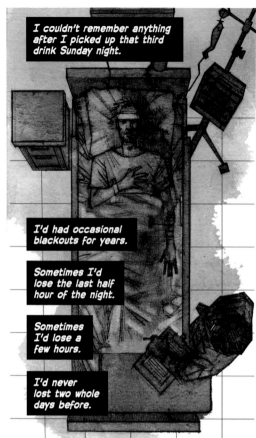

I couldn't remember anything after I picked up that third drink Sunday night.

I'd had occasional blackouts for years.

Sometimes I'd lose the last half hour of the night.

Sometimes I'd lose a few hours.

I'd never lost two whole days before.

They didn't want to let me go.

YOU KNOW HOW YOU GOT HERE LAST NIGHT? YOU HAD A CONVULSION, A FULL-SCALE GRAND MAL SEIZURE. EVER HAVE ONE OF THOSE BEFORE?

NO.

WELL, YOU'LL HAVE THEM AGAIN. IF YOU KEEP ON DRINKING, YOU'LL DIE OF IT IF YOU DON'T DIE OF SOMETHING ELSE FIRST.

STOP IT.

NO, I WON'T STOP IT. WHY THE HELL SHOULD I STOP IT?

I CAN'T BE POLITE AND CONSIDERATE OF YOUR FEELINGS AND CUT THROUGH YOUR BULLSHIT AT THE SAME TIME. LOOK AT ME. LISTEN TO ME. YOU'RE AN ALCOHOLIC. IF YOU DRINK, YOU'LL DIE.

I DON'T HAVE TO STAY. I'M NOT GOING TO DRINK.

EVERYBODY SAYS THAT.

IN MY CASE, IT'S TRUE. YOU HAVE TO LET ME SIGN OUT.

IF YOU DO, YOU'LL BE SIGNING OUT AMA. AGAINST MEDICAL ADVICE.

"THEN THAT'S WHAT I'LL DO."

NEXT TIME MAYBE YOU'LL LISTEN TO ADVICE.

THERE WON'T BE A NEXT TIME.

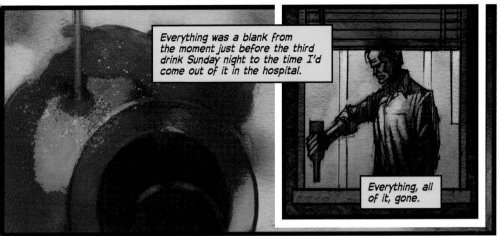

Everything was a blank from the moment just before the third drink Sunday night to the time I'd come out of it in the hospital.

Everything, all of it, gone.

I looked at my messages. Chance had called. The pimp who had killed Kim Dakkinen. He had left his service number.

I called Midtown North instead.

WHAT'S ON YOUR MIND, SCUDDER?

THAT PIMP'S BEEN TRYING TO REACH ME. CHANCE. IF YOU WANT, I CAN PROBABLY SET HIM UP.

WE'RE NOT LOOKING FOR HIM. HE WOUND UP COMING IN OF HIS OWN ACCORD. HE HAD A SLICK LAWYER WITH HIM AND HE WAS PRETTY SLICK HIMSELF.

HE HAD A SOLID ALIBI. AND THE CLERK WHO CHECKED CHARLES JONES INTO THE GALAXY CAN'T COME UP WITH A DESCRIPTION.

HE COULD HAVE HAD SOMEONE ELSE RENT THE ROOM.

YOU'RE RIGHT. HE ALSO COULD HAVE HAD SOMEONE KILL HER.

IS THAT WHAT YOU FIGURE HE DID?

I DON'T GET PAID TO FIGURE. I KNOW WE DON'T HAVE A CASE AGAINST THE SON OF A BITCH.

WHY WOULD HE CALL ME? DOES HE KNOW I STEERED YOU TO HIM?

HE DIDN'T HEAR IT FROM ME.
THEN WHAT DOES HE WANT FROM ME?
WHY DON'T YOU ASK HIM YOURSELF?
MAYBE I'LL DO THAT.
I called his service. A little less than a hour later the phone rang.
"IT'S CHANCE. I WANT TO THANK YOU FOR RETURNING MY CALL. I'D LIKE TO SPEAK WITH YOU. FACE TO FACE, THAT IS.
"I'M DOWNSTAIRS, IN YOUR LOBBY. COULD YOU COME DOWN?"
"ALL RIGHT."
"I DIDN'T DO IT. MAYBE I COULD HAVE, BUT I DIDN'T."
"IF YOU SAY SO."
"GOD DAMN, SHE ANYTHING MORE TO YOU THAN YOU LET ON THAT NIGHT?"
"NO."
"JUST A FRIEND OF A FRIEND?"
"THAT'S RIGHT."
Moisha's
ONETTE
COFFEE SHOP
YOU WENT TO BED WITH HER.
ANYTHING THAT HAPPENED BETWEN US IS MY BUSINESS.
I'M JUST GETTING A FIX ON WHERE YOU'RE COMING FROM.
I'M NOT COMING FROM ANYPLACE AND I'M NOT GOING ANYWHERE. I DID A PIECE OF WORK AND I WAS PAID IN FULL. YOU THINK IT MATTERS TO ME WHO KILLED KIM DAKKINEN? YOU THINK I GIVE A DAMN?

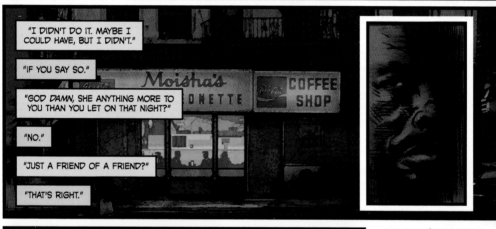

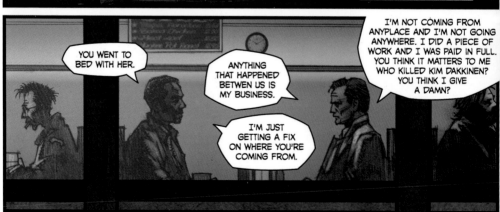

YES, I THINK IT MATTERS TO YOU.
I THINK YOU CARE WHO KILLED HER. THAT'S WHY I'M HERE.
SEE, WHAT I WANT IS TO HIRE YOU, MR. MATTHEW SCUDDER. I WANT YOU TO FIND OUT WHO KILLED HER.
WHAT'S IT TO YOU IF THE CASE STAYS ON THE BOOKS AS UNSOLVED?
MAYBE I'M CONCERNED ABOUT MY REPUTATION. SOMEBODY KILLED A WOMAN OF MINE.
SHE WASN'T YOURS WHEN SHE GOT KILLED.
WHO KNEW THAT? FAR AS THE WORLD KNOWS, ONE OF MY GIRLS GOT KILLED AND THE KILLER'S GETTING AWAY WITH IT.
WHY ME, CHANCE?
I'VE ASKED AROUND. A LOT OF FOLKS KNOW YOU AND MOST OF THEM SAID GOOD THINGS ABOUT YOU.
I'M NOT SOME AVENGING ANGEL WITH A FLAMING SWORD. I DON'T MUCH WANT THE CASE.
WHY NOT?
Because I want to sit in a dark corner and turn the world off. I want a drink, dammit.
Moisha's
LUNCHEONETTE
COFFEE SHOP
SCUDDER?
YOU WANT THE JOB OR NOT?
It was such a goddamned puzzle. I'd been controlling my drinking and it had worked fine.
Except when it didn't.

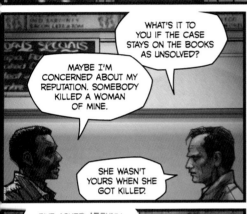

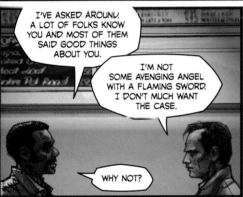

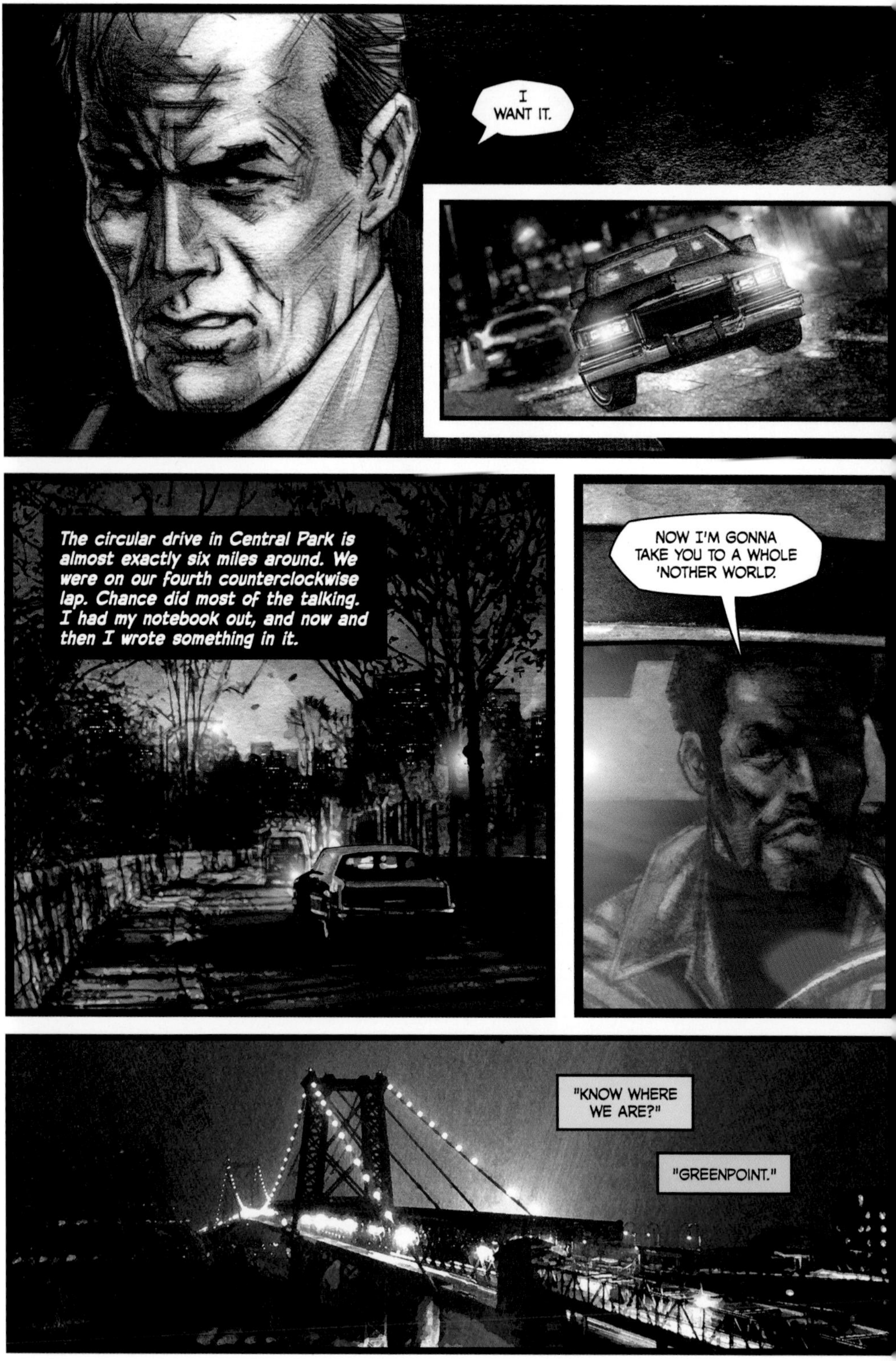
I WANT IT.
The circular drive in Central Park is almost exactly six miles around. We were on our fourth counterclockwise lap. Chance did most of the talking. I had my notebook out, and now and then I wrote something in it.
NOW I'M GONNA TAKE YOU TO A WHOLE 'NOTHER WORLD.
"KNOW WHERE WE ARE?"
"GREENPOINT."

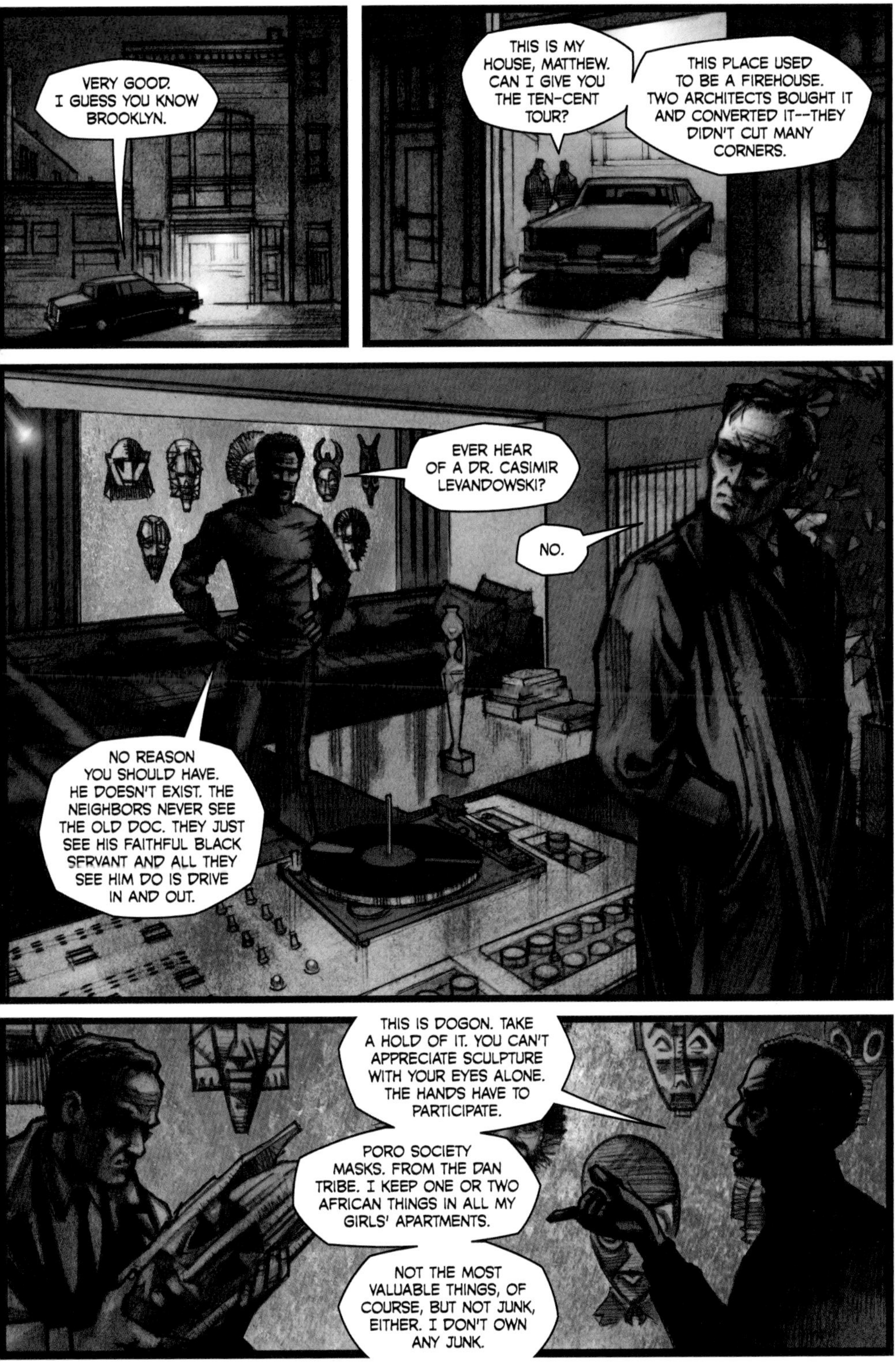
VERY GOOD. I GUESS YOU KNOW BROOKLYN.
THIS IS MY HOUSE, MATTHEW. CAN I GIVE YOU THE TEN-CENT TOUR?
THIS PLACE USED TO BE A FIREHOUSE. TWO ARCHITECTS BOUGHT IT AND CONVERTED IT--THEY DIDN'T CUT MANY CORNERS.
EVER HEAR OF A DR. CASIMIR LEVANDOWSKI?
NO.
NO REASON YOU SHOULD HAVE. HE DOESN'T EXIST. THE NEIGHBORS NEVER SEE THE OLD DOC. THEY JUST SEE HIS FAITHFUL BLACK SERVANT AND ALL THEY SEE HIM DO IS DRIVE IN AND OUT.
THIS IS DOGON. TAKE A HOLD OF IT. YOU CAN'T APPRECIATE SCULPTURE WITH YOUR EYES ALONE. THE HANDS HAVE TO PARTICIPATE.
PORO SOCIETY MASKS. FROM THE DAN TRIBE. I KEEP ONE OR TWO AFRICAN THINGS IN ALL MY GIRLS' APARTMENTS.
NOT THE MOST VALUABLE THINGS, OF COURSE, BUT NOT JUNK, EITHER. I DON'T OWN ANY JUNK.

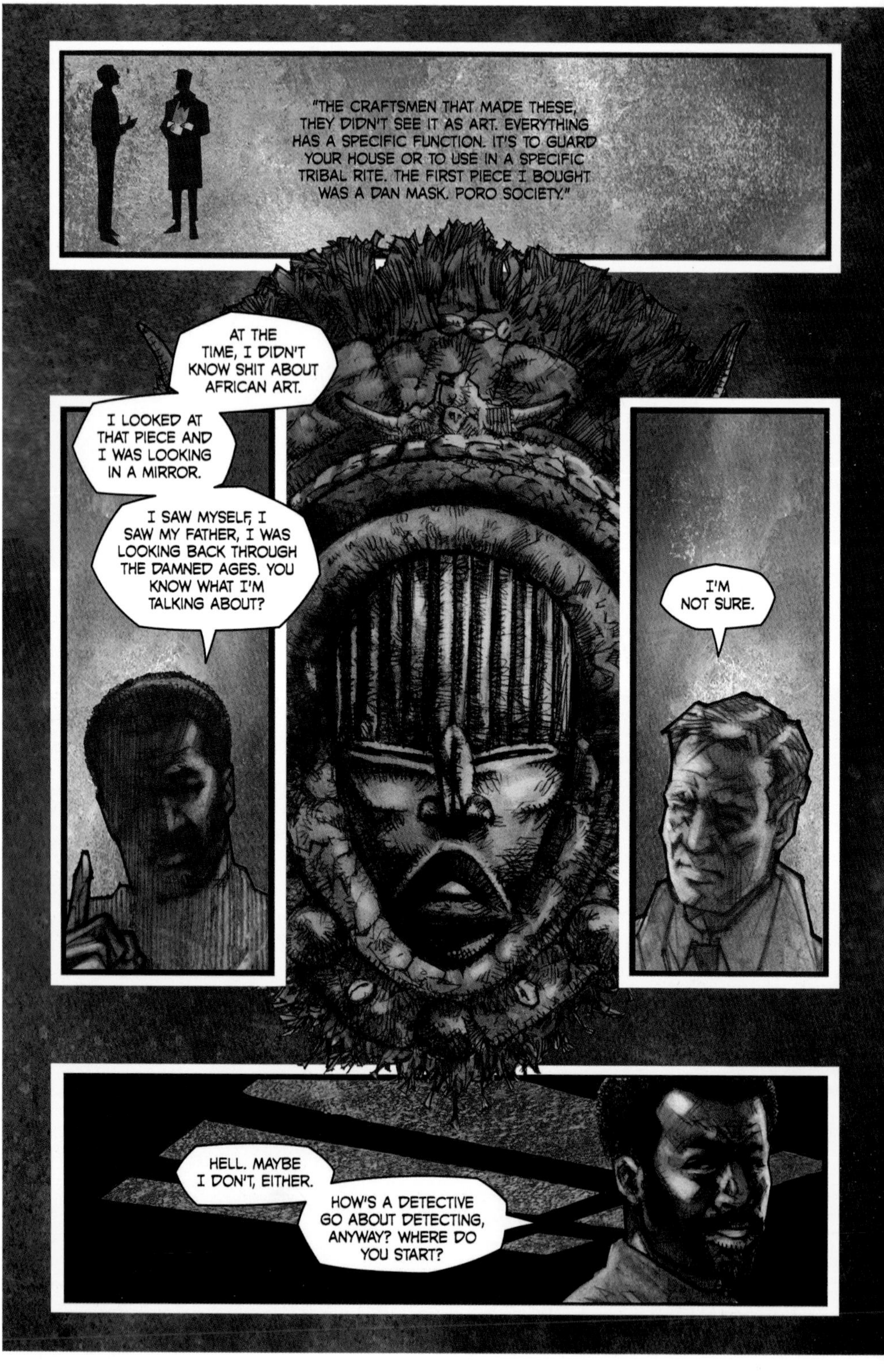
"THE CRAFTSMEN THAT MADE THESE, THEY DIDN'T SEE IT AS ART. EVERYTHING HAS A SPECIFIC FUNCTION. IT'S TO GUARD YOUR HOUSE OR TO USE IN A SPECIFIC TRIBAL RITE. THE FIRST PIECE I BOUGHT WAS A DAN MASK. PORO SOCIETY."
AT THE TIME, I DIDN'T KNOW SHIT ABOUT AFRICAN ART.
I LOOKED AT THAT PIECE AND I WAS LOOKING IN A MIRROR.
I SAW MYSELF, I SAW MY FATHER, I WAS LOOKING BACK THROUGH THE DAMNED AGES. YOU KNOW WHAT I'M TALKING ABOUT?
I'M NOT SURE.
HELL. MAYBE I DON'T, EITHER.
HOW'S A DETECTIVE GO ABOUT DETECTING, ANYWAY? WHERE DO YOU START?

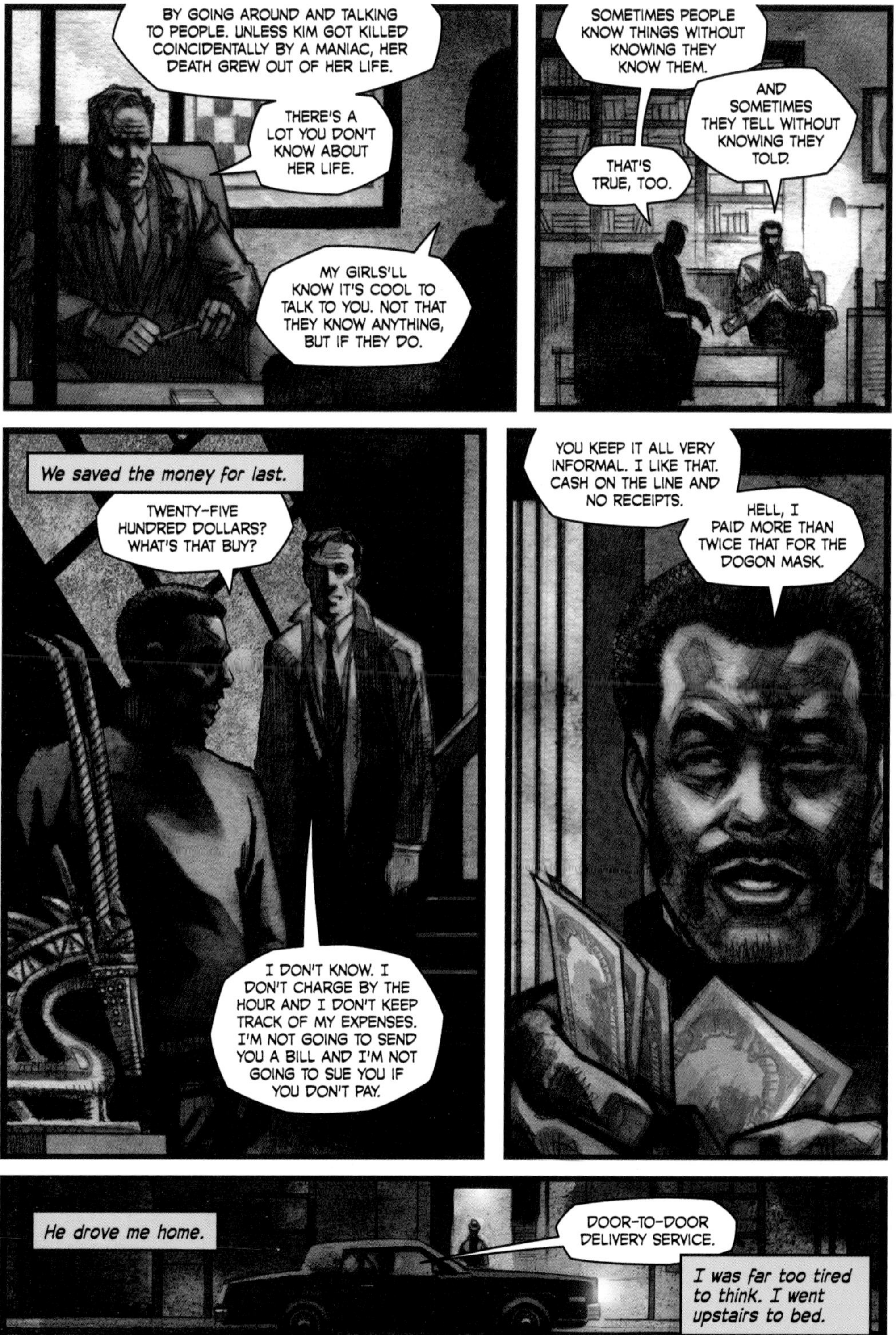
BY GOING AROUND AND TALKING TO PEOPLE. UNLESS KIM GOT KILLED COINCIDENTALLY BY A MANIAC, HER DEATH GREW OUT OF HER LIFE.
THERE'S A LOT YOU DON'T KNOW ABOUT HER LIFE.
MY GIRLS'LL KNOW IT'S COOL TO TALK TO YOU. NOT THAT THEY KNOW ANYTHING, BUT IF THEY DO.
SOMETIMES PEOPLE KNOW THINGS WITHOUT KNOWING THEY KNOW THEM.
THAT'S TRUE, TOO.
AND SOMETIMES THEY TELL WITHOUT KNOWING THEY TOLD.
We saved the money for last.
TWENTY-FIVE HUNDRED DOLLARS? WHAT'S THAT BUY?
I DON'T KNOW. I DON'T CHARGE BY THE HOUR AND I DON'T KEEP TRACK OF MY EXPENSES. I'M NOT GOING TO SEND YOU A BILL AND I'M NOT GOING TO SUE YOU IF YOU DON'T PAY.
YOU KEEP IT ALL VERY INFORMAL. I LIKE THAT. CASH ON THE LINE AND NO RECEIPTS.
HELL, I PAID MORE THAN TWICE THAT FOR THE DOGON MASK.
He drove me home.
DOOR-TO-DOOR DELIVERY SERVICE.
I was far too tired to think. I went upstairs to bed.

The next night, I went over to Mid-town North. I had an appointment with Detective Durkin. I told him I'd like to see whatever he could show me on the Kim Dakkinen killing.

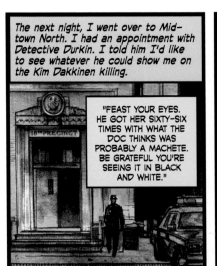

"FEAST YOUR EYES. HE GOT HER SIXTY-SIX TIMES WITH WHAT THE DOC THINKS WAS PROBABLY A MACHETE. BE GRATEFUL YOU'RE SEEING IT IN BLACK AND WHITE."

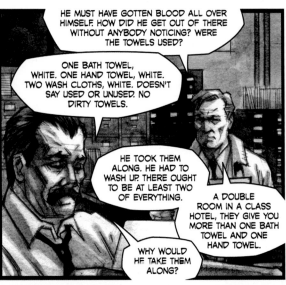

HE MUST HAVE GOTTEN BLOOD ALL OVER HIMSELF. HOW DID HE GET OUT OF THERE WITHOUT ANYBODY NOTICING? WERE THE TOWELS USED?

ONE BATH TOWEL, WHITE. ONE HAND TOWEL, WHITE. TWO WASH CLOTHS, WHITE. DOESN'T SAY USED OR UNUSED. NO DIRTY TOWELS.

HE TOOK THEM ALONG. HE HAD TO WASH UP. THERE OUGHT TO BE AT LEAST TWO OF EVERYTHING.

A DOUBLE ROOM IN A CLASS HOTEL, THEY GIVE YOU MORE THAN ONE BATH TOWEL AND ONE HAND TOWEL.

WHY WOULD HE TAKE THEM ALONG?

"MAYBE TO WRAP THE MACHETE IN."

We went through the file together.

NOW YOU KNOW WHAT WE KNOW. IT'S A WASTE OF TIME WORRYING ABOUT IT, BUT I SHOULDA NOTICED THE MISSING TOWELS. THAT'S SOMETHING I SHOULD HAVE THOUGHT OF.

YOU GOT SOMEPLACE YOU GOTTA BE?

They could have called it Last Stop Before Detox.

I went to the bar to get our drinks, a double vodka for him, ginger ale for myself.

HE'S YOUR CLIENT, RIGHT? CHANCE?

YOU THINK THERE'S A CHANCE IN THE WORLD HE DIDN'T KILL HER? OR SET HER UP AND HIRE IT DONE?

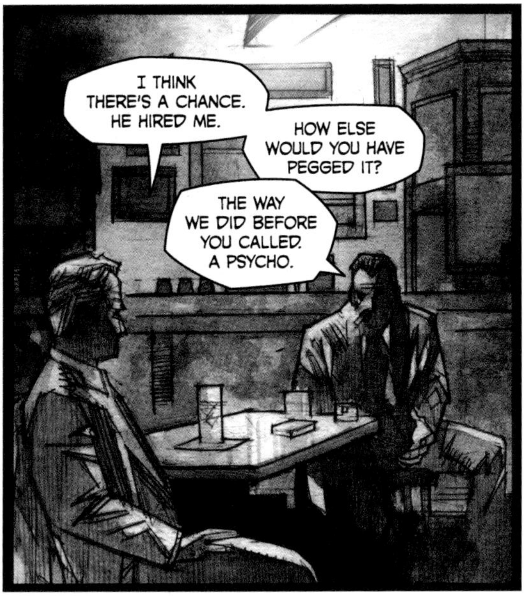
I THINK THERE'S A CHANCE. HE HIRED ME.
HOW ELSE WOULD YOU HAVE PEGGED IT?
THE WAY WE DID BEFORE YOU CALLED A PSYCHO.

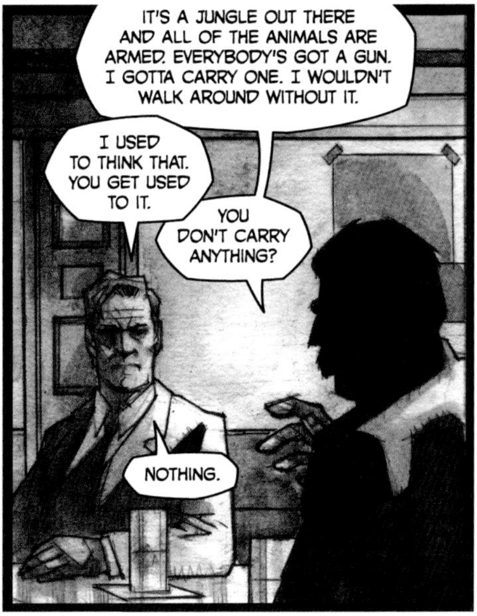
IT'S A JUNGLE OUT THERE AND ALL OF THE ANIMALS ARE ARMED. EVERYBODY'S GOT A GUN. I GOTTA CARRY ONE. I WOULDN'T WALK AROUND WITHOUT IT.
I USED TO THINK THAT. YOU GET USED TO IT.
YOU DON'T CARRY ANYTHING?
NOTHING.

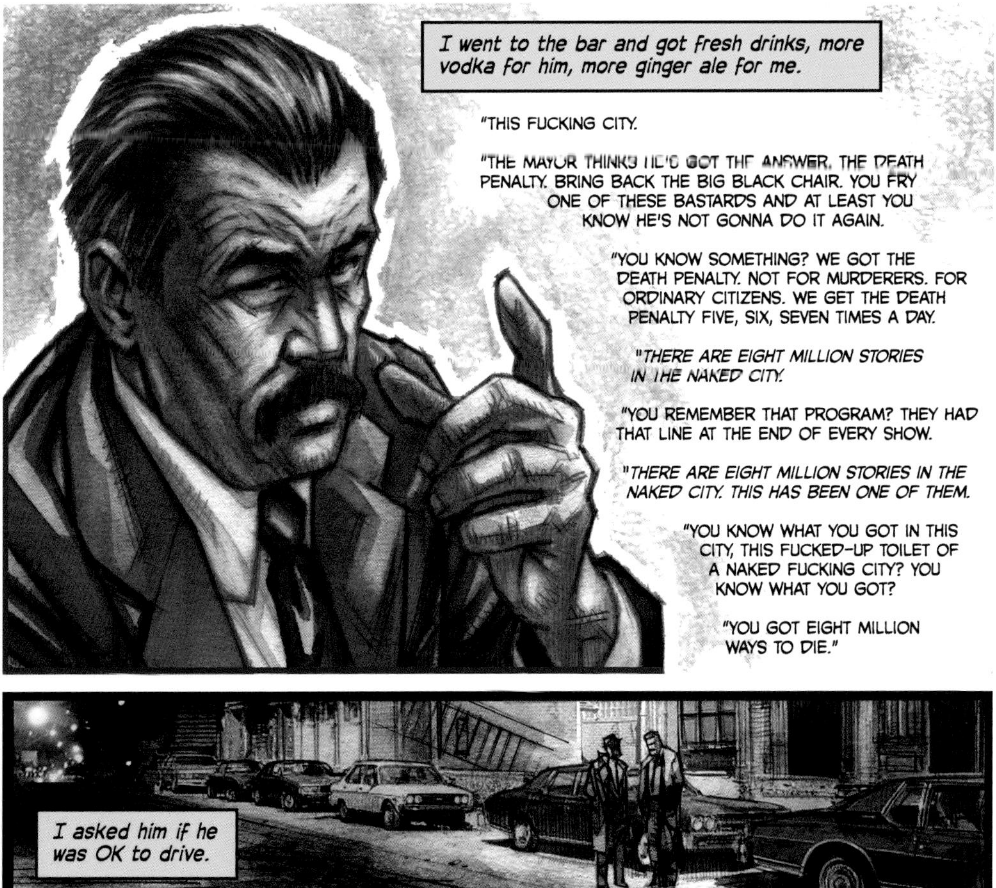
I went to the bar and got fresh drinks, more vodka for him, more ginger ale for me.
"THIS FUCKING CITY.
"THE MAYOR THINKS HE'S GOT THE ANSWER. THE DEATH PENALTY. BRING BACK THE BIG BLACK CHAIR. YOU FRY ONE OF THESE BASTARDS AND AT LEAST YOU KNOW HE'S NOT GONNA DO IT AGAIN.
"YOU KNOW SOMETHING? WE GOT THE DEATH PENALTY. NOT FOR MURDERERS. FOR ORDINARY CITIZENS. WE GET THE DEATH PENALTY FIVE, SIX, SEVEN TIMES A DAY.
"*THERE ARE EIGHT MILLION STORIES IN THE NAKED CITY.*
"YOU REMEMBER THAT PROGRAM? THEY HAD THAT LINE AT THE END OF EVERY SHOW.
"*THERE ARE EIGHT MILLION STORIES IN THE NAKED CITY. THIS HAS BEEN ONE OF THEM.*
"YOU KNOW WHAT YOU GOT IN THIS CITY, THIS FUCKED-UP TOILET OF A NAKED FUCKING CITY? YOU KNOW WHAT YOU GOT?
"YOU GOT EIGHT MILLION WAYS TO DIE."

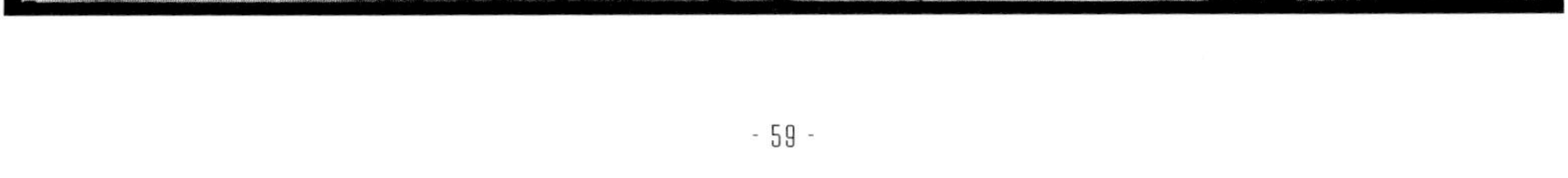
I asked him if he was OK to drive.

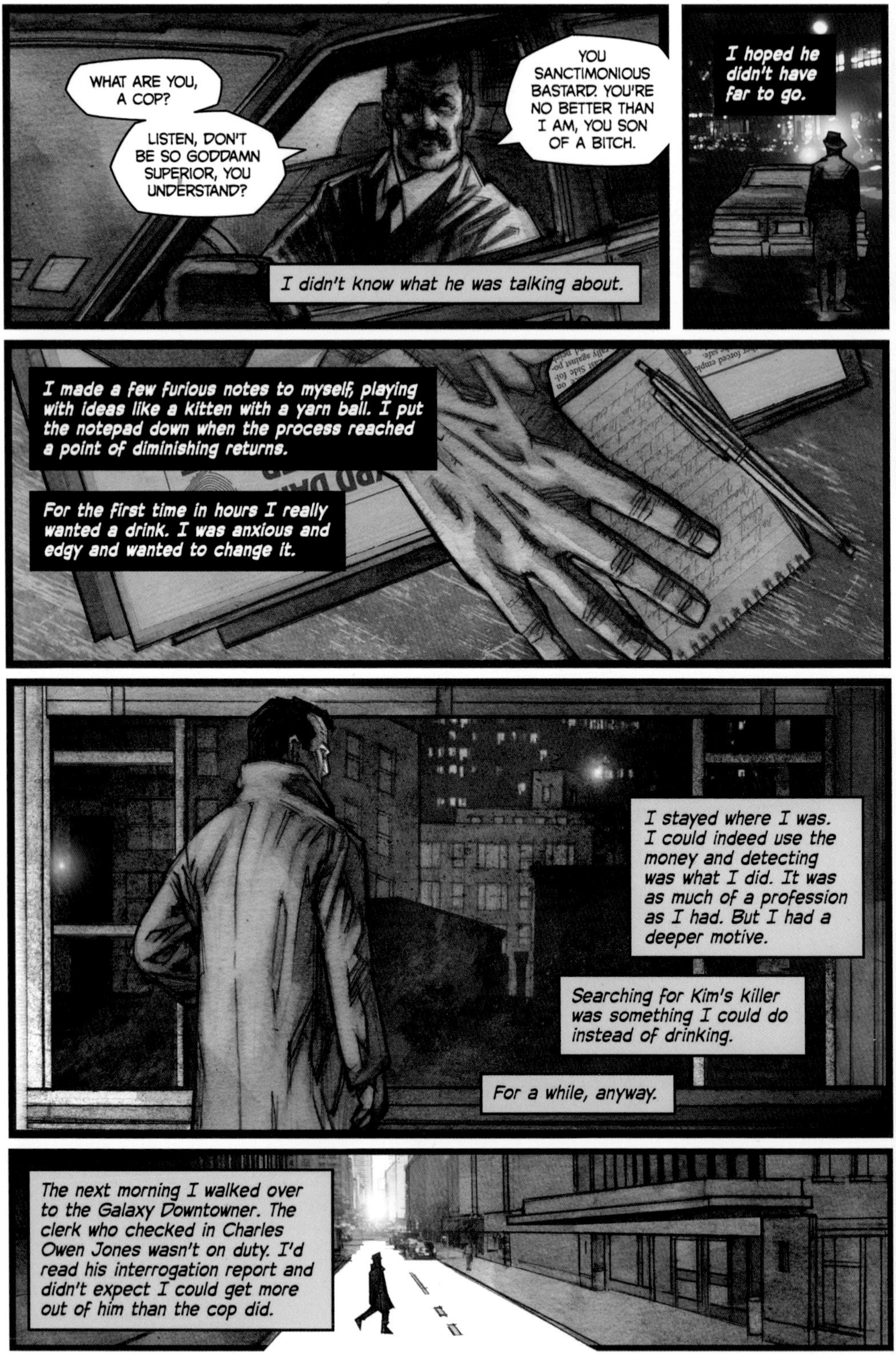
WHAT ARE YOU, A COP?
LISTEN, DON'T BE SO GODDAMN SUPERIOR, YOU UNDERSTAND?
YOU SANCTIMONIOUS BASTARD. YOU'RE NO BETTER THAN I AM, YOU SON OF A BITCH.
I didn't know what he was talking about.
I hoped he didn't have far to go.
I made a few furious notes to myself, playing with ideas like a kitten with a yarn ball. I put the notepad down when the process reached a point of diminishing returns.
For the first time in hours I really wanted a drink. I was anxious and edgy and wanted to change it.
I stayed where I was. I could indeed use the money and detecting was what I did. It was as much of a profession as I had. But I had a deeper motive.
Searching for Kim's killer was something I could do instead of drinking.
For a while, anyway.
The next morning I walked over to the Galaxy Downtowner. The clerk who checked in Charles Owen Jones wasn't on duty. I'd read his interrogation report and didn't expect I could get more out of him than the cop did.

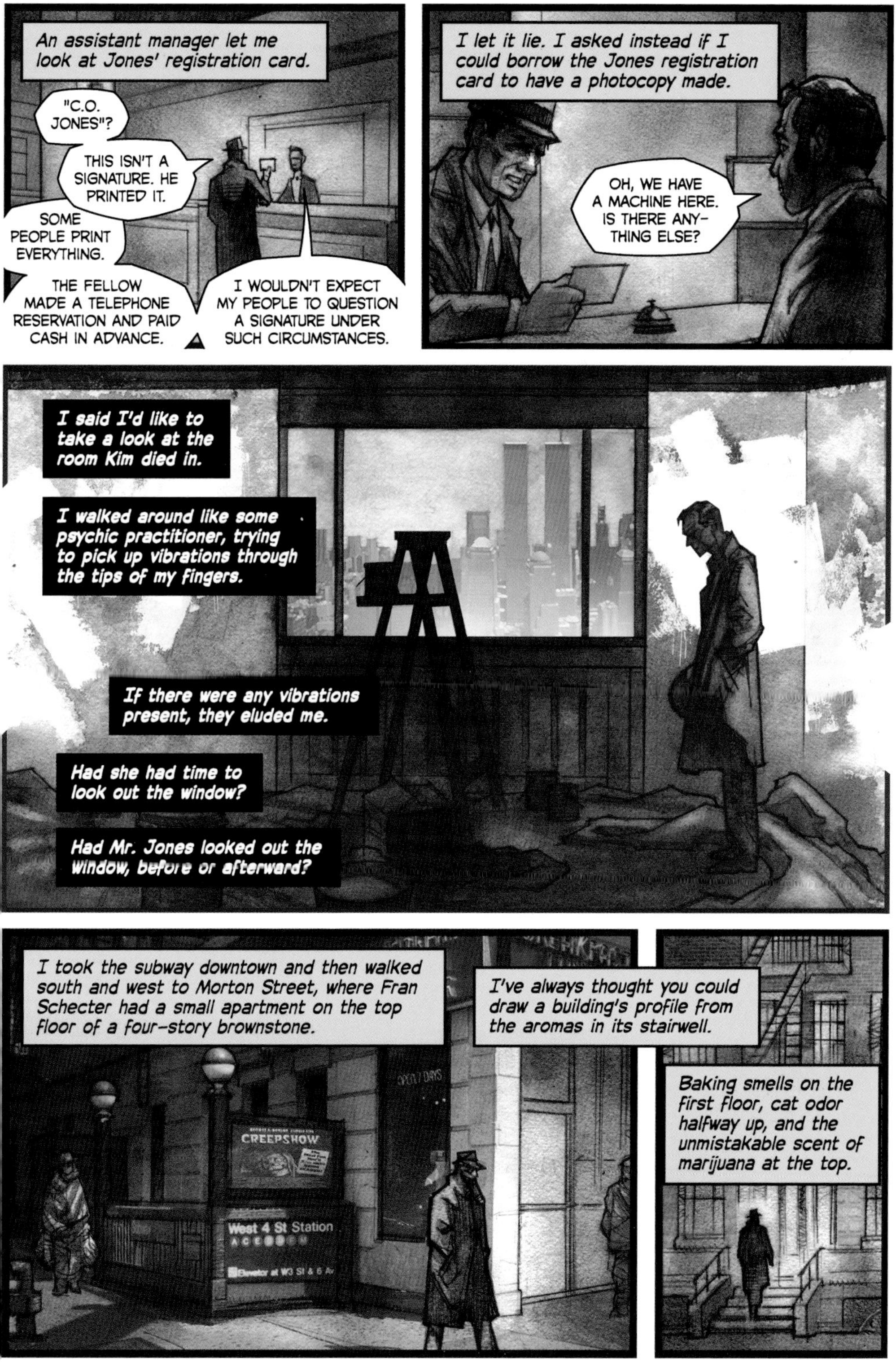

An assistant manager let me look at Jones' registration card.
"C.O. JONES"?
THIS ISN'T A SIGNATURE. HE PRINTED IT.
SOME PEOPLE PRINT EVERYTHING.
THE FELLOW MADE A TELEPHONE RESERVATION AND PAID CASH IN ADVANCE.
I WOULDN'T EXPECT MY PEOPLE TO QUESTION A SIGNATURE UNDER SUCH CIRCUMSTANCES.
I let it lie. I asked instead if I could borrow the Jones registration card to have a photocopy made.
OH, WE HAVE A MACHINE HERE. IS THERE ANYTHING ELSE?
I said I'd like to take a look at the room Kim died in.
I walked around like some psychic practitioner, trying to pick up vibrations through the tips of my fingers.
If there were any vibrations present, they eluded me.
Had she had time to look out the window?
Had Mr. Jones looked out the window, before or afterward?
I took the subway downtown and then walked south and west to Morton Street, where Fran Schecter had a small apartment on the top floor of a four-story brownstone.
CREEPSHOW
West 4 St Station
Elevator at W3 St & 6 Av
I've always thought you could draw a building's profile from the aromas in its stairwell.
Baking smells on the first floor, cat odor halfway up, and the unmistakable scent of marijuana at the top.

"I MET KIM A FEW TIMES. SOMETIMES CHANCE'LL TAKE TWO GIRLS AT ONCE OUT TO DINNER OR A SHOW. I GUESS I MET EVERYONE AT ONE TIME OR ANOTHER.

"MATT, I DON'T WANT TO HASSLE YOU, BUT COULD I TELL SOMEBODY IT WOULD BE COOL TO COME OVER IN AN HOUR?"

"NO PROBLEM."

"HE'S A REAL NICE GUY. THEY THINK THEY'RE FRIENDS OF MINE. I'M NOT A HOOKER. I'M A GIRLFRIEND. THEY GIVE ME MONEY BECAUSE I GOT RENT TO PAY, AND I'M A POOR LITTLE VILLAGE CHICK WHO WANTS TO MAKE IT AS AN ACTRESS. I HAVEN'T BOUGHT GRASS IN AGES. YOU KNOW WHO GETS THE BEST GRASS? WALL STREET GUYS. I KIND OF LIKE TO SMOKE."

"I GUESSED THAT."

"DO YOU EVER SMOKE, MATT?"

"NO."

"YOU DON'T SMOKE AND YOU DON'T DRINK, THAT'S TERRIFIC. CAN I GET YOU ANOTHER DIET SODA?"

"NO. DO YOU THINK KIM HAD A BOYFRIEND? SOMEONE SPECIAL?"

"SURE, I CAN DIG IT. SOMEBODY WHO WASN'T A JOHN, AND THAT'S WHY SHE WANTED TO SPLIT WITH CHANCE. THAT WHAT YOU MEAN? AND THEN HE KILLED HER."

"CHANCE?"

"ARE YOU CRAZY? NO. THE BOYFRIEND FROM SCARSDALE. 'CAUSE HE'S ON THE SPOT. IT'S KICKY BEING IN LOVE WITH A HOOKER AND HAVING HER IN LOVE WITH YOU, BUT YOU DON'T WANT ANYONE TURNING YOUR LIFE AROUND. KIM SAYS, HEY, I'M FREE NOW, TIME TO DITCH YOUR WIFE AND KIDS AND WE'LL RUN INTO THE SUNSET, AND THE SUNSET'S SOMETHING HE WATCHES FROM THE TERRACE AT THE COUNTRY CLUB AND HE WANTS TO KEEP IT THAT WAY. NEXT THING YOU KNOW, ZIP, SHE'S DEAD AND HE'S BACK IN LARCHMONT."

"IT WAS SCARSDALE A MINUTE AGO."

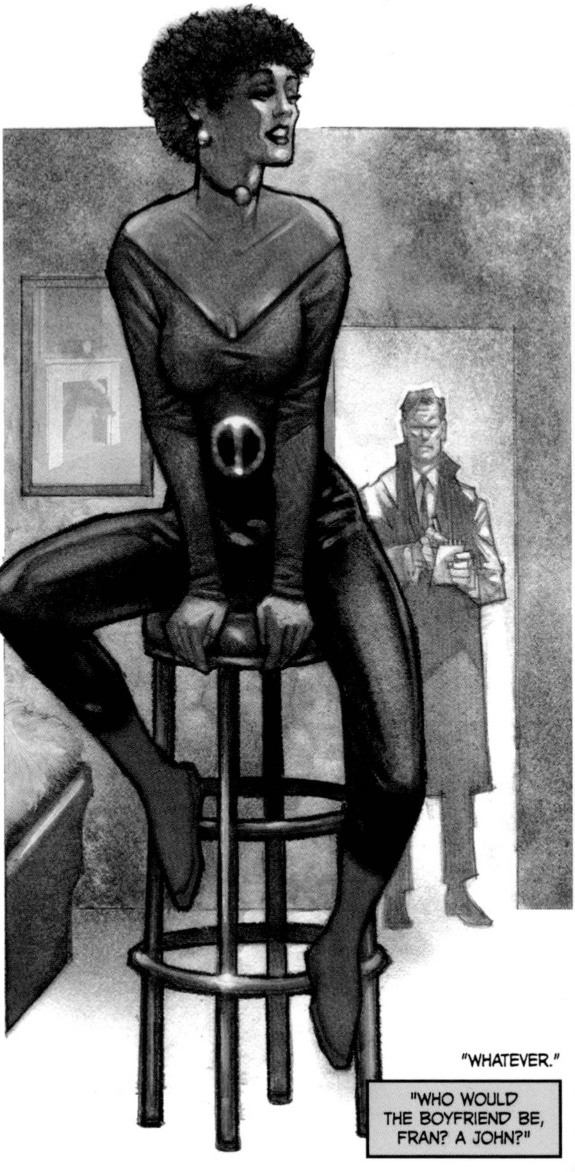
"WHATEVER."
"WHO WOULD THE BOYFRIEND BE, FRAN? A JOHN?"

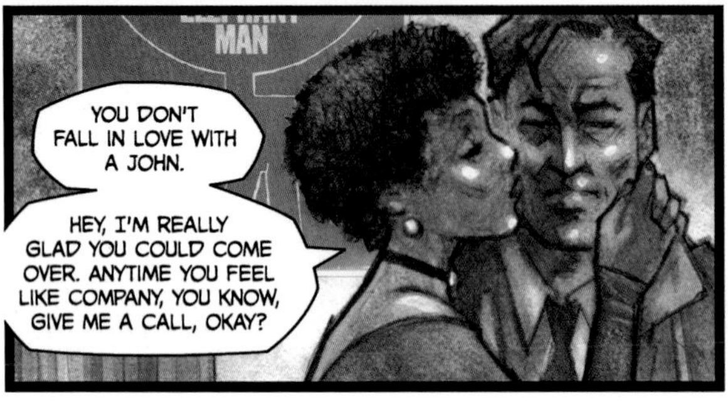
MAN
YOU DON'T FALL IN LOVE WITH A JOHN.
HEY, I'M REALLY GLAD YOU COULD COME OVER. ANYTIME YOU FEEL LIKE COMPANY, YOU KNOW, GIVE ME A CALL, OKAY?

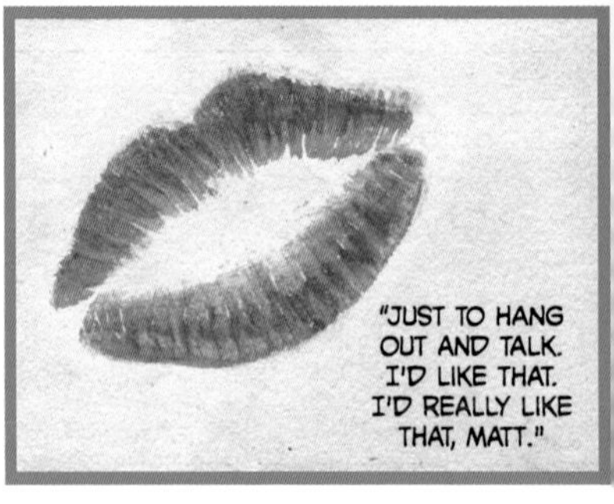
"JUST TO HANG OUT AND TALK. I'D LIKE THAT. I'D REALLY LIKE THAT, MATT."

Next stop: Donna Campion's apartment on East Seventeenth Street.

"YOU'RE TRYING TO FIND OUT WHO KILLED THE DAIRY QUEEN."

"THE DAIRY QUEEN?"

"SHE LOOKED LIKE A BEAUTY QUEEN, AND THEN I LEARNED SHE WAS FROM WISCONSIN, AND I THOUGHT OF ALL THAT ROBUST MILK-FED INNOCENCE. SHE WAS A SORT OF REGAL MILKMAID.

"THAT'S MY IMAGINATION TALKING. I REALLY DIDN'T KNOW HER."

"DID YOU EVER MEET HER BOYFRIEND?"

"I DIDN'T KNOW SHE HAD ONE."

"HOW LONG HAVE YOU BEEN WITH CHANCE?"

"GOING ON THREE YEARS.

"I HAVE EVERYTHING I WANT. ALL I EVER WANTED WAS TO BE LEFT ALONE, TO HAVE A DECENT PLACE TO LIVE AND TIME TO DO MY WORK. I'M TALKING ABOUT MY POETRY."

"CHANCE TAKES ALL THE MONEY YOU EARN. DOESN'T THAT BOTHER YOU?"

IT'S NOT REAL MONEY ANYWAY. FAST MONEY DOESN'T LAST. IF IT DID, ALL THE DRUG DEALERS WOULD RUN THE STOCK EXCHANGE.

I JUST WANTED TO MAKE POEMS.

WHAT DID KIM WANT TO DO?

"GOD KNOWS."

I THINK SHE WAS INVOLVED WITH SOMEBODY. I THINK THAT'S WHAT GOT HER KILLED.

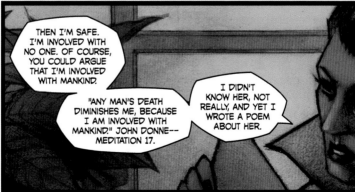

THEN I'M SAFE. I'M INVOLVED WITH NO ONE. OF COURSE, YOU COULD ARGUE THAT I'M INVOLVED WITH MANKIND.

"ANY MAN'S DEATH DIMINISHES ME, BECAUSE I AM INVOLVED WITH MANKIND." JOHN DONNE-- MEDITATION 17.

I DIDN'T KNOW HER, NOT REALLY, AND YET I WROTE A POEM ABOUT HER.

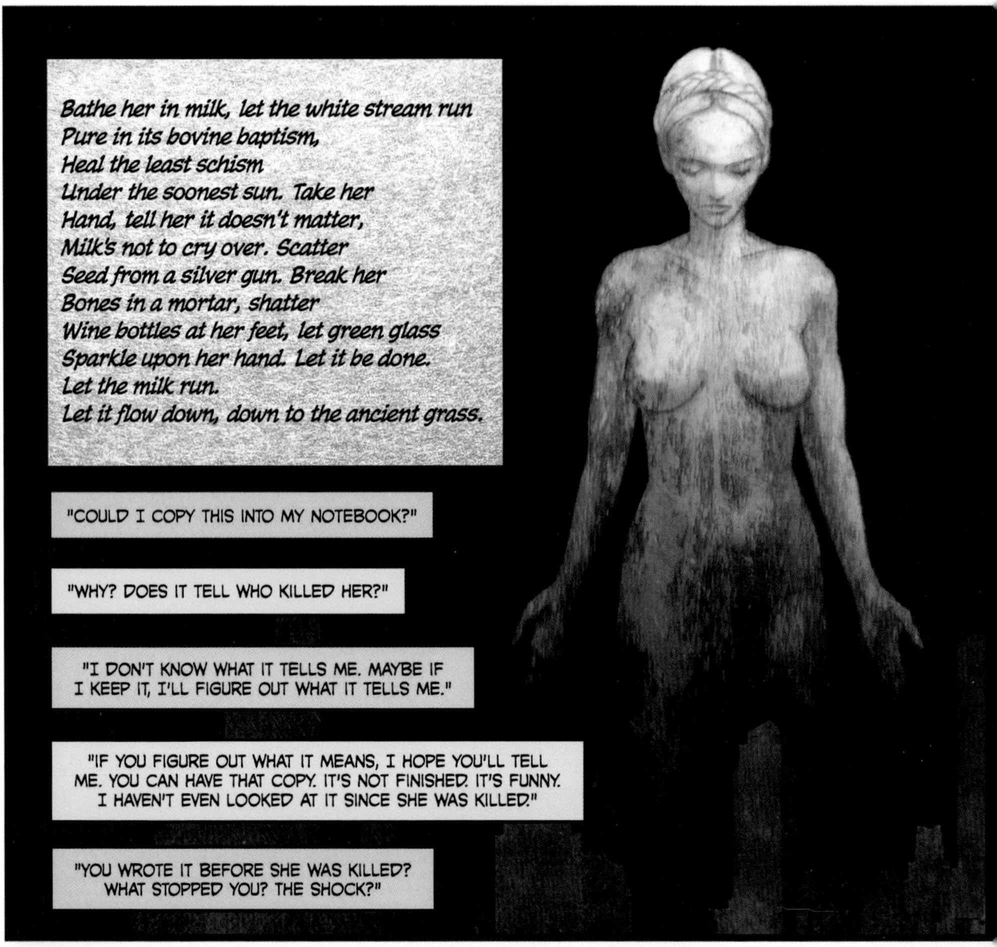
*Bathe her in milk, let the white stream run
Pure in its bovine baptism,
Heal the least schism
Under the soonest sun. Take her
Hand, tell her it doesn't matter,
Milk's not to cry over. Scatter
Seed from a silver gun. Break her
Bones in a mortar, shatter
Wine bottles at her feet, let green glass
Sparkle upon her hand. Let it be done.
Let the milk run.
Let it flow down, down to the ancient grass.*
"COULD I COPY THIS INTO MY NOTEBOOK?"
"WHY? DOES IT TELL WHO KILLED HER?"
"I DON'T KNOW WHAT IT TELLS ME. MAYBE IF I KEEP IT, I'LL FIGURE OUT WHAT IT TELLS ME."
"IF YOU FIGURE OUT WHAT IT MEANS, I HOPE YOU'LL TELL ME. YOU CAN HAVE THAT COPY. IT'S NOT FINISHED. IT'S FUNNY. I HAVEN'T EVEN LOOKED AT IT SINCE SHE WAS KILLED."
"YOU WROTE IT BEFORE SHE WAS KILLED? WHAT STOPPED YOU? THE SHOCK?"

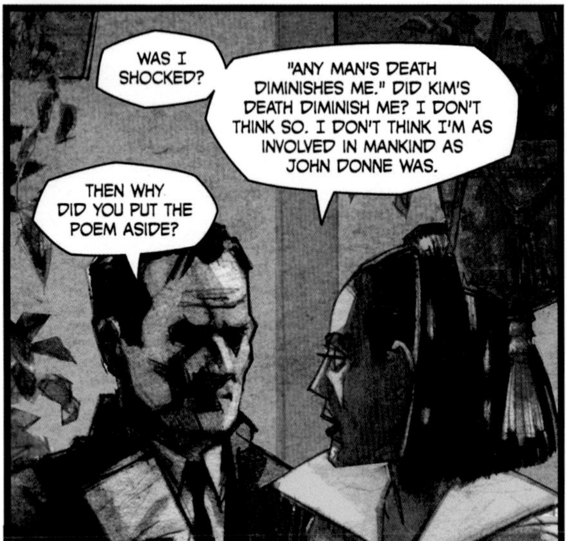
WAS I SHOCKED?
"ANY MAN'S DEATH DIMINISHES ME." DID KIM'S DEATH DIMINISH ME? I DON'T THINK SO. I DON'T THINK I'M AS INVOLVED IN MANKIND AS JOHN DONNE WAS.
THEN WHY DID YOU PUT THE POEM ASIDE?

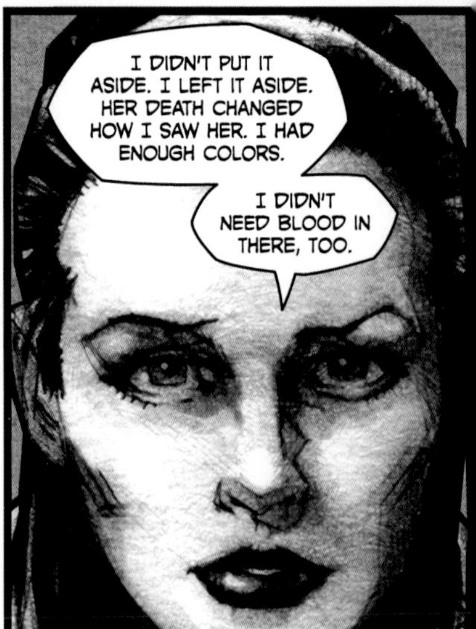
I DIDN'T PUT IT ASIDE. I LEFT IT ASIDE. HER DEATH CHANGED HOW I SAW HER. I HAD ENOUGH COLORS.
I DIDN'T NEED BLOOD IN THERE, TOO.

I took a cab to Kim's building on Thirty-Seventh. As I paid the driver I realized I hadn't made it to the bank. Tomorrow was Saturday, so I'd have Chance's money all weekend.

I lightened the load some by slipping five bucks to the doorman for a key to Kim's apartment.

I spent over an hour there.

Who would get all of this?

Would her parents fly in from Wisconsin and take possession of the fur jacket, the high school ring, the ivory bracelet?

Kim's kitten.

I'd seen no traces of the animal, no litter pan in the bathroom. Someone must've taken it.

When I got back to my hotel, I found Kim's key with my pocket change. I hadn't remembered to return it to the doorman, and he hadn't thought to ask me for it.

HEY, MATT. IT'S DURKIN. I HOPE I DIDN'T GET OUT OF LINE THERE LAST NIGHT.

ONCE IN A WHILE, THE WHOLE BUSINESS GETS TO ME, YOU KNOW WHAT I MEAN? MOST OF THE TIME I LOVE THE JOB, BUT EVERY NOW AND THEN I HAVE TO GET ALL OF THAT SHIT OUT OF MY SYSTEM.

SURE. FORGET IT.

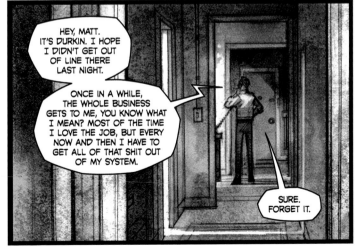

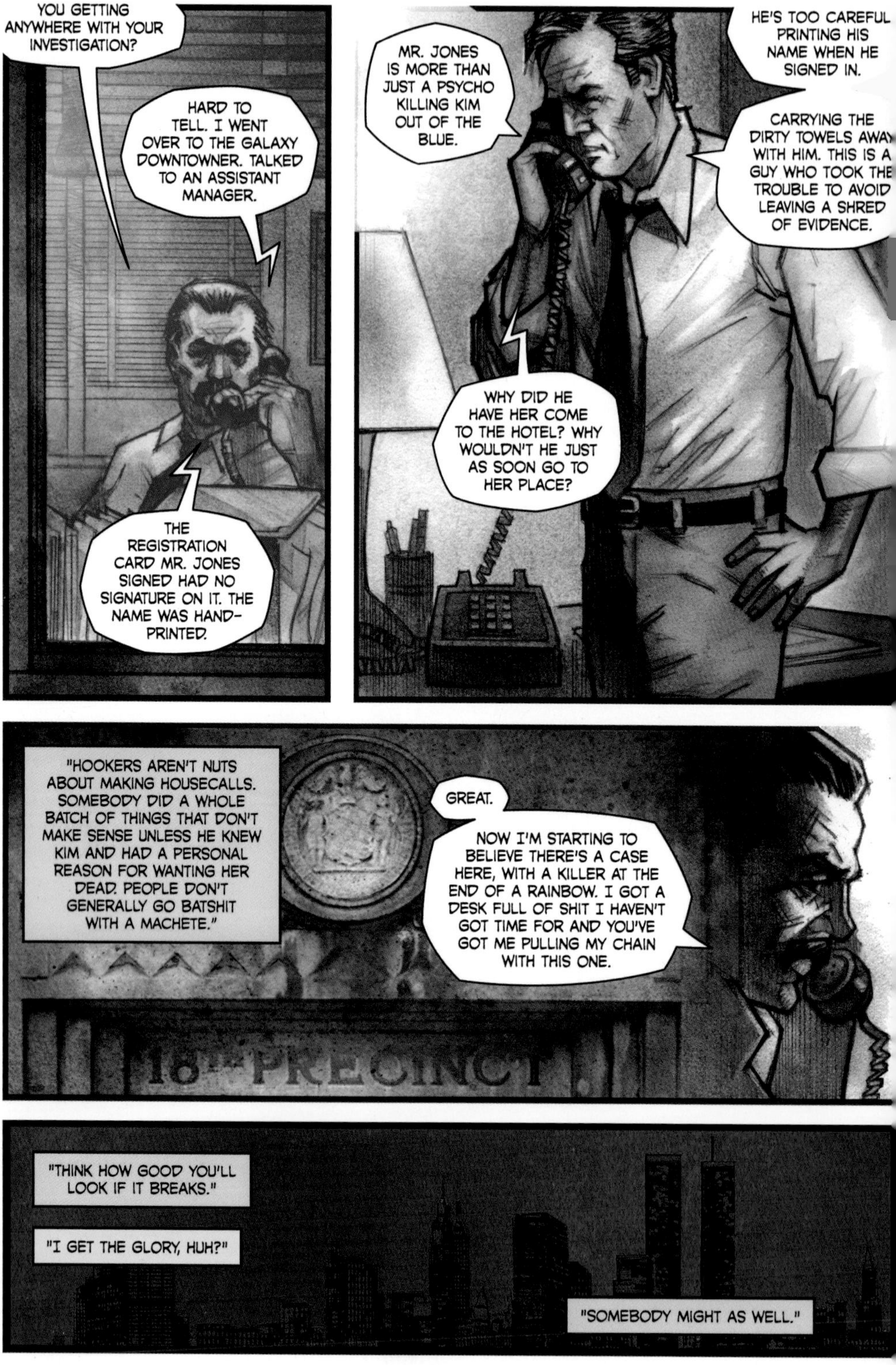
YOU GETTING ANYWHERE WITH YOUR INVESTIGATION?
HARD TO TELL. I WENT OVER TO THE GALAXY DOWNTOWNER. TALKED TO AN ASSISTANT MANAGER.
THE REGISTRATION CARD MR. JONES SIGNED HAD NO SIGNATURE ON IT. THE NAME WAS HAND-PRINTED.
MR. JONES IS MORE THAN JUST A PSYCHO KILLING KIM OUT OF THE BLUE.
HE'S TOO CAREFUL PRINTING HIS NAME WHEN HE SIGNED IN.
CARRYING THE DIRTY TOWELS AWAY WITH HIM. THIS IS A GUY WHO TOOK THE TROUBLE TO AVOID LEAVING A SHRED OF EVIDENCE.
WHY DID HE HAVE HER COME TO THE HOTEL? WHY WOULDN'T HE JUST AS SOON GO TO HER PLACE?
"HOOKERS AREN'T NUTS ABOUT MAKING HOUSECALLS. SOMEBODY DID A WHOLE BATCH OF THINGS THAT DON'T MAKE SENSE UNLESS HE KNEW KIM AND HAD A PERSONAL REASON FOR WANTING HER DEAD. PEOPLE DON'T GENERALLY GO BATSHIT WITH A MACHETE."
GREAT.
NOW I'M STARTING TO BELIEVE THERE'S A CASE HERE, WITH A KILLER AT THE END OF A RAINBOW. I GOT A DESK FULL OF SHIT I HAVEN'T GOT TIME FOR AND YOU'VE GOT ME PULLING MY CHAIN WITH THIS ONE.
18TH PRECINCT
"THINK HOW GOOD YOU'LL LOOK IF IT BREAKS."
"I GET THE GLORY, HUH?"
"SOMEBODY MIGHT AS WELL."

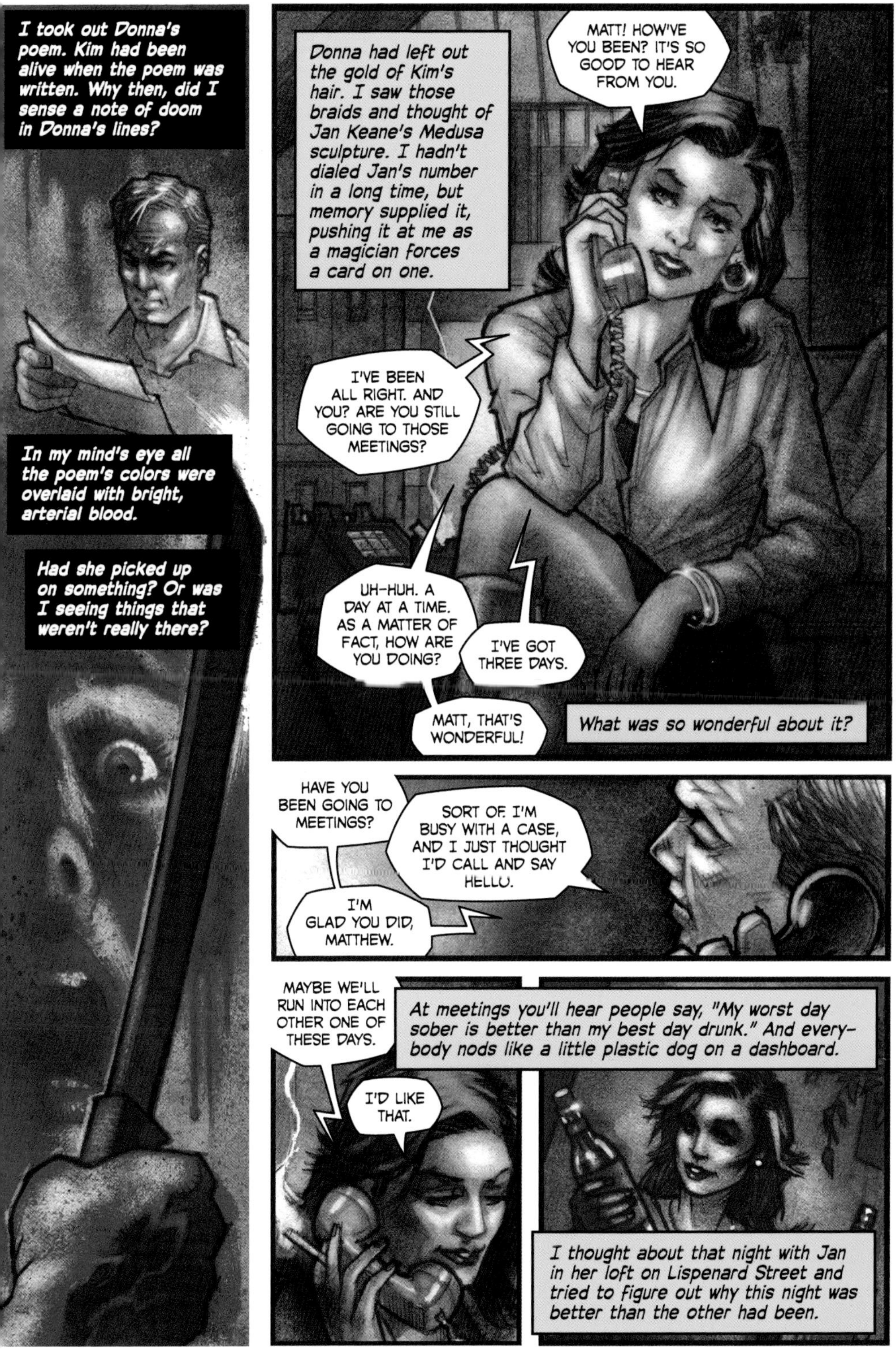
I took out Donna's poem. Kim had been alive when the poem was written. Why then, did I sense a note of doom in Donna's lines?
In my mind's eye all the poem's colors were overlaid with bright, arterial blood.
Had she picked up on something? Or was I seeing things that weren't really there?
Donna had left out the gold of Kim's hair. I saw those braids and thought of Jan Keane's Medusa sculpture. I hadn't dialed Jan's number in a long time, but memory supplied it, pushing it at me as a magician forces a card on one.
MATT! HOW'VE YOU BEEN? IT'S SO GOOD TO HEAR FROM YOU.
I'VE BEEN ALL RIGHT. AND YOU? ARE YOU STILL GOING TO THOSE MEETINGS?
UH-HUH. A DAY AT A TIME. AS A MATTER OF FACT, HOW ARE YOU DOING?
I'VE GOT THREE DAYS.
MATT, THAT'S WONDERFUL!
What was so wonderful about it?
HAVE YOU BEEN GOING TO MEETINGS?
SORT OF. I'M BUSY WITH A CASE, AND I JUST THOUGHT I'D CALL AND SAY HELLO.
I'M GLAD YOU DID, MATTHEW.
MAYBE WE'LL RUN INTO EACH OTHER ONE OF THESE DAYS.
I'D LIKE THAT.
At meetings you'll hear people say, "My worst day sober is better than my best day drunk." And everybody nods like a little plastic dog on a dashboard.
I thought about that night with Jan in her loft on Lispenard Street and tried to figure out why this night was better than the other had been.

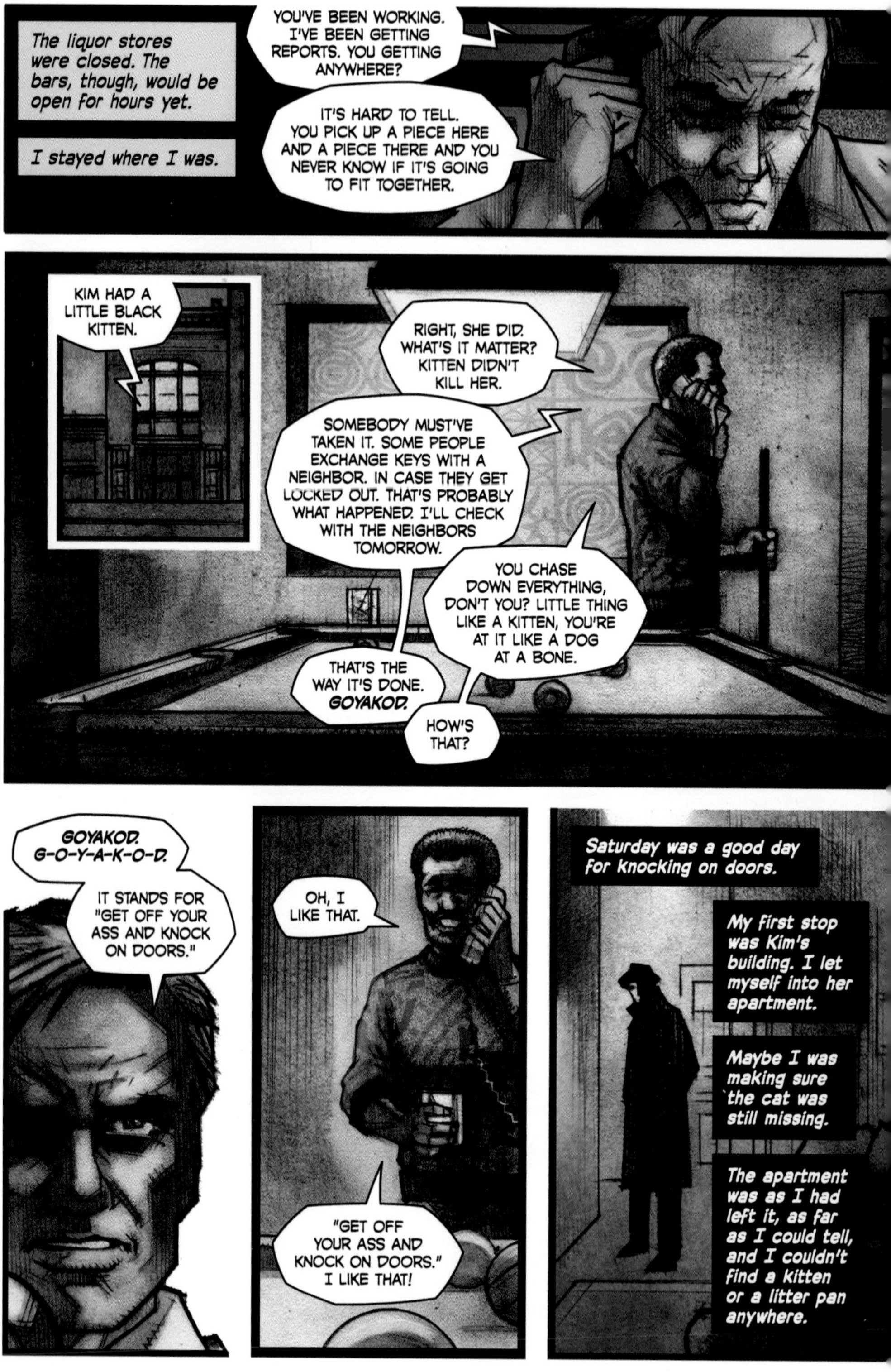

The liquor stores were closed. The bars, though, would be open for hours yet.
I stayed where I was.
YOU'VE BEEN WORKING. I'VE BEEN GETTING REPORTS. YOU GETTING ANYWHERE?
IT'S HARD TO TELL. YOU PICK UP A PIECE HERE AND A PIECE THERE AND YOU NEVER KNOW IF IT'S GOING TO FIT TOGETHER.
KIM HAD A LITTLE BLACK KITTEN.
RIGHT, SHE DID. WHAT'S IT MATTER? KITTEN DIDN'T KILL HER.
SOMEBODY MUST'VE TAKEN IT. SOME PEOPLE EXCHANGE KEYS WITH A NEIGHBOR. IN CASE THEY GET LOCKED OUT. THAT'S PROBABLY WHAT HAPPENED. I'LL CHECK WITH THE NEIGHBORS TOMORROW.
YOU CHASE DOWN EVERYTHING, DON'T YOU? LITTLE THING LIKE A KITTEN, YOU'RE AT IT LIKE A DOG AT A BONE.
THAT'S THE WAY IT'S DONE. ***GOYAKOD.***
HOW'S THAT?
GOYAKOD. G-O-Y-A-K-O-D.
IT STANDS FOR "GET OFF YOUR ASS AND KNOCK ON DOORS."
OH, I LIKE THAT.
"GET OFF YOUR ASS AND KNOCK ON DOORS." I LIKE THAT!
Saturday was a good day for knocking on doors.
My first stop was Kim's building. I let myself into her apartment.
Maybe I was making sure the cat was still missing.
The apartment was as I had left it, as far as I could tell, and I couldn't find a kitten or a litter pan anywhere.

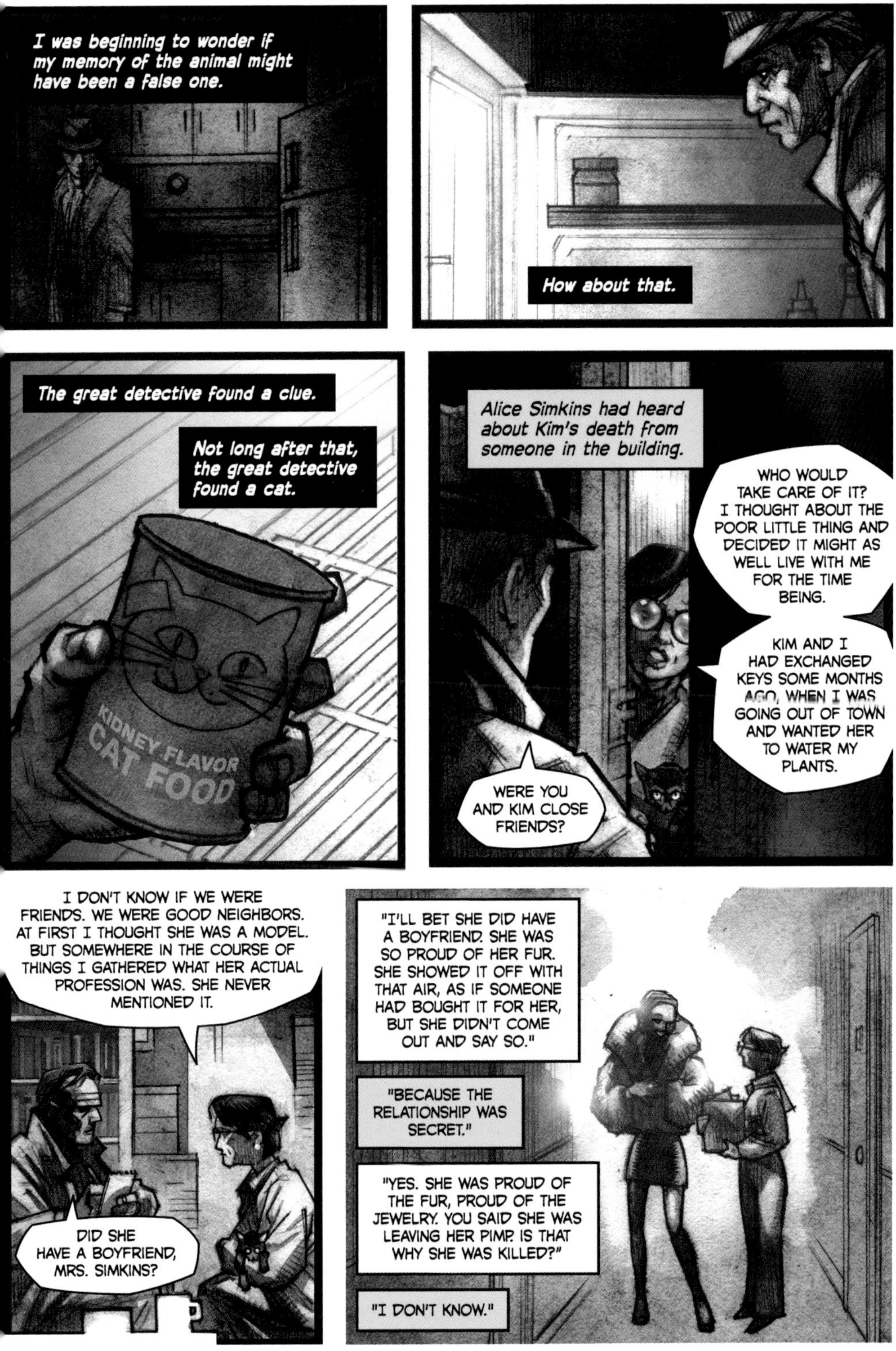
I was beginning to wonder if my memory of the animal might have been a false one.
How about that.
The great detective found a clue.
Not long after that, the great detective found a cat.
KIDNEY FLAVOR CAT FOOD
Alice Simkins had heard about Kim's death from someone in the building.
WHO WOULD TAKE CARE OF IT? I THOUGHT ABOUT THE POOR LITTLE THING AND DECIDED IT MIGHT AS WELL LIVE WITH ME FOR THE TIME BEING.
WERE YOU AND KIM CLOSE FRIENDS?
KIM AND I HAD EXCHANGED KEYS SOME MONTHS AGO, WHEN I WAS GOING OUT OF TOWN AND WANTED HER TO WATER MY PLANTS.
I DON'T KNOW IF WE WERE FRIENDS. WE WERE GOOD NEIGHBORS. AT FIRST I THOUGHT SHE WAS A MODEL. BUT SOMEWHERE IN THE COURSE OF THINGS I GATHERED WHAT HER ACTUAL PROFESSION WAS. SHE NEVER MENTIONED IT.
DID SHE HAVE A BOYFRIEND, MRS. SIMKINS?
"I'LL BET SHE DID HAVE A BOYFRIEND. SHE WAS SO PROUD OF HER FUR. SHE SHOWED IT OFF WITH THAT AIR, AS IF SOMEONE HAD BOUGHT IT FOR HER, BUT SHE DIDN'T COME OUT AND SAY SO."
"BECAUSE THE RELATIONSHIP WAS SECRET."
"YES. SHE WAS PROUD OF THE FUR, PROUD OF THE JEWELRY. YOU SAID SHE WAS LEAVING HER PIMP. IS THAT WHY SHE WAS KILLED?"
"I DON'T KNOW."

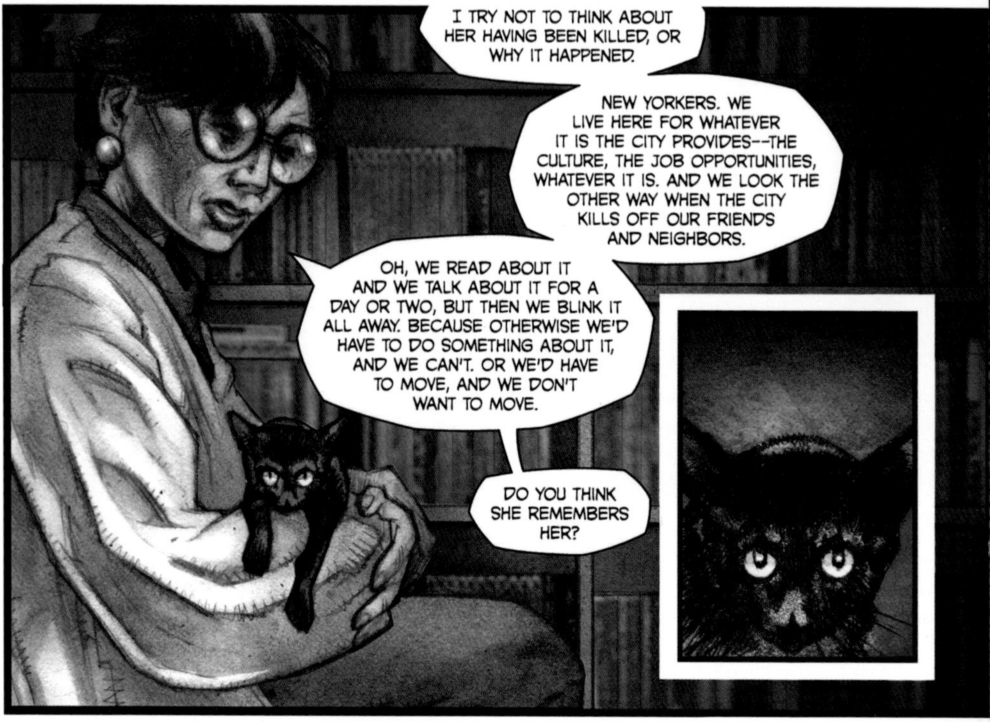

I TRY NOT TO THINK ABOUT HER HAVING BEEN KILLED, OR WHY IT HAPPENED.
NEW YORKERS. WE LIVE HERE FOR WHATEVER IT IS THE CITY PROVIDES--THE CULTURE, THE JOB OPPORTUNITIES, WHATEVER IT IS. AND WE LOOK THE OTHER WAY WHEN THE CITY KILLS OFF OUR FRIENDS AND NEIGHBORS.
OH, WE READ ABOUT IT AND WE TALK ABOUT IT FOR A DAY OR TWO, BUT THEN WE BLINK IT ALL AWAY. BECAUSE OTHERWISE WE'D HAVE TO DO SOMETHING ABOUT IT, AND WE CAN'T. OR WE'D HAVE TO MOVE, AND WE DON'T WANT TO MOVE.
DO YOU THINK SHE REMEMBERS HER?

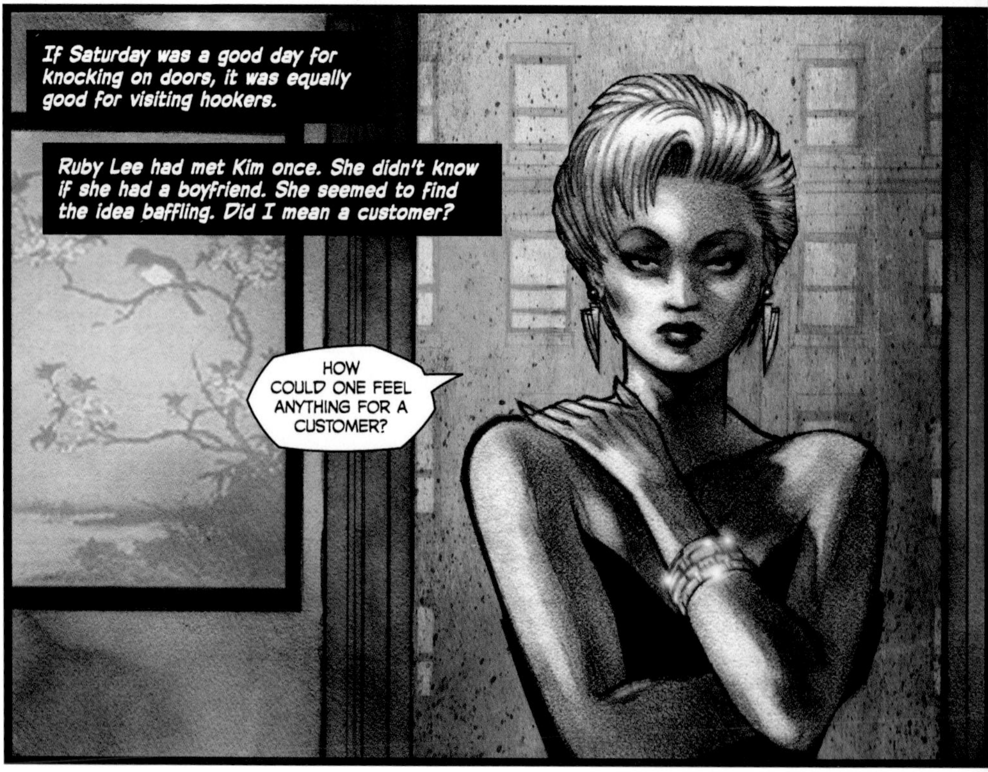

If Saturday was a good day for knocking on doors, it was equally good for visiting hookers.
Ruby Lee had met Kim once. She didn't know if she had a boyfriend. She seemed to find the idea baffling. Did I mean a customer?
HOW COULD ONE FEEL ANYTHING FOR A CUSTOMER?

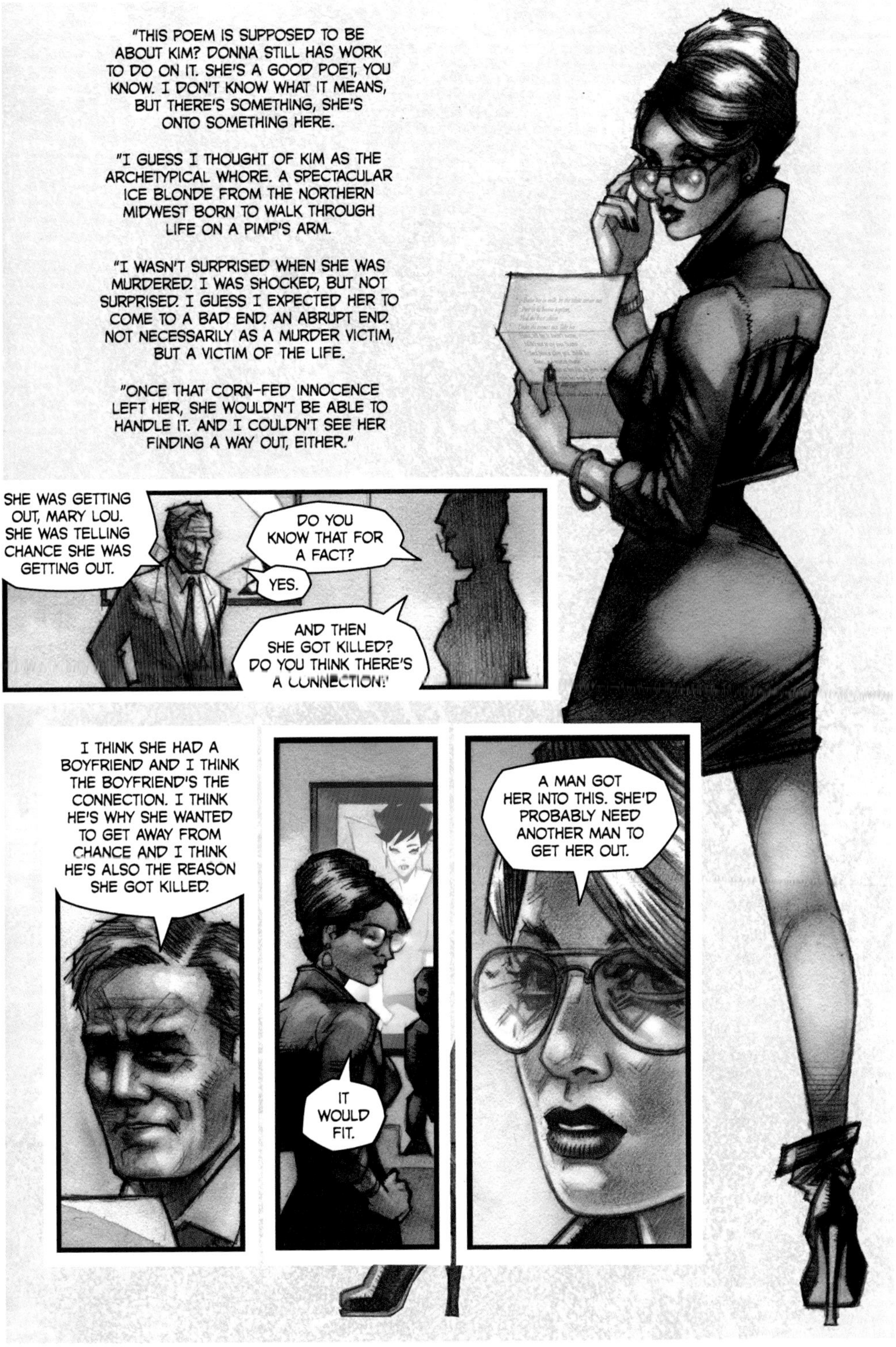
"THIS POEM IS SUPPOSED TO BE ABOUT KIM? DONNA STILL HAS WORK TO DO ON IT. SHE'S A GOOD POET, YOU KNOW. I DON'T KNOW WHAT IT MEANS, BUT THERE'S SOMETHING, SHE'S ONTO SOMETHING HERE.
"I GUESS I THOUGHT OF KIM AS THE ARCHETYPICAL WHORE. A SPECTACULAR ICE BLONDE FROM THE NORTHERN MIDWEST BORN TO WALK THROUGH LIFE ON A PIMP'S ARM.
"I WASN'T SURPRISED WHEN SHE WAS MURDERED. I WAS SHOCKED, BUT NOT SURPRISED. I GUESS I EXPECTED HER TO COME TO A BAD END. AN ABRUPT END. NOT NECESSARILY AS A MURDER VICTIM, BUT A VICTIM OF THE LIFE.
"ONCE THAT CORN-FED INNOCENCE LEFT HER, SHE WOULDN'T BE ABLE TO HANDLE IT. AND I COULDN'T SEE HER FINDING A WAY OUT, EITHER."
SHE WAS GETTING OUT, MARY LOU. SHE WAS TELLING CHANCE SHE WAS GETTING OUT.
DO YOU KNOW THAT FOR A FACT?
YES.
AND THEN SHE GOT KILLED? DO YOU THINK THERE'S A CONNECTION?
I THINK SHE HAD A BOYFRIEND AND I THINK THE BOYFRIEND'S THE CONNECTION. I THINK HE'S WHY SHE WANTED TO GET AWAY FROM CHANCE AND I THINK HE'S ALSO THE REASON SHE GOT KILLED.
IT WOULD FIT.
A MAN GOT HER INTO THIS. SHE'D PROBABLY NEED ANOTHER MAN TO GET HER OUT.

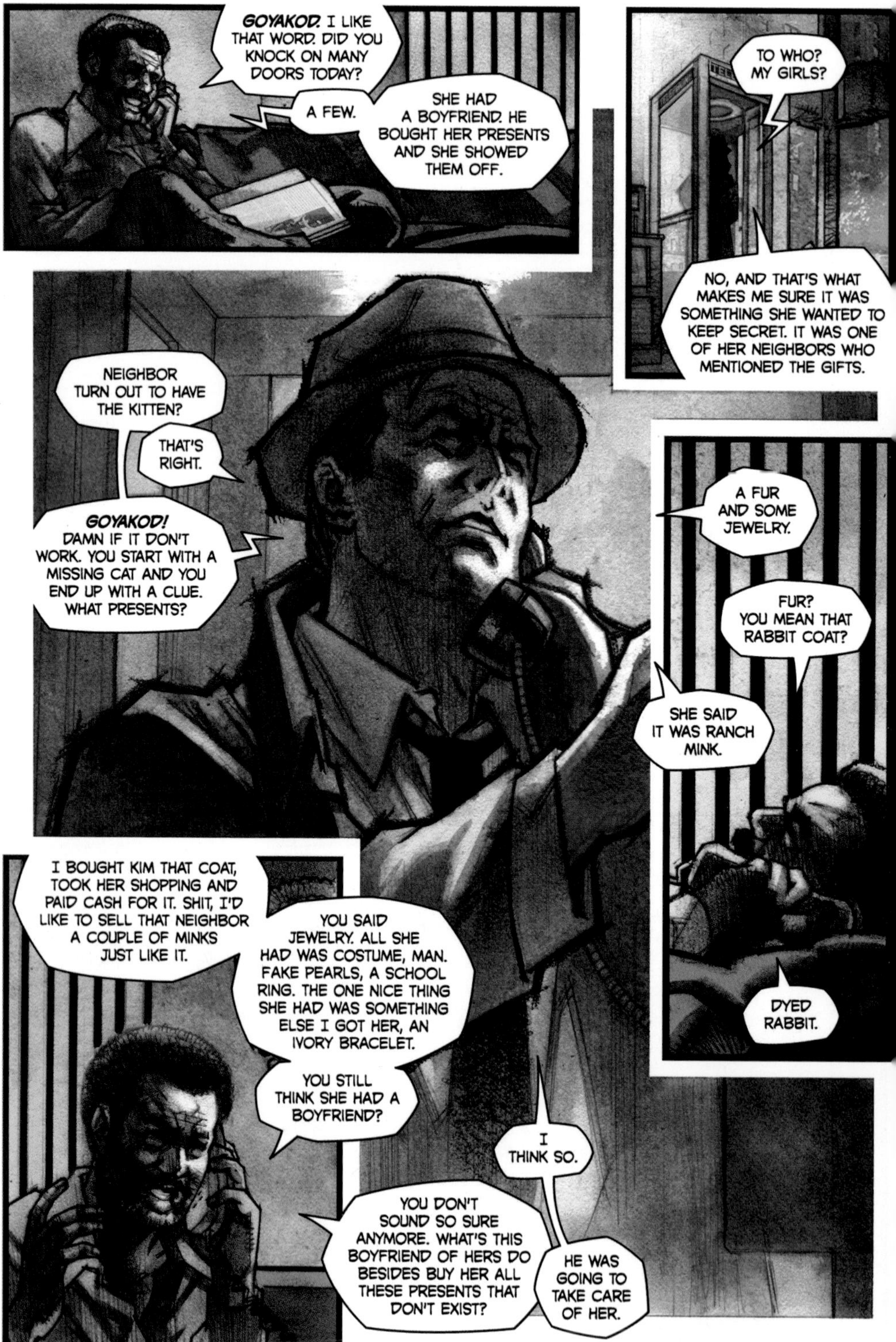
GOYAKOD. I LIKE THAT WORD. DID YOU KNOCK ON MANY DOORS TODAY?
A FEW.
SHE HAD A BOYFRIEND. HE BOUGHT HER PRESENTS AND SHE SHOWED THEM OFF.
TO WHO? MY GIRLS?
NO, AND THAT'S WHAT MAKES ME SURE IT WAS SOMETHING SHE WANTED TO KEEP SECRET. IT WAS ONE OF HER NEIGHBORS WHO MENTIONED THE GIFTS.
NEIGHBOR TURN OUT TO HAVE THE KITTEN?
THAT'S RIGHT.
GOYAKOD! DAMN IF IT DON'T WORK. YOU START WITH A MISSING CAT AND YOU END UP WITH A CLUE. WHAT PRESENTS?
A FUR AND SOME JEWELRY.
FUR? YOU MEAN THAT RABBIT COAT?
SHE SAID IT WAS RANCH MINK.
DYED RABBIT.
I BOUGHT KIM THAT COAT, TOOK HER SHOPPING AND PAID CASH FOR IT. SHIT, I'D LIKE TO SELL THAT NEIGHBOR A COUPLE OF MINKS JUST LIKE IT.
YOU SAID JEWELRY. ALL SHE HAD WAS COSTUME, MAN. FAKE PEARLS, A SCHOOL RING. THE ONE NICE THING SHE HAD WAS SOMETHING ELSE I GOT HER, AN IVORY BRACELET.
YOU STILL THINK SHE HAD A BOYFRIEND?
I THINK SO.
YOU DON'T SOUND SO SURE ANYMORE. WHAT'S THIS BOYFRIEND OF HERS DO BESIDES BUY HER ALL THESE PRESENTS THAT DON'T EXIST?
HE WAS GOING TO TAKE CARE OF HER.

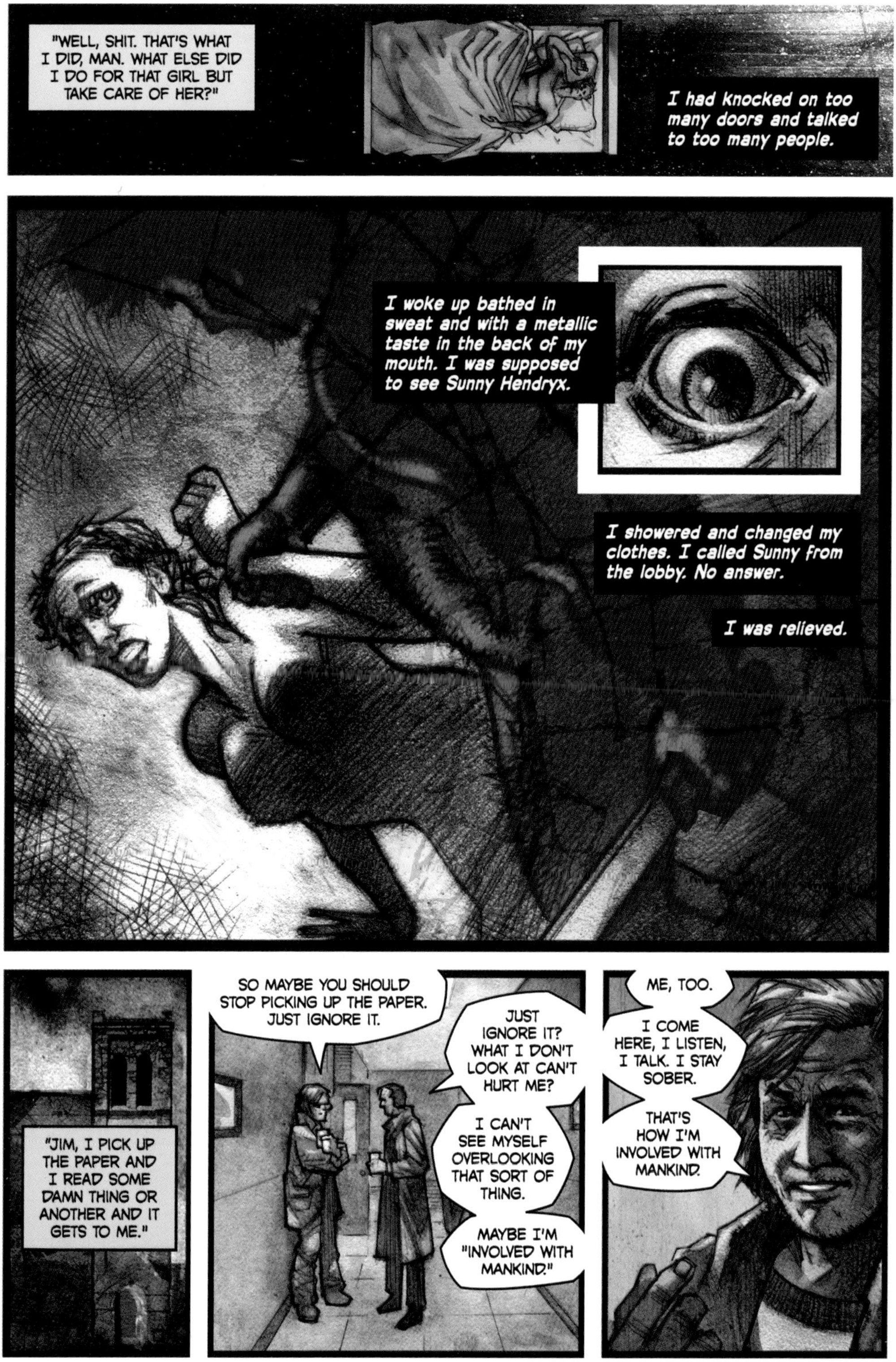
"WELL, SHIT. THAT'S WHAT I DID, MAN. WHAT ELSE DID I DO FOR THAT GIRL BUT TAKE CARE OF HER?"
I had knocked on too many doors and talked to too many people.
I woke up bathed in sweat and with a metallic taste in the back of my mouth. I was supposed to see Sunny Hendryx.
I showered and changed my clothes. I called Sunny from the lobby. No answer.
I was relieved.
"JIM, I PICK UP THE PAPER AND I READ SOME DAMN THING OR ANOTHER AND IT GETS TO ME."
SO MAYBE YOU SHOULD STOP PICKING UP THE PAPER. JUST IGNORE IT.
JUST IGNORE IT? WHAT I DON'T LOOK AT CAN'T HURT ME?
I CAN'T SEE MYSELF OVERLOOKING THAT SORT OF THING.
MAYBE I'M "INVOLVED WITH MANKIND."
ME, TOO.
I COME HERE, I LISTEN, I TALK. I STAY SOBER.
THAT'S HOW I'M INVOLVED WITH MANKIND.

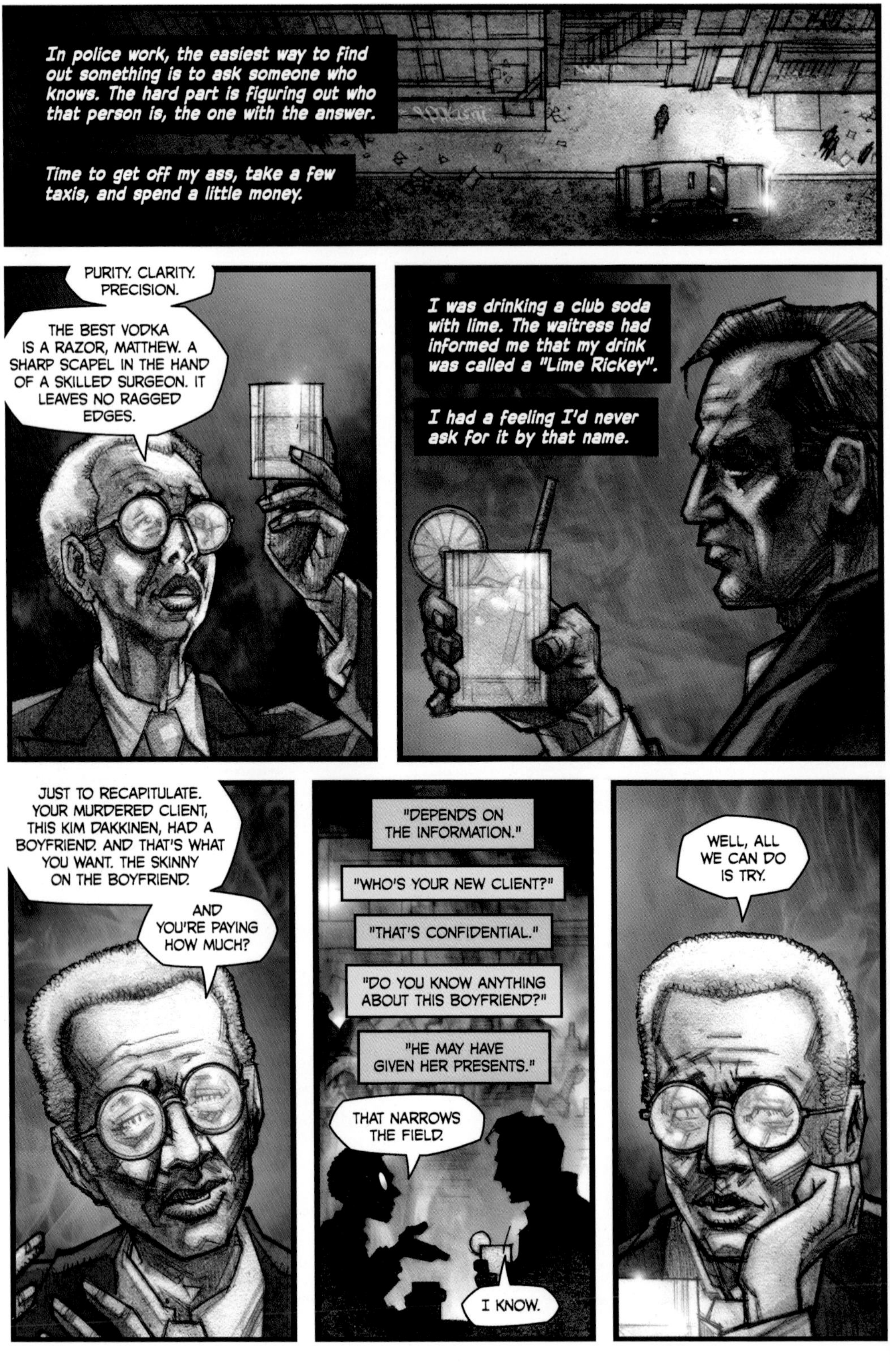
In police work, the easiest way to find out something is to ask someone who knows. The hard part is figuring out who that person is, the one with the answer.
Time to get off my ass, take a few taxis, and spend a little money.
PURITY. CLARITY. PRECISION.
THE BEST VODKA IS A RAZOR, MATTHEW. A SHARP SCAPEL IN THE HAND OF A SKILLED SURGEON. IT LEAVES NO RAGGED EDGES.
I was drinking a club soda with lime. The waitress had informed me that my drink was called a "Lime Rickey".
I had a feeling I'd never ask for it by that name.
JUST TO RECAPITULATE. YOUR MURDERED CLIENT, THIS KIM DAKKINEN, HAD A BOYFRIEND. AND THAT'S WHAT YOU WANT. THE SKINNY ON THE BOYFRIEND.
AND YOU'RE PAYING HOW MUCH?
"DEPENDS ON THE INFORMATION."
"WHO'S YOUR NEW CLIENT?"
"THAT'S CONFIDENTIAL."
"DO YOU KNOW ANYTHING ABOUT THIS BOYFRIEND?"
"HE MAY HAVE GIVEN HER PRESENTS."
THAT NARROWS THE FIELD.
I KNOW.
WELL, ALL WE CAN DO IS TRY.

And so I'd been doing that.

No one knew anything.

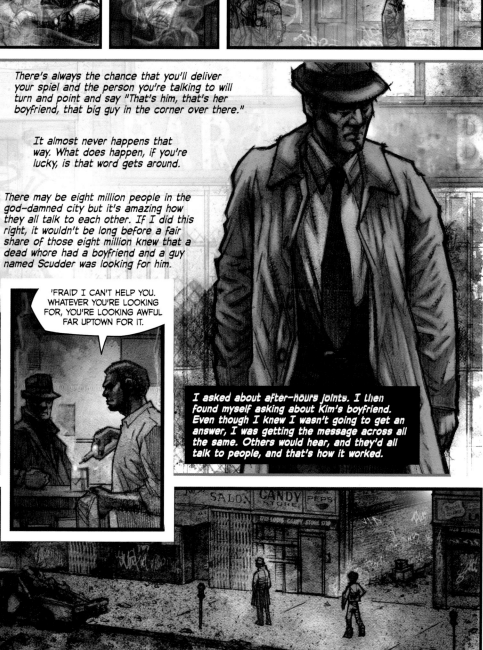

There's always the chance that you'll deliver your spiel and the person you're talking to will turn and point and say "That's him, that's her boyfriend, that big guy in the corner over there."

It almost never happens that way. What does happen, if you're lucky, is that word gets around.

There may be eight million people in the god-damned city but it's amazing how they all talk to each other. If I did this right, it wouldn't be long before a fair share of those eight million knew that a dead whore had a boyfriend and a guy named Scudder was looking for him.

'FRAID I CAN'T HELP YOU. WHATEVER YOU'RE LOOKING FOR, YOU'RE LOOKING AWFUL FAR UPTOWN FOR IT.

I asked about after-hours joints. I then found myself asking about Kim's boyfriend. Even though I knew I wasn't going to get an answer, I was getting the message across all the same. Others would hear, and they'd all talk to people, and that's how it worked.

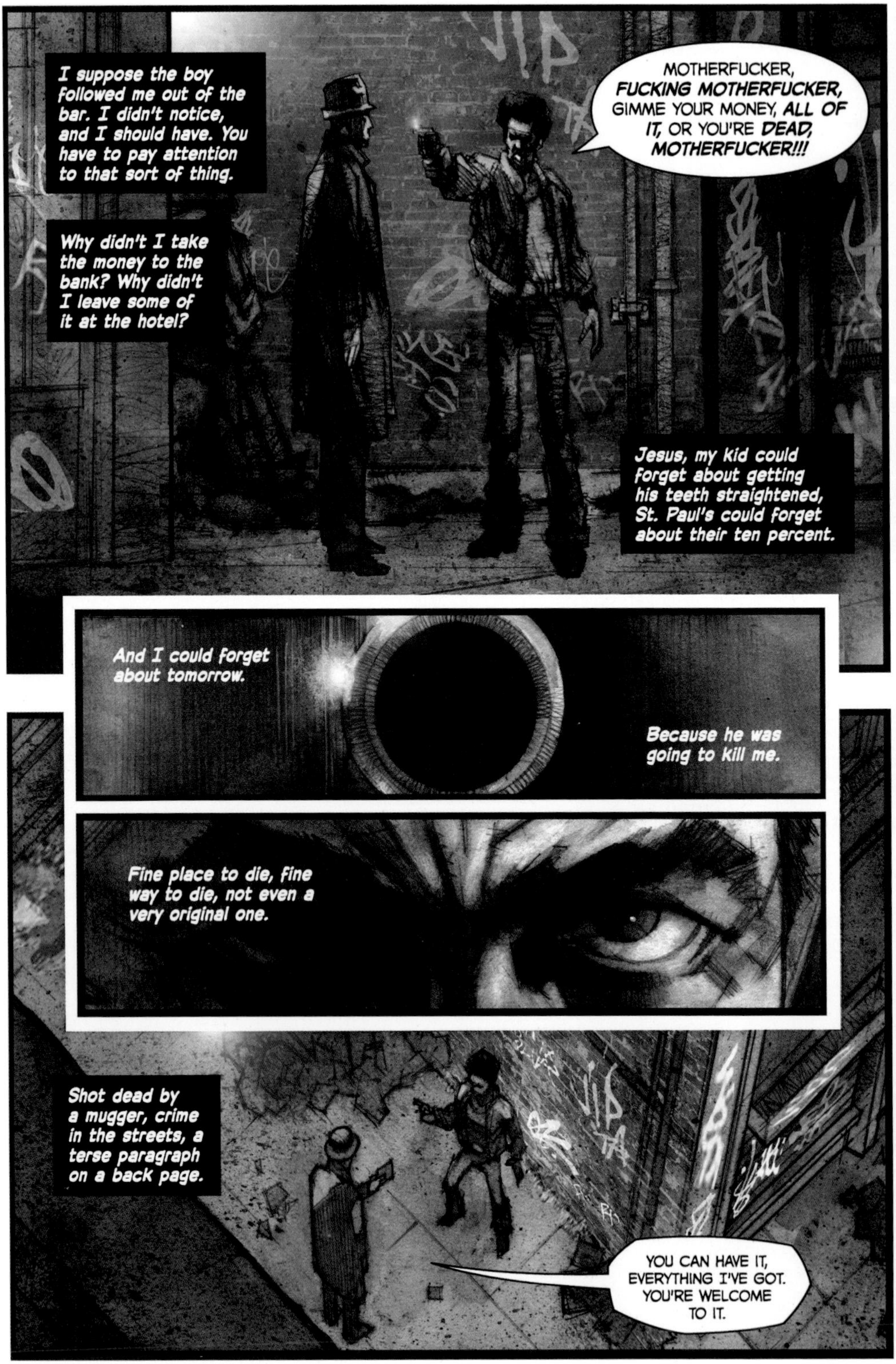
I suppose the boy followed me out of the bar. I didn't notice, and I should have. You have to pay attention to that sort of thing.
Why didn't I take the money to the bank? Why didn't I leave some of it at the hotel?
MOTHERFUCKER, FUCKING MOTHERFUCKER, GIMME YOUR MONEY, ALL OF IT, OR YOU'RE DEAD, MOTHERFUCKER!!!
Jesus, my kid could forget about getting his teeth straightened, St. Paul's could forget about their ten percent.
And I could forget about tomorrow.
Because he was going to kill me.
Fine place to die, fine way to die, not even a very original one.
Shot dead by a mugger, crime in the streets, a terse paragraph on a back page.
YOU CAN HAVE IT, EVERYTHING I'VE GOT. YOU'RE WELCOME TO IT.

I'M SORRY.

VERY SORRY, I'LL GET IT.

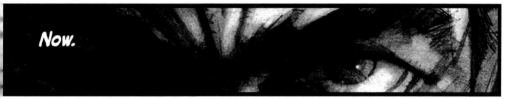

Now.

BLAM

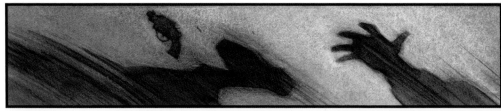

He came off the
wall, his eyes
full of murder.

I grabbed that
son-of-a-bitch...

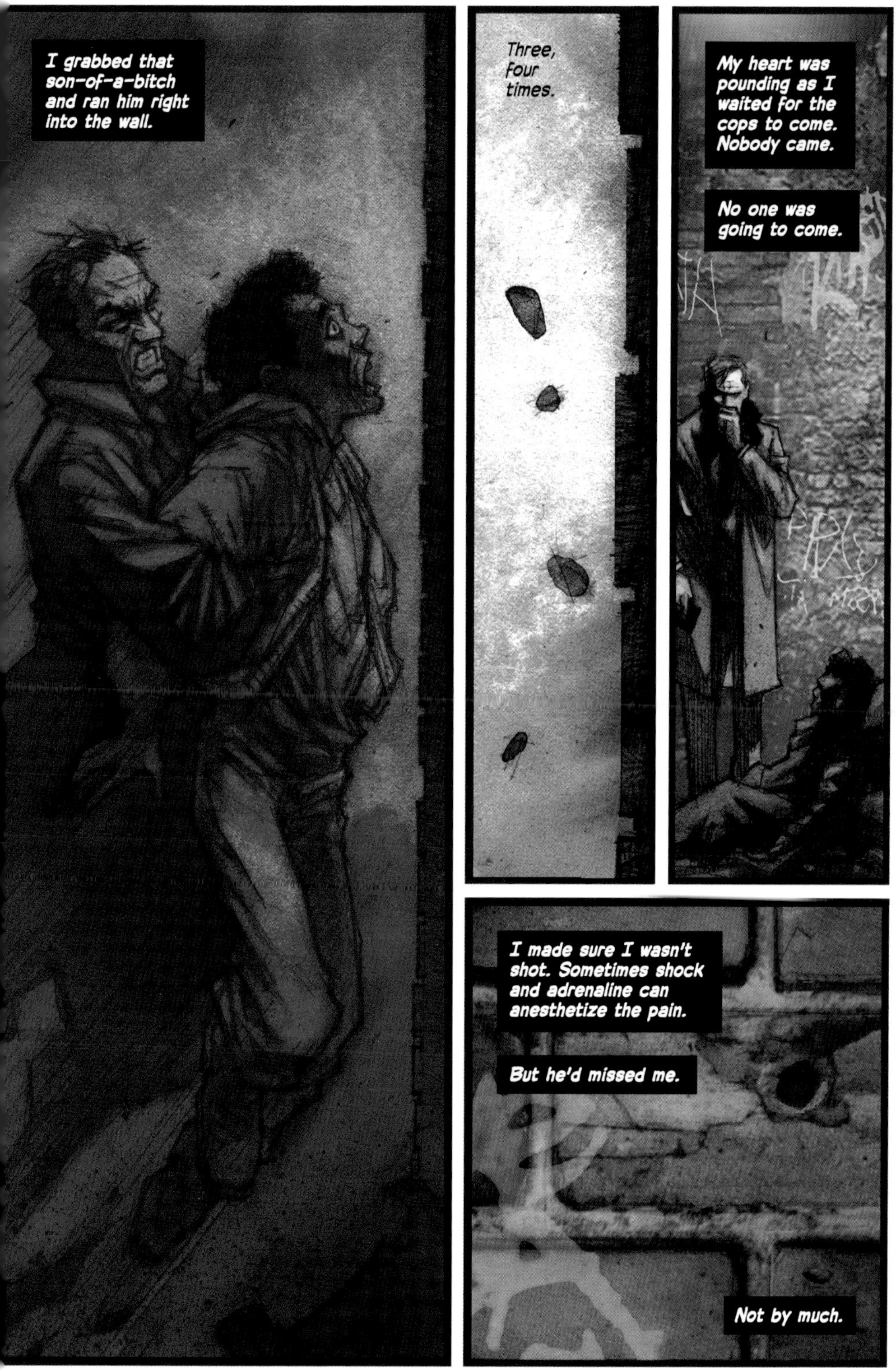
I grabbed that son-of-a-bitch and ran him right into the wall.
Three, Four times.
My heart was pounding as I waited for the cops to come. Nobody came.
No one was going to come.
I made sure I wasn't shot. Sometimes shock and adrenaline can anesthetize the pain.
But he'd missed me.
Not by much.

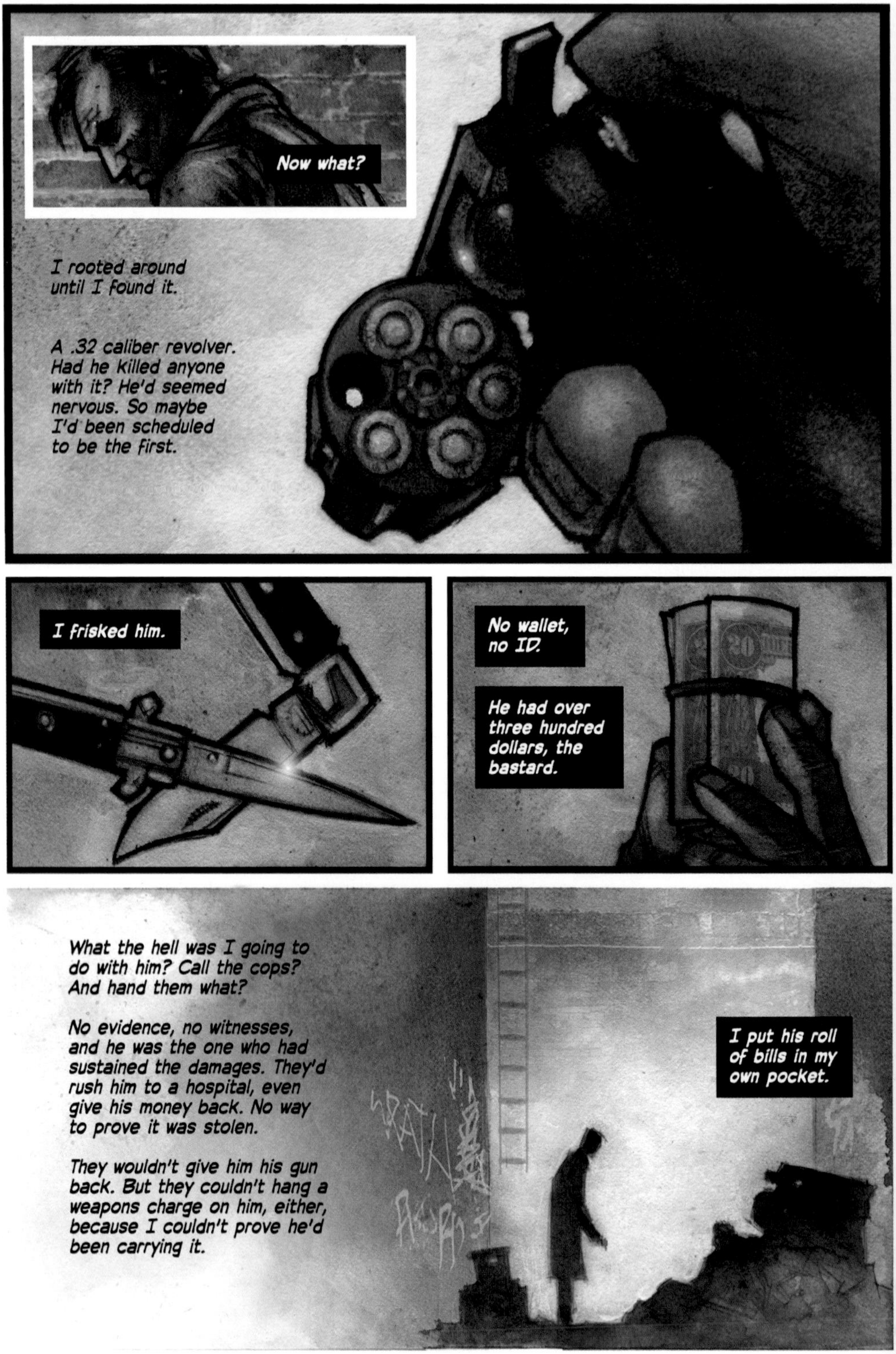
Now what?
I rooted around until I found it.
A .32 caliber revolver. Had he killed anyone with it? He'd seemed nervous. So maybe I'd been scheduled to be the first.
I frisked him.
No wallet, no ID.
He had over three hundred dollars, the bastard.
What the hell was I going to do with him? Call the cops? And hand them what?
No evidence, no witnesses, and he was the one who had sustained the damages. They'd rush him to a hospital, even give his money back. No way to prove it was stolen.
They wouldn't give him his gun back. But they couldn't hang a weapons charge on him, either, because I couldn't prove he'd been carrying it.
I put his roll of bills in my own pocket.

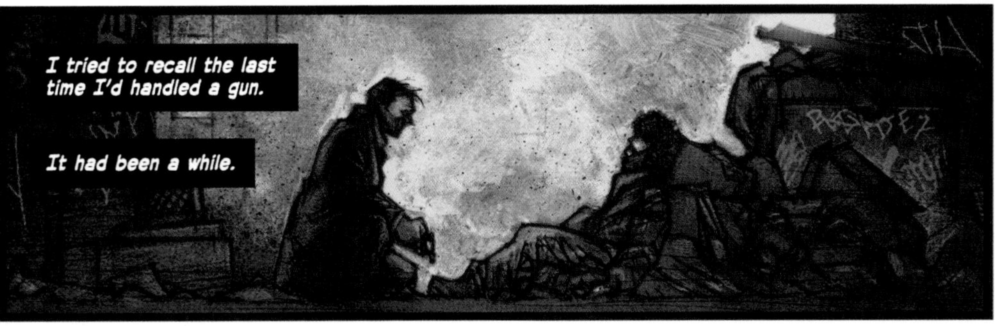
I tried to recall the last time I'd handled a gun.
It had been a while.

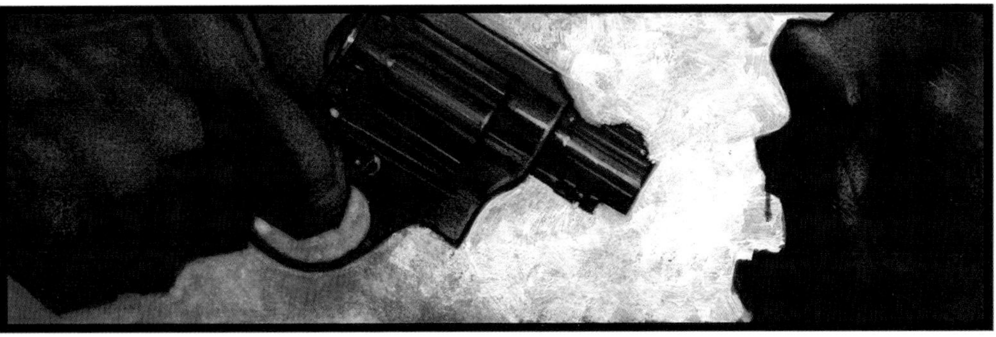

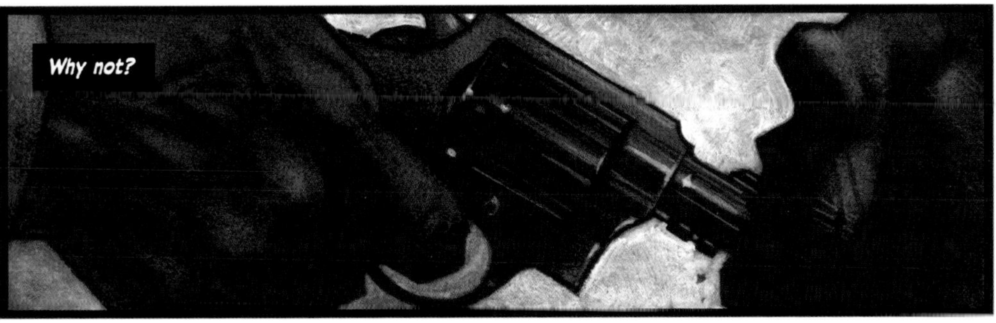
Why not?

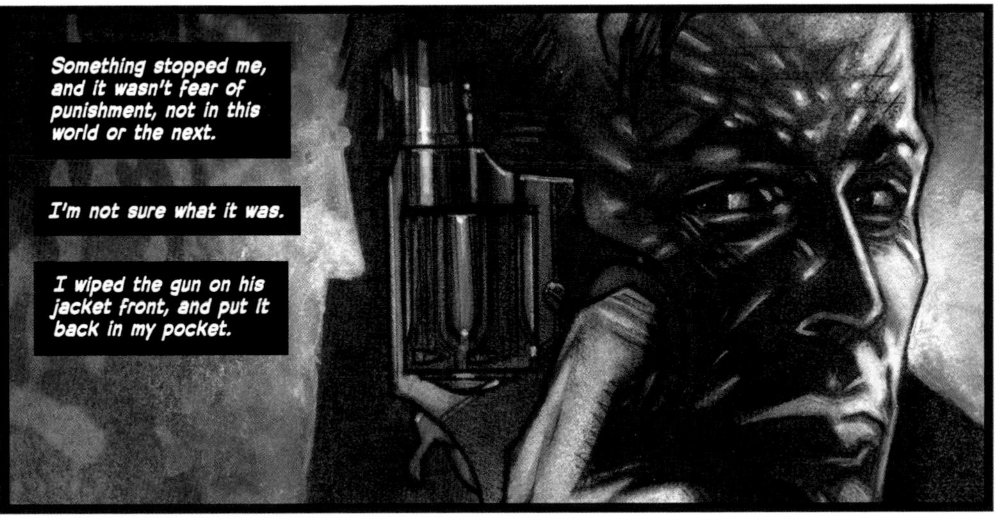
Something stopped me, and it wasn't fear of punishment, not in this world or the next.
I'm not sure what it was.
I wiped the gun on his jacket front, and put it back in my pocket.

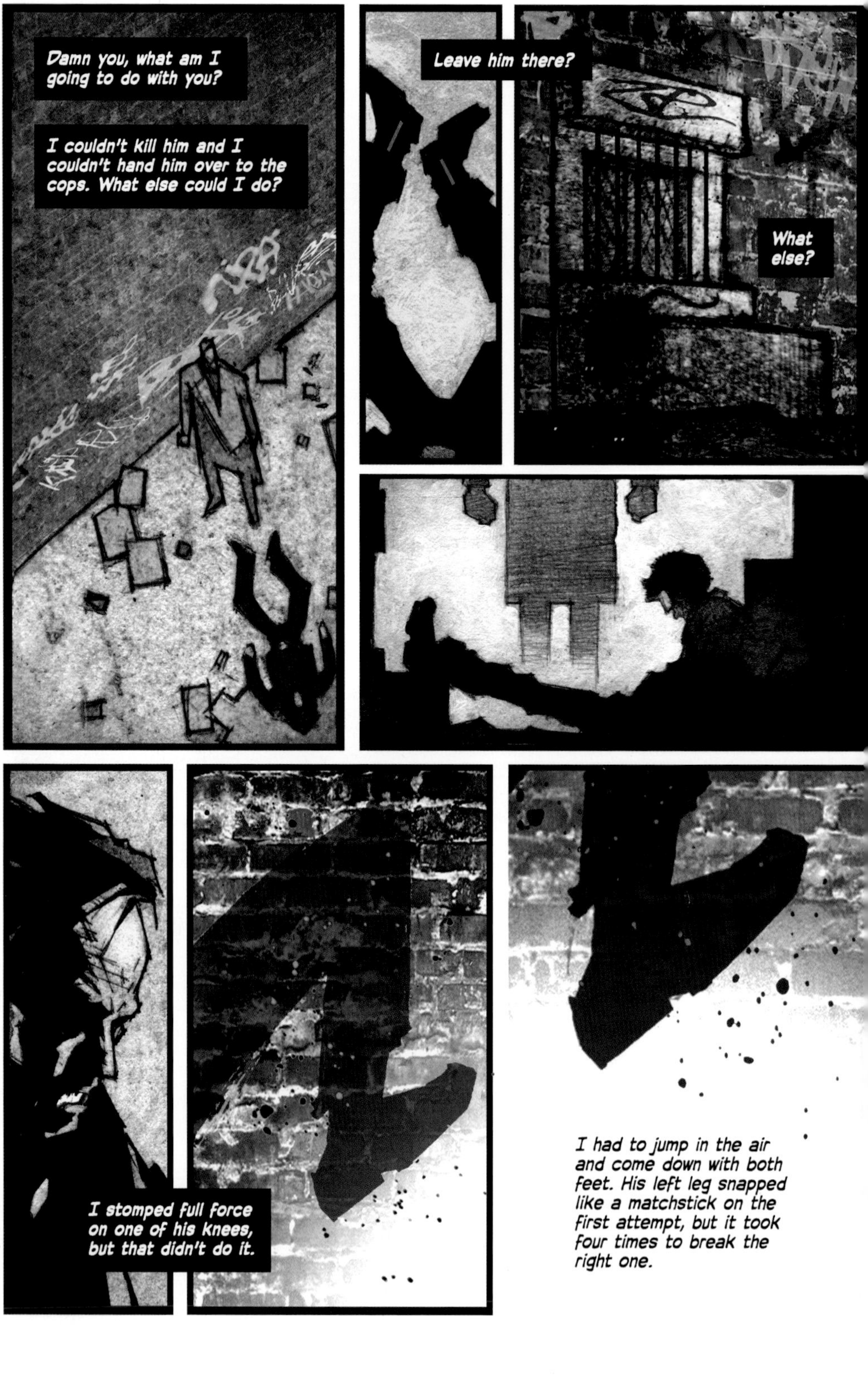
Damn you, what am I going to do with you?
I couldn't kill him and I couldn't hand him over to the cops. What else could I do?
Leave him there?
What else?
I stomped full force on one of his knees, but that didn't do it.
I had to jump in the air and come down with both feet. His left leg snapped like a matchstick on the first attempt, but it took four times to break the right one.

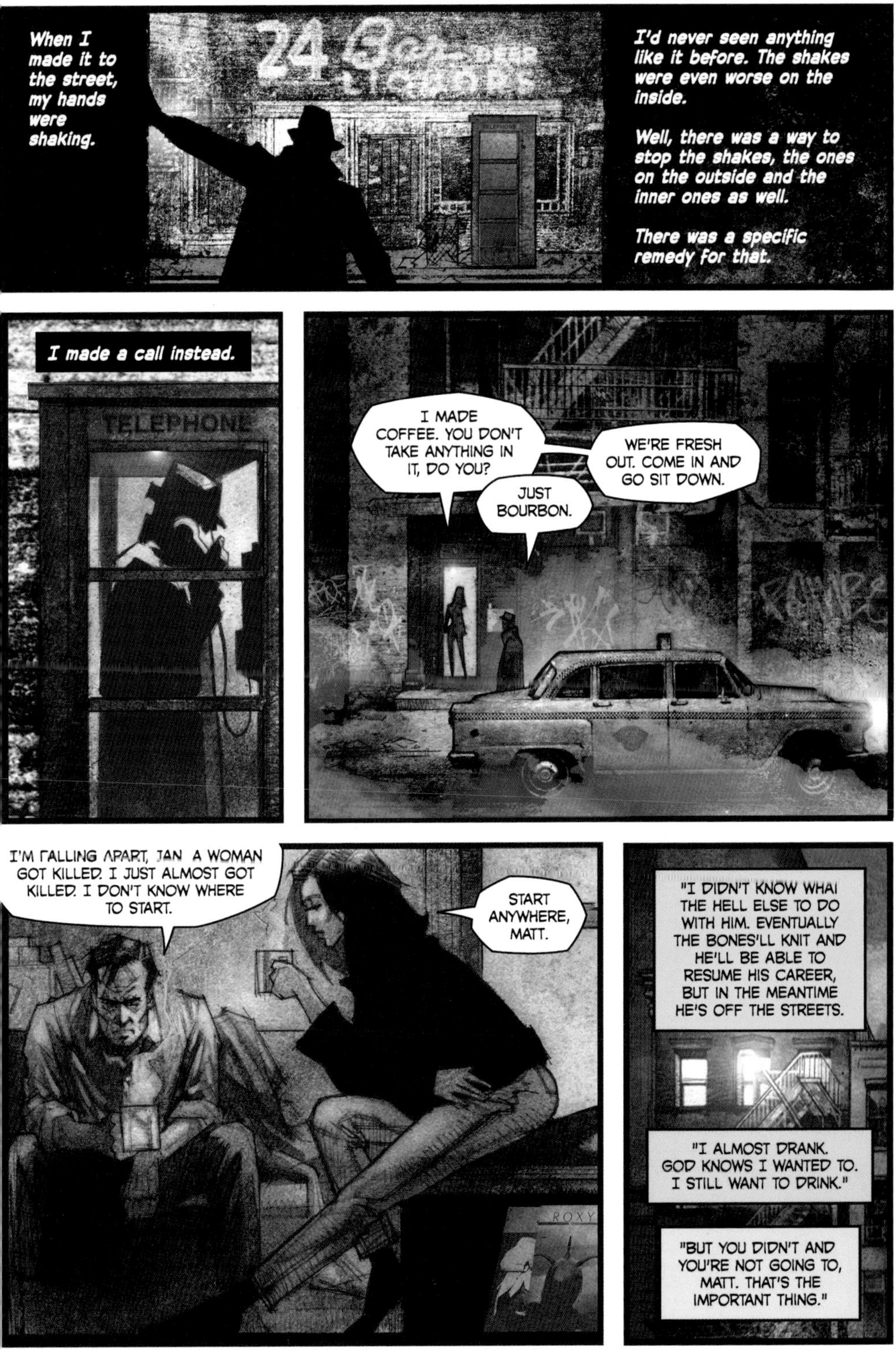
When I made it to the street, my hands were shaking.
I'd never seen anything like it before. The shakes were even worse on the inside.
Well, there was a way to stop the shakes, the ones on the outside and the inner ones as well.
There was a specific remedy for that.
I made a call instead.
TELEPHONE
I MADE COFFEE. YOU DON'T TAKE ANYTHING IN IT, DO YOU?
JUST BOURBON.
WE'RE FRESH OUT. COME IN AND GO SIT DOWN.
I'M FALLING APART, JAN. A WOMAN GOT KILLED. I JUST ALMOST GOT KILLED. I DON'T KNOW WHERE TO START.
START ANYWHERE, MATT.
"I DIDN'T KNOW WHAT THE HELL ELSE TO DO WITH HIM. EVENTUALLY THE BONES'LL KNIT AND HE'LL BE ABLE TO RESUME HIS CAREER, BUT IN THE MEANTIME HE'S OFF THE STREETS.
"I ALMOST DRANK. GOD KNOWS I WANTED TO. I STILL WANT TO DRINK."
"BUT YOU DIDN'T AND YOU'RE NOT GOING TO, MATT. THAT'S THE IMPORTANT THING."

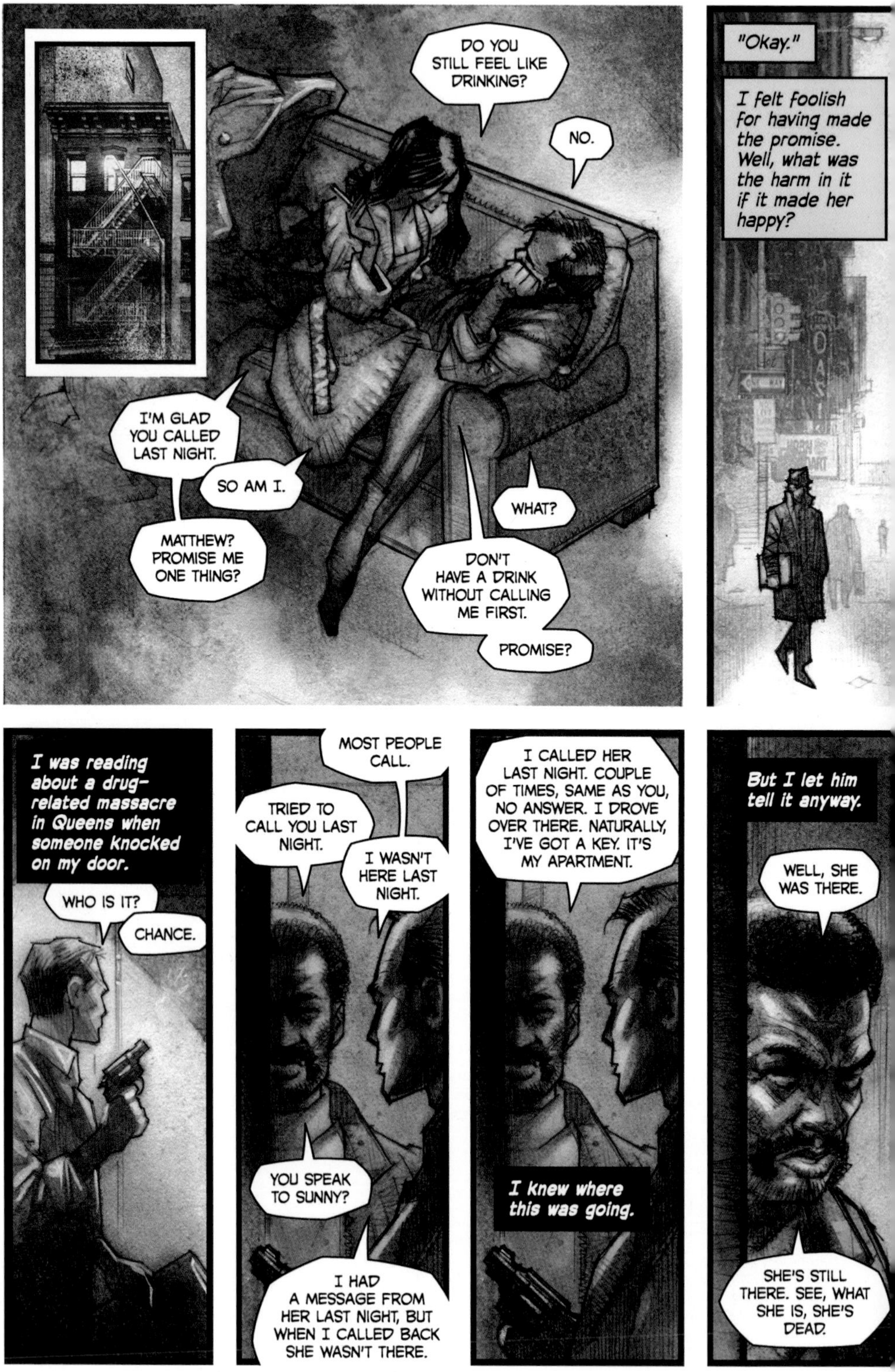
DO YOU STILL FEEL LIKE DRINKING?
NO.
I'M GLAD YOU CALLED LAST NIGHT.
SO AM I.
MATTHEW? PROMISE ME ONE THING?
WHAT?
DON'T HAVE A DRINK WITHOUT CALLING ME FIRST.
PROMISE?
"Okay."
I felt foolish for having made the promise. Well, what was the harm in it if it made her happy?
I was reading about a drug-related massacre in Queens when someone knocked on my door.
WHO IS IT?
CHANCE.
MOST PEOPLE CALL.
TRIED TO CALL YOU LAST NIGHT.
I WASN'T HERE LAST NIGHT.
YOU SPEAK TO SUNNY?
I HAD A MESSAGE FROM HER LAST NIGHT, BUT WHEN I CALLED BACK SHE WASN'T THERE.
I CALLED HER LAST NIGHT. COUPLE OF TIMES, SAME AS YOU, NO ANSWER. I DROVE OVER THERE. NATURALLY, I'VE GOT A KEY. IT'S MY APARTMENT.
I knew where this was going.
But I let him tell it anyway.
WELL, SHE WAS THERE.
SHE'S STILL THERE. SEE, WHAT SHE IS, SHE'S DEAD.

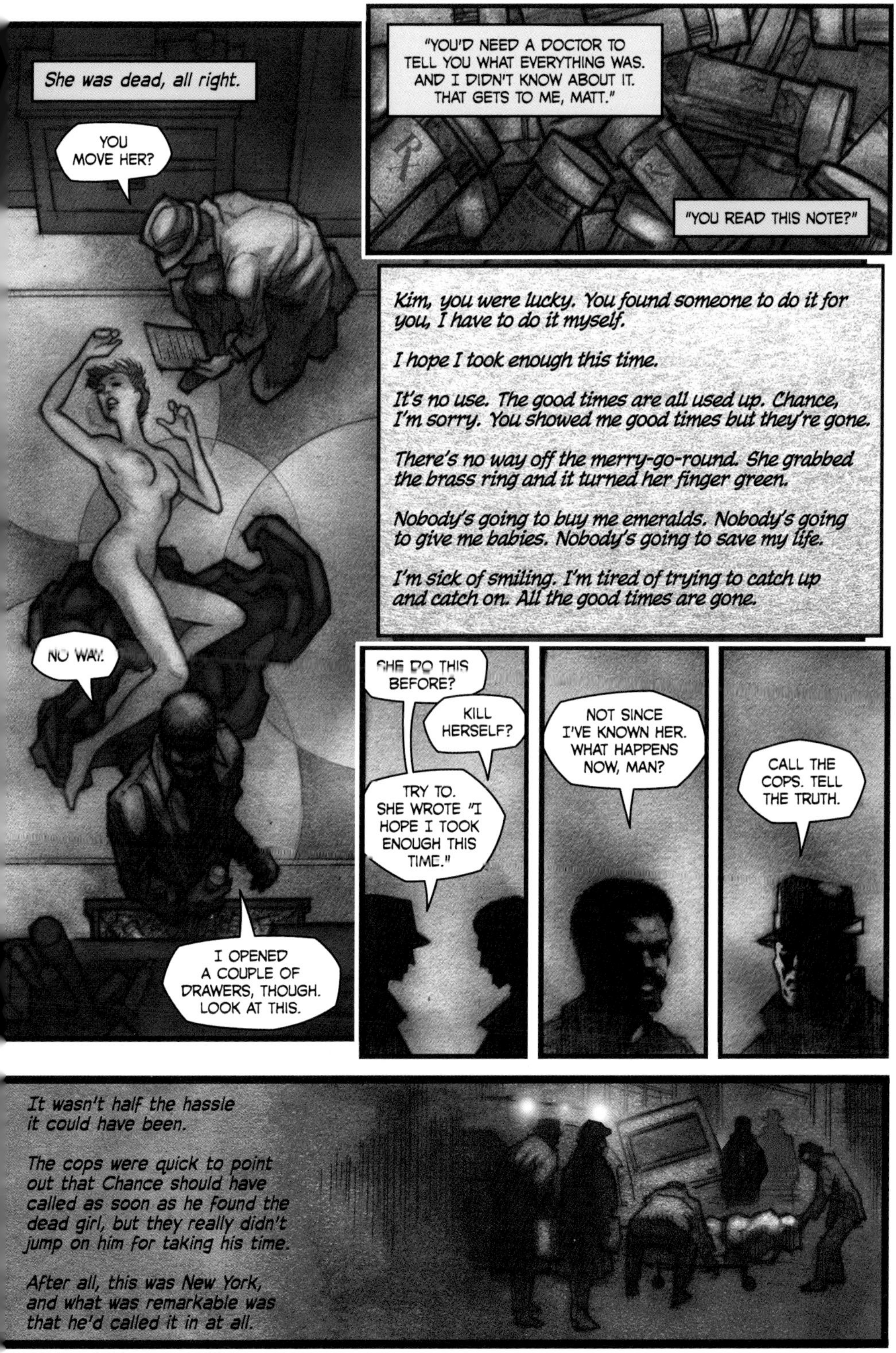

She was dead, all right.
YOU MOVE HER?
NO WAY.
I OPENED A COUPLE OF DRAWERS, THOUGH. LOOK AT THIS.
"YOU'D NEED A DOCTOR TO TELL YOU WHAT EVERYTHING WAS. AND I DIDN'T KNOW ABOUT IT. THAT GETS TO ME, MATT."
"YOU READ THIS NOTE?"
Kim, you were lucky. You found someone to do it for you, I have to do it myself.
I hope I took enough this time.
It's no use. The good times are all used up. Chance, I'm sorry. You showed me good times but they're gone.
There's no way off the merry-go-round. She grabbed the brass ring and it turned her finger green.
Nobody's going to buy me emeralds. Nobody's going to give me babies. Nobody's going to save my life.
I'm sick of smiling. I'm tired of trying to catch up and catch on. All the good times are gone.
SHE DO THIS BEFORE?
KILL HERSELF?
TRY TO. SHE WROTE "I HOPE I TOOK ENOUGH THIS TIME."
NOT SINCE I'VE KNOWN HER. WHAT HAPPENS NOW, MAN?
CALL THE COPS. TELL THE TRUTH.
It wasn't half the hassle it could have been.
The cops were quick to point out that Chance should have called as soon as he found the dead girl, but they really didn't jump on him for taking his time.
After all, this was New York, and what was remarkable was that he'd called it in at all.

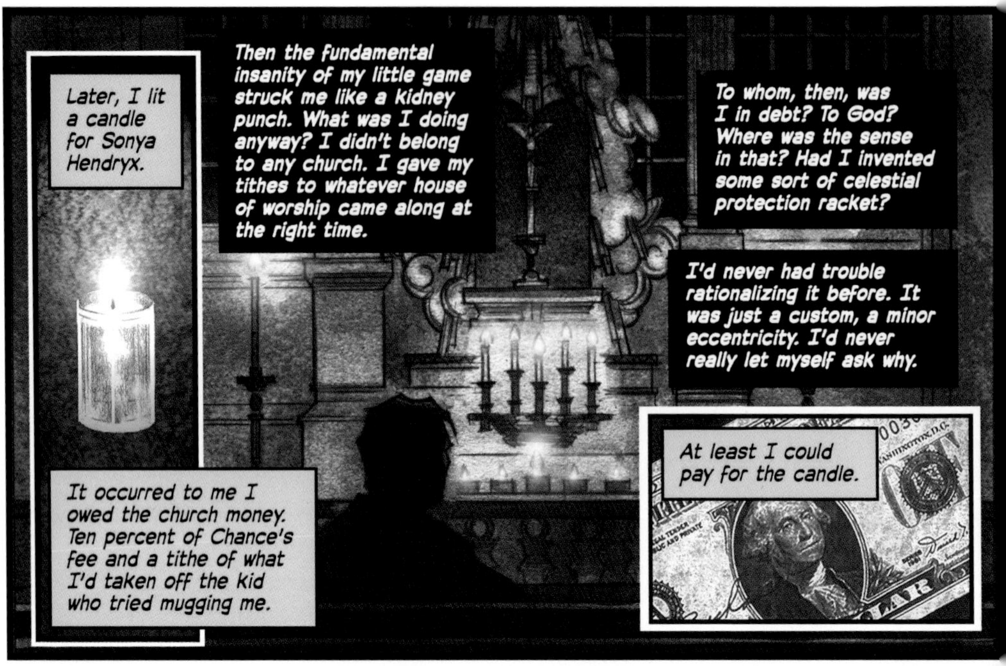
Later, I lit a candle for Sonya Hendryx.
Then the fundamental insanity of my little game struck me like a kidney punch. What was I doing anyway? I didn't belong to any church. I gave my tithes to whatever house of worship came along at the right time.
To whom, then, was I in debt? To God? Where was the sense in that? Had I invented some sort of celestial protection racket?
I'd never had trouble rationalizing it before. It was just a custom, a minor eccentricity. I'd never really let myself ask why.
It occurred to me I owed the church money. Ten percent of Chance's fee and a tithe of what I'd taken off the kid who tried mugging me.
At least I could pay for the candle.

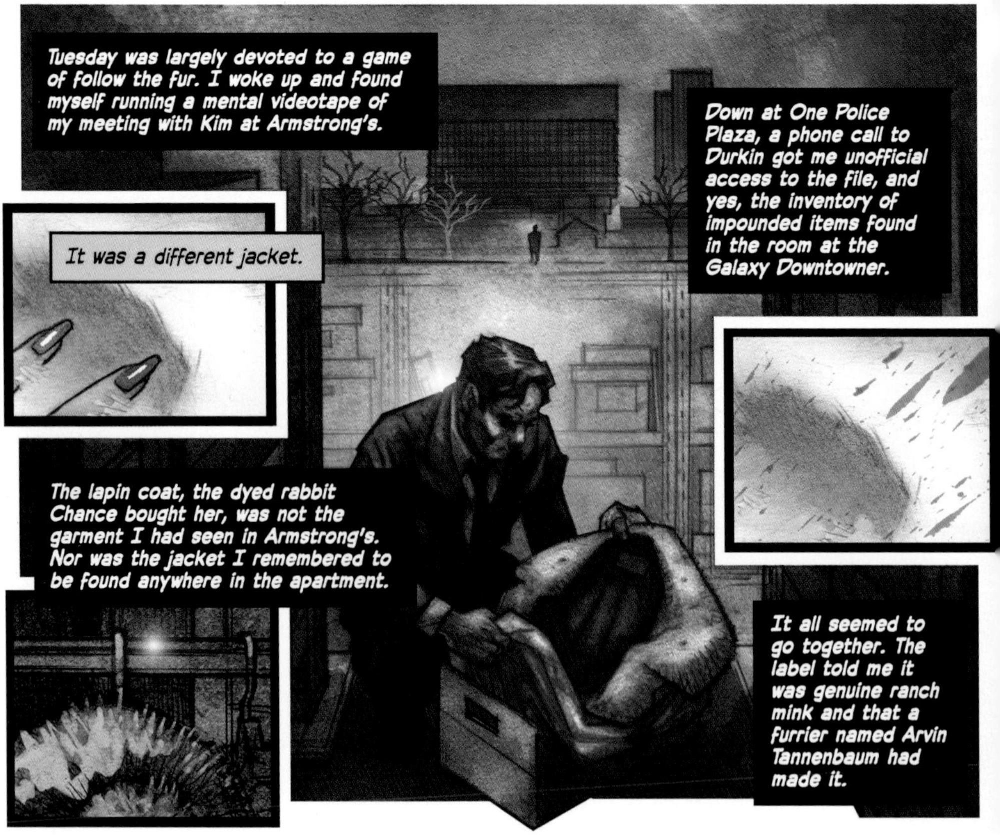
Tuesday was largely devoted to a game of follow the fur. I woke up and found myself running a mental videotape of my meeting with Kim at Armstrong's.
It was a different jacket.
The lapin coat, the dyed rabbit Chance bought her, was not the garment I had seen in Armstrong's. Nor was the jacket I remembered to be found anywhere in the apartment.
Down at One Police Plaza, a phone call to Durkin got me unofficial access to the file, and yes, the inventory of impounded items found in the room at the Galaxy Downtowner.
It all seemed to go together. The label told me it was genuine ranch mink and that a furrier named Arvin Tannenbaum had made it.

The Tannenbaum Firm was on the third floor of a loft building on West Twenty-Ninth, right in the heart of the fur district. A check of their sales records revealed the purchase of a mink jacket six weeks previously by Kim Dakkinen, and the sales slip led us to the right salesman.

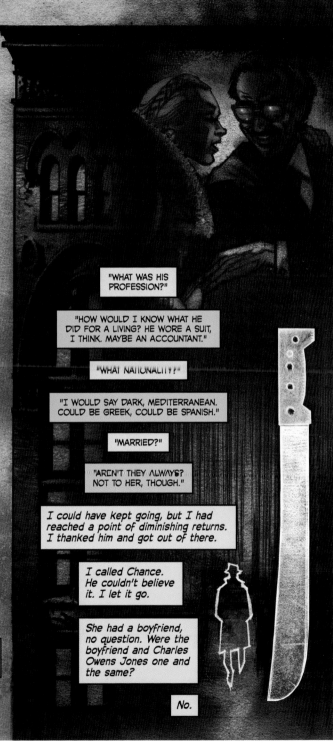

VERY PRETTY GIRL. YOU KNOW, I READ HER NAME IN THE NEWSPAPER. TERRIBLE THING.

SHE WAS WITH A GENTLEMAN. HE PAID CASH FOR THE COAT. NOT UNUSUAL IN THIS BUSINESS.

"A LUXURY GIFT FOR A LUXURY FRIEND. USUALLY THE CUSTOMER IS HAPPIER IF NO RECORD OF THE TRANSACTION EXISTS. THUS PAYMENT IN CASH, THUS THE SALES SLIP NOT IN THE BUYER'S NAME BUT IN MISS DAKKINEN'S."

The sale had come to just under twenty-five hundred dollars with the tax. A lot of cash to carry, but not unheard of. I asked him to describe the gentleman.

"THIRTY-EIGHT, FORTY YEARS OLD, I SUPPOSE. I HAVE A SENSE OF HIM BUT I CAN'T PICTURE HIM."

"WHAT WAS HIS PROFESSION?"

"HOW WOULD I KNOW WHAT HE DID FOR A LIVING? HE WORE A SUIT, I THINK. MAYBE AN ACCOUNTANT."

"WHAT NATIONALITY?"

"I WOULD SAY DARK, MEDITERRANEAN. COULD BE GREEK, COULD BE SPANISH."

"MARRIED?"

"AREN'T THEY ALWAYS? NOT TO HER, THOUGH."

I could have kept going, but I had reached a point of diminishing returns. I thanked him and got out of there.

I called Chance. He couldn't believe it. I let it go.

She had a boyfriend, no question. Were the boyfriend and Charles Owens Jones one and the same?

No.

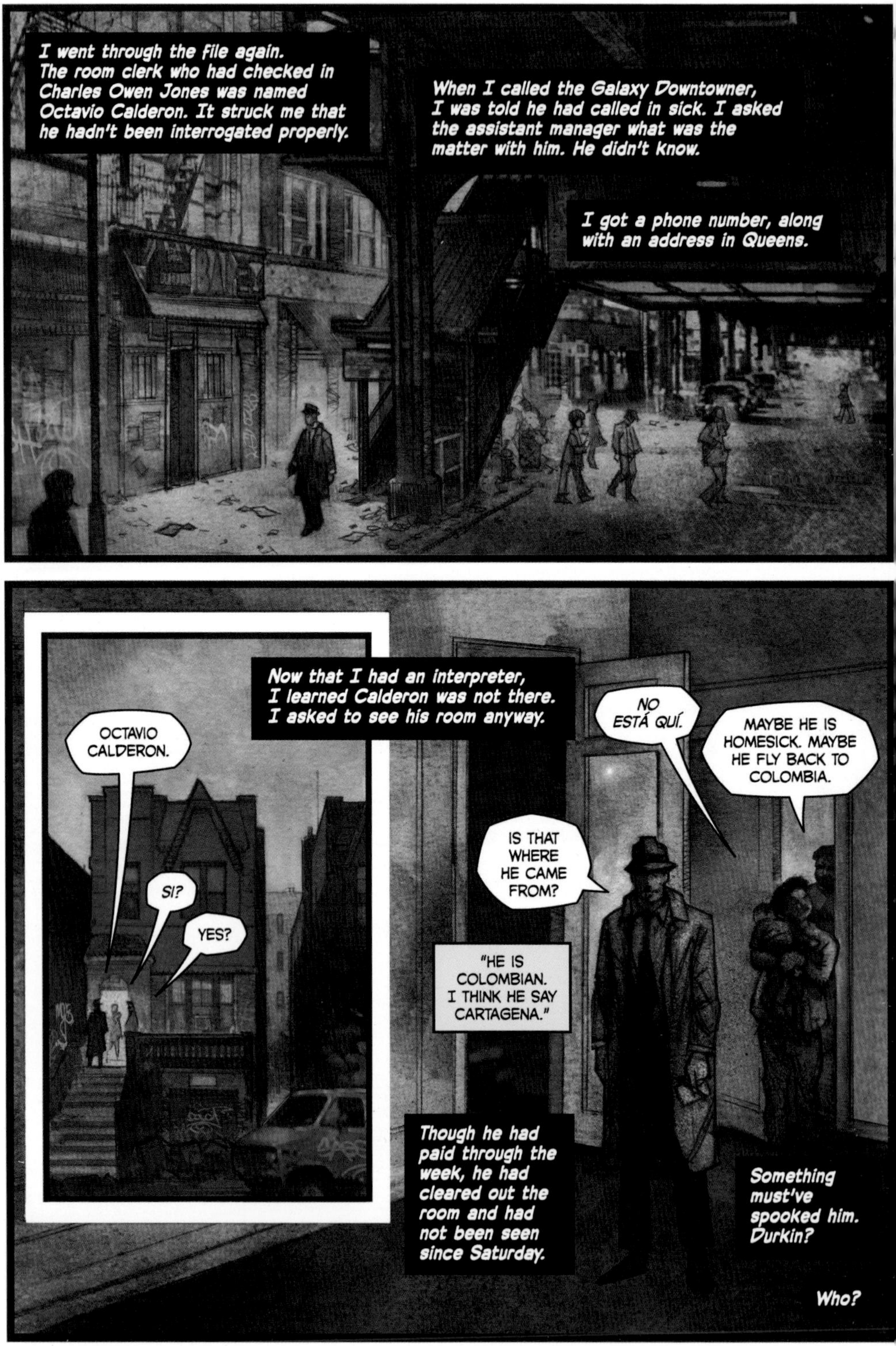
I went through the file again. The room clerk who had checked in Charles Owen Jones was named Octavio Calderon. It struck me that he hadn't been interrogated properly.
When I called the Galaxy Downtowner, I was told he had called in sick. I asked the assistant manager what was the matter with him. He didn't know.
I got a phone number, along with an address in Queens.
OCTAVIO CALDERON.
SI?
YES?
Now that I had an interpreter, I learned Calderon was not there. I asked to see his room anyway.
NO ESTÁ QUÍ.
MAYBE HE IS HOMESICK. MAYBE HE FLY BACK TO COLOMBIA.
IS THAT WHERE HE CAME FROM?
"HE IS COLOMBIAN. I THINK HE SAY CARTAGENA."
Though he had paid through the week, he had cleared out the room and had not been seen since Saturday.
Something must've spooked him. Durkin?
Who?

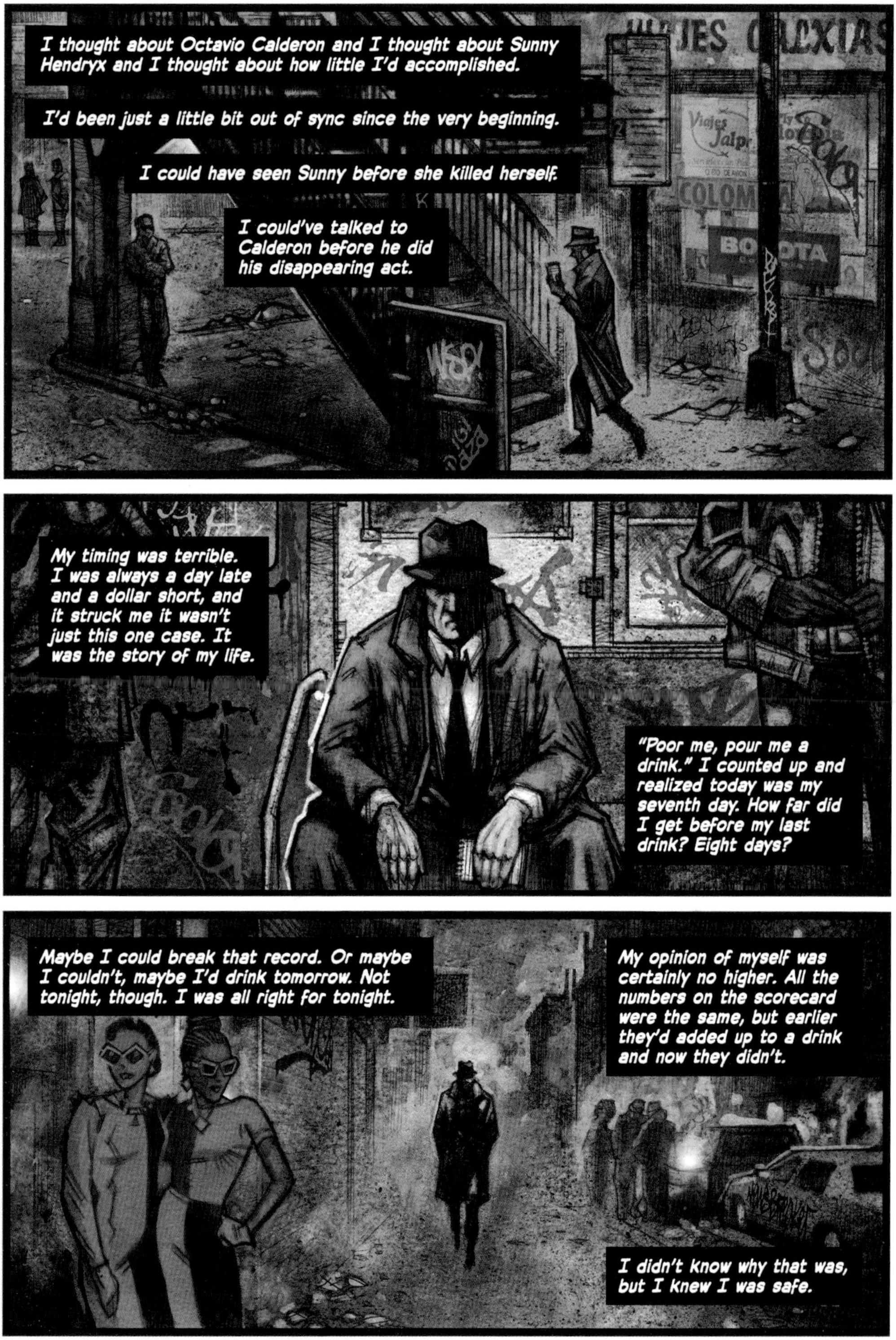

I thought about Octavio Calderon and I thought about Sunny Hendryx and I thought about how little I'd accomplished.
I'd been just a little bit out of sync since the very beginning.
I could have seen Sunny before she killed herself.
I could've talked to Calderon before he did his disappearing act.
My timing was terrible. I was always a day late and a dollar short, and it struck me it wasn't just this one case. It was the story of my life.
"Poor me, pour me a drink." I counted up and realized today was my seventh day. How far did I get before my last drink? Eight days?
Maybe I could break that record. Or maybe I couldn't, maybe I'd drink tomorrow. Not tonight, though. I was all right for tonight.
My opinion of myself was certainly no higher. All the numbers on the scorecard were the same, but earlier they'd added up to a drink and now they didn't.
I didn't know why that was, but I knew I was safe.

Back at the hotel, there was a message at the desk to call Danny Boy Bell.

MATT, I THINK YOU SHOULD COME UP AND LET ME BUY YOU A GINGER ALE.

THAT'S WHAT I THINK YOU SHOULD DO.

I didn't really think Danny Boy would set me up.

But you never know who might be drinking at Poogan's.

"I'VE GOT TWO THINGS FOR YOU. A MESSAGE AND AN OPINION. THE MESSAGE FIRST. IT'S A WARNING. YOU SHOULD FORGET ABOUT THE DAKKINEN GIRL."

"WHO'S THE MESSAGE FROM, DANNY?"

"SOMEBODY TALKED TO SOMEBODY WHO TALKED TO SOMEBODY WHO TALKED TO ME. SOMEONE WHO SAID, AND I QUOTE, 'YOU'VE GOT SOME PAIR OF BALLS.' YOU WANT THE OPINION?"

"SURE."

THE OPINION IS I THINK YOU SHOULD HEED THE MESSAGE. EITHER I'M GETTING OLD IN A HURRY OR THIS TOWN HAS GOTTEN NASTIER IN THE PAST COUPLE OF YEARS. THEY USED TO NEED MORE OF A REASON TO KILL. YOU KNOW WHAT I MEAN?

ABOUT DAKKINEN--I COULD PASS A MESSAGE BACK UP THE LINE.

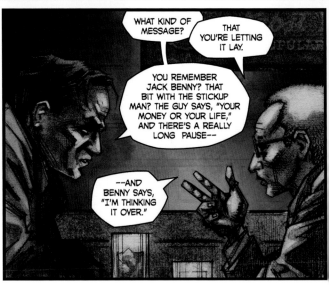

WHAT KIND OF MESSAGE?

THAT YOU'RE LETTING IT LAY.

YOU REMEMBER JACK BENNY? THAT BIT WITH THE STICKUP MAN? THE GUY SAYS, "YOUR MONEY OR YOUR LIFE," AND THERE'S A REALLY LONG PAUSE--

--AND BENNY SAYS, "I'M THINKING IT OVER."

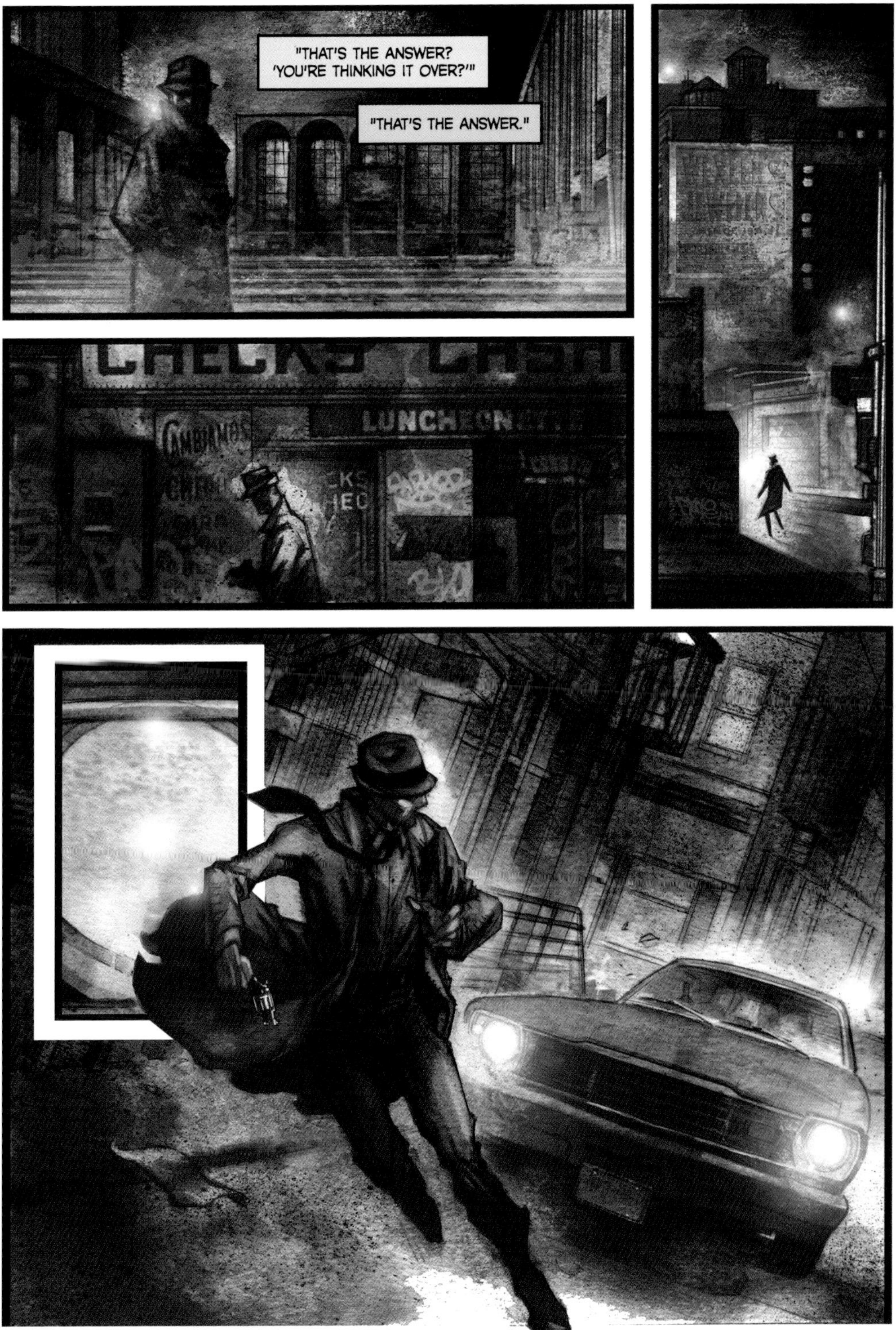
"THAT'S THE ANSWER?
'YOU'RE THINKING IT OVER?'"
"THAT'S THE ANSWER."

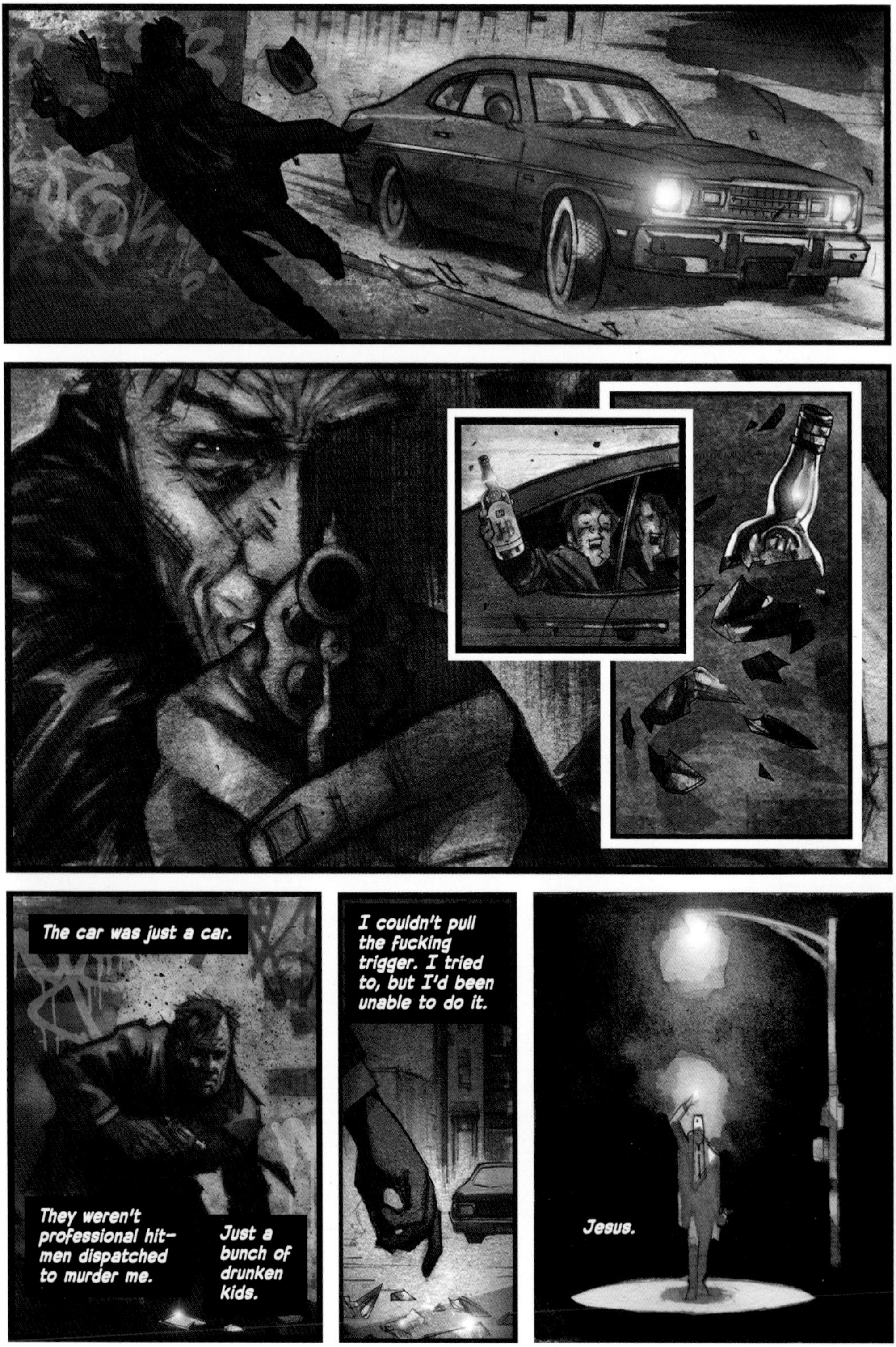
The car was just a car.
They weren't professional hit-men dispatched to murder me.
Just a bunch of drunken kids.
I couldn't pull the fucking trigger. I tried to, but I'd been unable to do it.
Jesus.

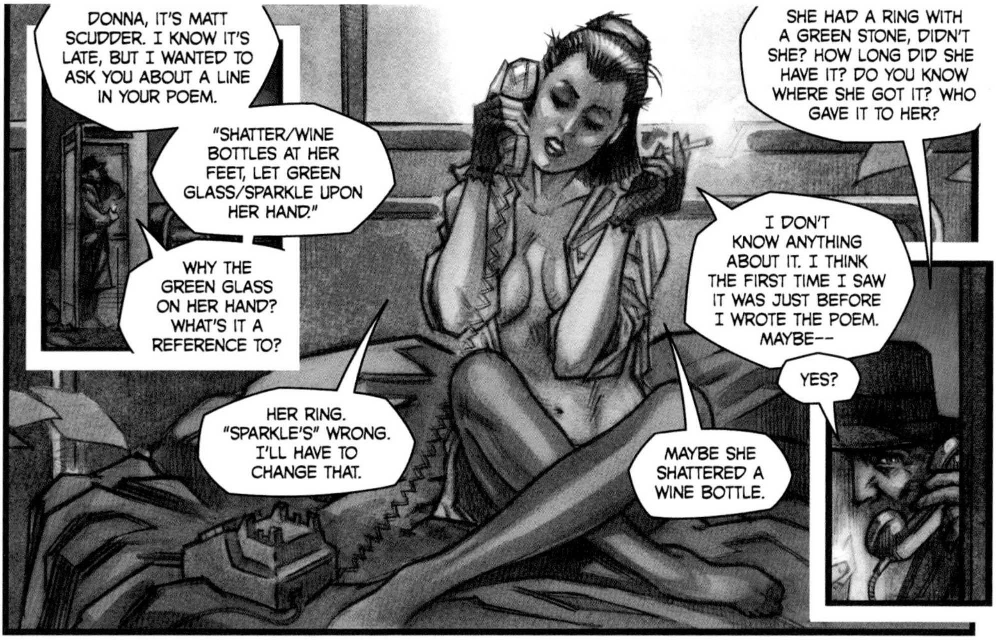
DONNA, IT'S MATT SCUDDER. I KNOW IT'S LATE, BUT I WANTED TO ASK YOU ABOUT A LINE IN YOUR POEM.
"SHATTER/WINE BOTTLES AT HER FEET, LET GREEN GLASS/SPARKLE UPON HER HAND."
WHY THE GREEN GLASS ON HER HAND? WHAT'S IT A REFERENCE TO?
HER RING. "SPARKLE'S" WRONG. I'LL HAVE TO CHANGE THAT.
MAYBE SHE SHATTERED A WINE BOTTLE.
SHE HAD A RING WITH A GREEN STONE, DIDN'T SHE? HOW LONG DID SHE HAVE IT? DO YOU KNOW WHERE SHE GOT IT? WHO GAVE IT TO HER?
I DON'T KNOW ANYTHING ABOUT IT. I THINK THE FIRST TIME I SAW IT WAS JUST BEFORE I WROTE THE POEM. MAYBE--
YES?

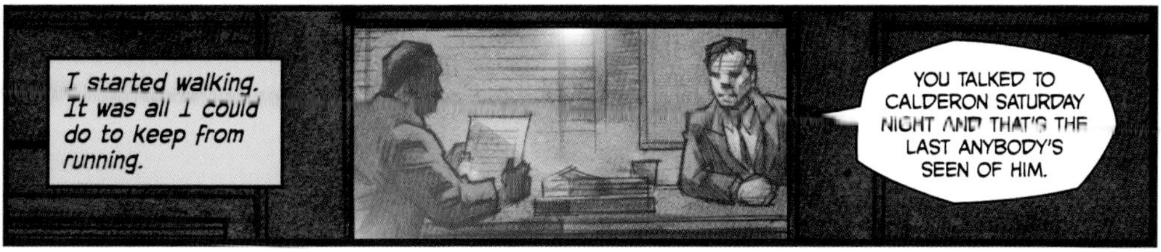
I started walking. It was all I could do to keep from running.
YOU TALKED TO CALDERON SATURDAY NIGHT AND THAT'S THE LAST ANYBODY'S SEEN OF HIM.

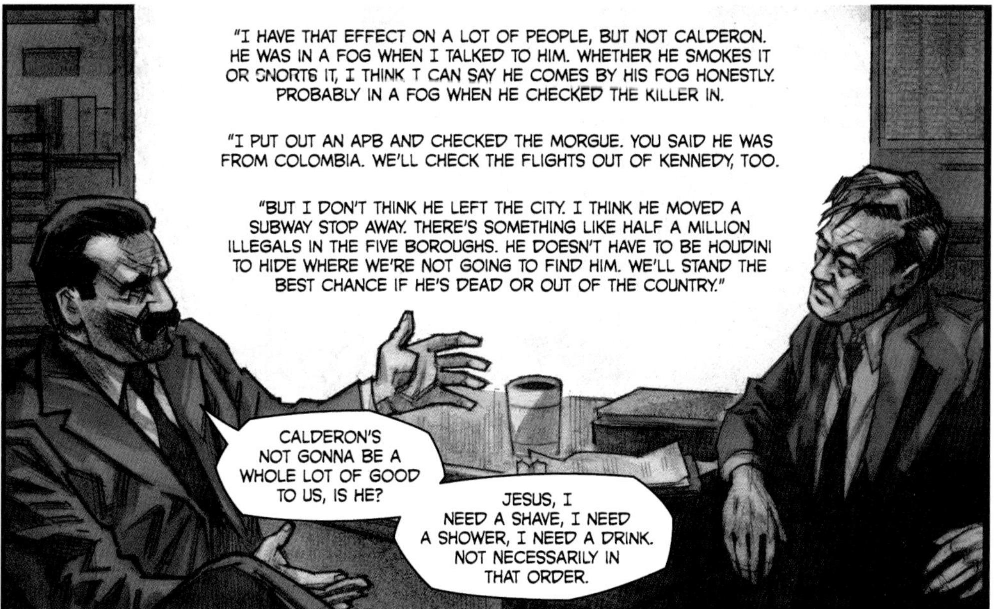
"I HAVE THAT EFFECT ON A LOT OF PEOPLE, BUT NOT CALDERON. HE WAS IN A FOG WHEN I TALKED TO HIM. WHETHER HE SMOKES IT OR SNORTS IT, I THINK I CAN SAY HE COMES BY HIS FOG HONESTLY. PROBABLY IN A FOG WHEN HE CHECKED THE KILLER IN.
"I PUT OUT AN APB AND CHECKED THE MORGUE. YOU SAID HE WAS FROM COLOMBIA. WE'LL CHECK THE FLIGHTS OUT OF KENNEDY, TOO.
"BUT I DON'T THINK HE LEFT THE CITY. I THINK HE MOVED A SUBWAY STOP AWAY. THERE'S SOMETHING LIKE HALF A MILLION ILLEGALS IN THE FIVE BOROUGHS. HE DOESN'T HAVE TO BE HOUDINI TO HIDE WHERE WE'RE NOT GOING TO FIND HIM. WE'LL STAND THE BEST CHANCE IF HE'S DEAD OR OUT OF THE COUNTRY."
CALDERON'S NOT GONNA BE A WHOLE LOT OF GOOD TO US, IS HE?
JESUS, I NEED A SHAVE, I NEED A SHOWER, I NEED A DRINK. NOT NECESSARILY IN THAT ORDER.

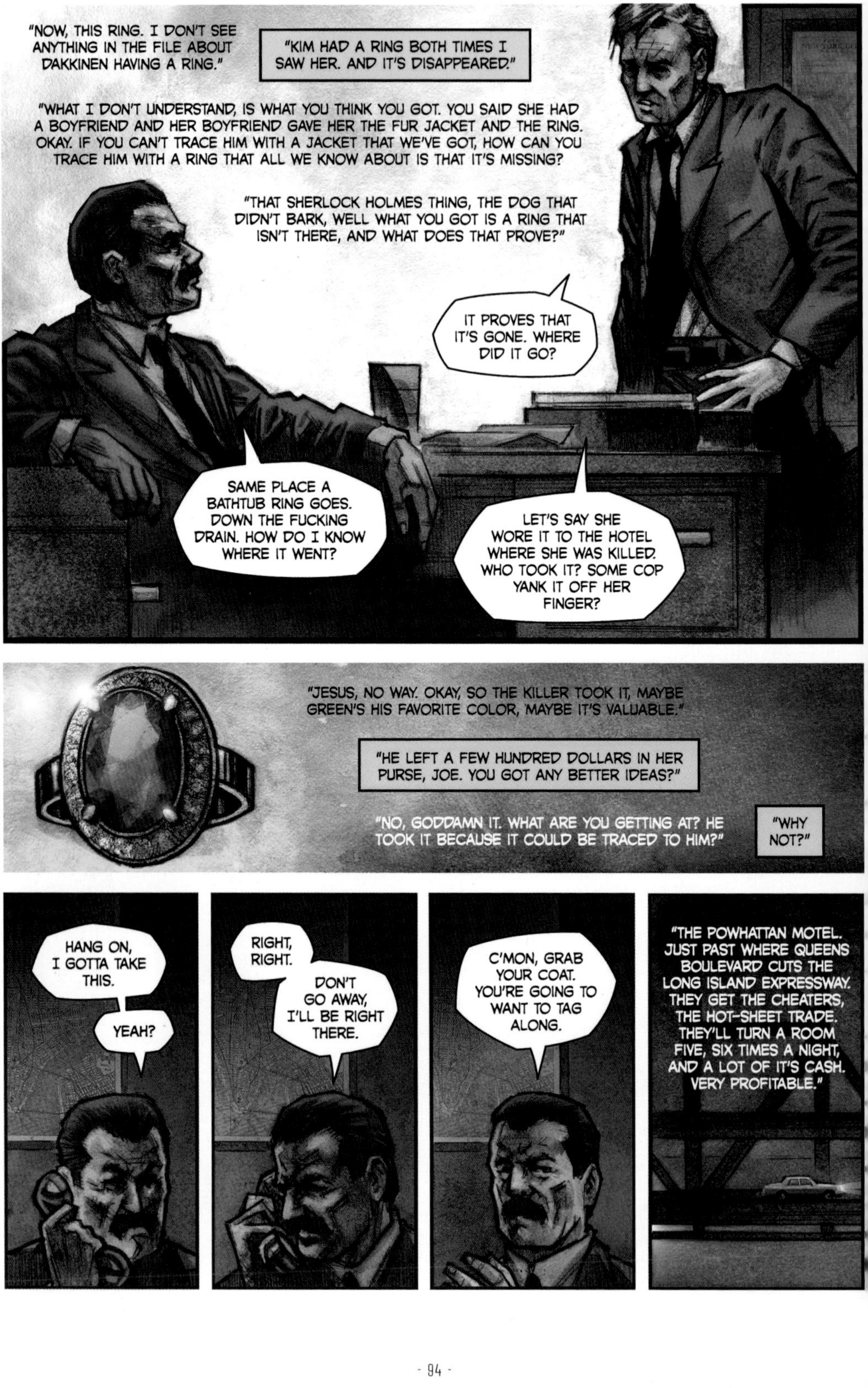

"NOW, THIS RING. I DON'T SEE ANYTHING IN THE FILE ABOUT DAKKINEN HAVING A RING."
"KIM HAD A RING BOTH TIMES I SAW HER. AND IT'S DISAPPEARED."
"WHAT I DON'T UNDERSTAND, IS WHAT YOU THINK YOU GOT. YOU SAID SHE HAD A BOYFRIEND AND HER BOYFRIEND GAVE HER THE FUR JACKET AND THE RING. OKAY. IF YOU CAN'T TRACE HIM WITH A JACKET THAT WE'VE GOT, HOW CAN YOU TRACE HIM WITH A RING THAT ALL WE KNOW ABOUT IS THAT IT'S MISSING?
"THAT SHERLOCK HOLMES THING, THE DOG THAT DIDN'T BARK, WELL WHAT YOU GOT IS A RING THAT ISN'T THERE, AND WHAT DOES THAT PROVE?"
IT PROVES THAT IT'S GONE. WHERE DID IT GO?
SAME PLACE A BATHTUB RING GOES. DOWN THE FUCKING DRAIN. HOW DO I KNOW WHERE IT WENT?
LET'S SAY SHE WORE IT TO THE HOTEL WHERE SHE WAS KILLED. WHO TOOK IT? SOME COP YANK IT OFF HER FINGER?
"JESUS, NO WAY. OKAY, SO THE KILLER TOOK IT, MAYBE GREEN'S HIS FAVORITE COLOR, MAYBE IT'S VALUABLE."
"HE LEFT A FEW HUNDRED DOLLARS IN HER PURSE, JOE. YOU GOT ANY BETTER IDEAS?"
"NO, GODDAMN IT. WHAT ARE YOU GETTING AT? HE TOOK IT BECAUSE IT COULD BE TRACED TO HIM?"
"WHY NOT?"
HANG ON, I GOTTA TAKE THIS.
YEAH?
RIGHT, RIGHT.
DON'T GO AWAY, I'LL BE RIGHT THERE.
C'MON, GRAB YOUR COAT. YOU'RE GOING TO WANT TO TAG ALONG.
"THE POWHATTAN MOTEL. JUST PAST WHERE QUEENS BOULEVARD CUTS THE LONG ISLAND EXPRESSWAY. THEY GET THE CHEATERS, THE HOT-SHEET TRADE. THEY'LL TURN A ROOM FIVE, SIX TIMES A NIGHT, AND A LOT OF IT'S CASH. VERY PROFITABLE."

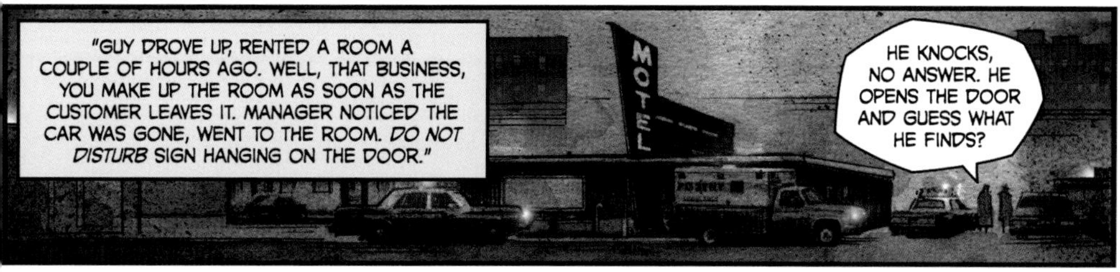
"GUY DROVE UP, RENTED A ROOM A COUPLE OF HOURS AGO. WELL, THAT BUSINESS, YOU MAKE UP THE ROOM AS SOON AS THE CUSTOMER LEAVES IT. MANAGER NOTICED THE CAR WAS GONE, WENT TO THE ROOM. *DO NOT DISTURB* SIGN HANGING ON THE DOOR."
MOTEL
HE KNOCKS, NO ANSWER. HE OPENS THE DOOR AND GUESS WHAT HE FINDS?

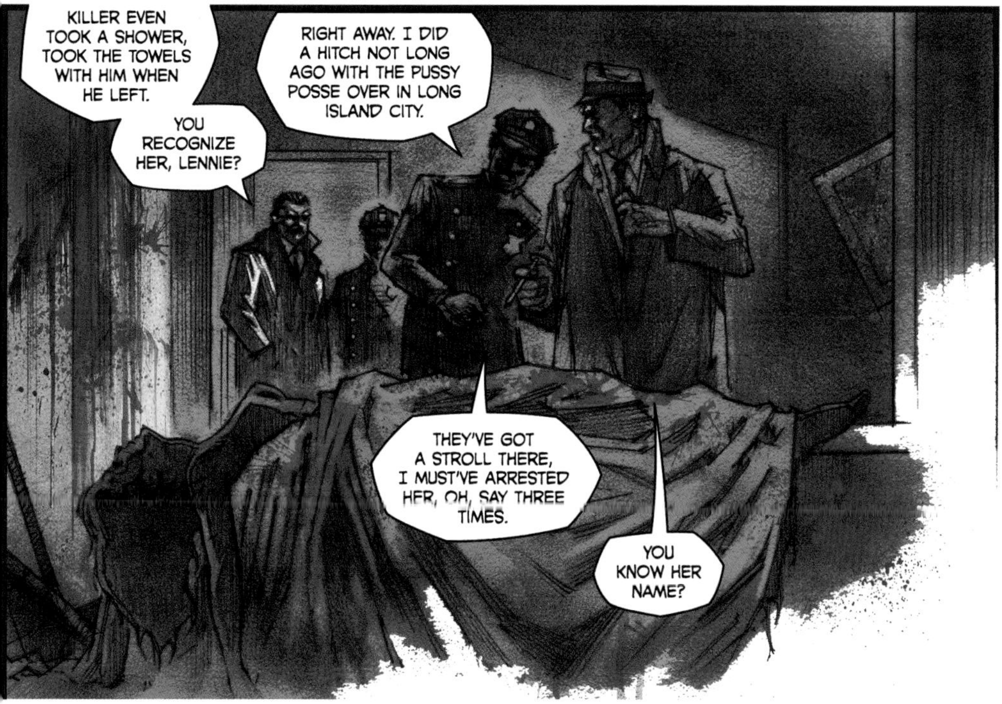
KILLER EVEN TOOK A SHOWER, TOOK THE TOWELS WITH HIM WHEN HE LEFT.
YOU RECOGNIZE HER, LENNIE?
RIGHT AWAY. I DID A HITCH NOT LONG AGO WITH THE PUSSY POSSE OVER IN LONG ISLAND CITY.
THEY'VE GOT A STROLL THERE, I MUST'VE ARRESTED HER, OH, SAY THREE TIMES.
YOU KNOW HER NAME?

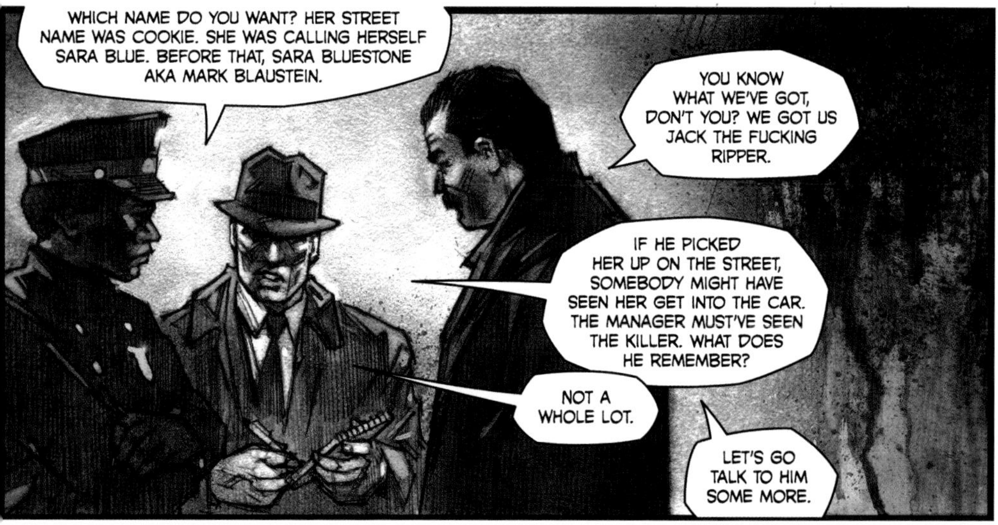
WHICH NAME DO YOU WANT? HER STREET NAME WAS COOKIE. SHE WAS CALLING HERSELF SARA BLUE. BEFORE THAT, SARA BLUESTONE AKA MARK BLAUSTEIN.
YOU KNOW WHAT WE'VE GOT, DON'T YOU? WE GOT US JACK THE FUCKING RIPPER.
IF HE PICKED HER UP ON THE STREET, SOMEBODY MIGHT HAVE SEEN HER GET INTO THE CAR. THE MANAGER MUST'VE SEEN THE KILLER. WHAT DOES HE REMEMBER?
NOT A WHOLE LOT.
LET'S GO TALK TO HIM SOME MORE.

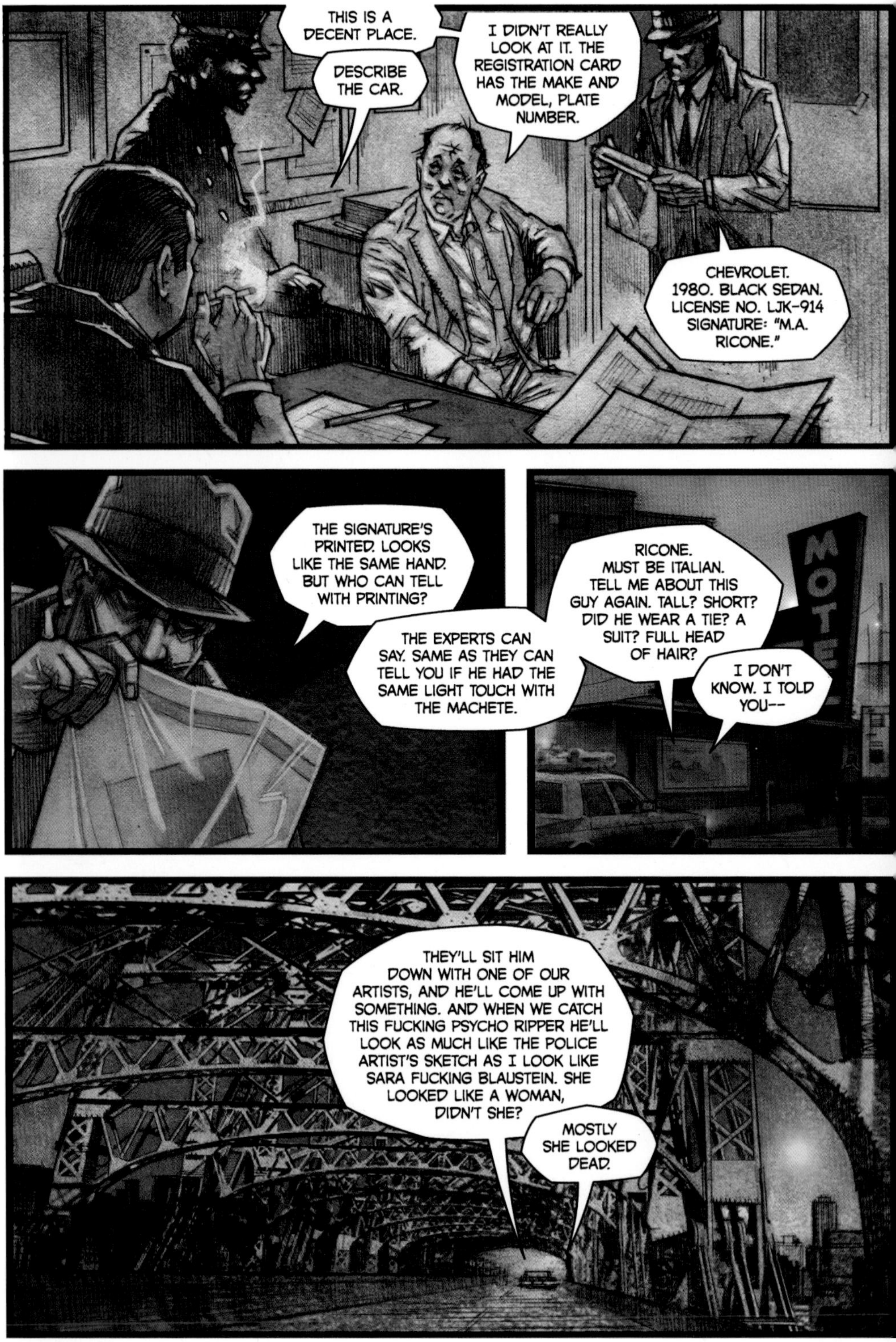
THIS IS A DECENT PLACE.
DESCRIBE THE CAR.
I DIDN'T REALLY LOOK AT IT. THE REGISTRATION CARD HAS THE MAKE AND MODEL, PLATE NUMBER.
CHEVROLET. 1980. BLACK SEDAN. LICENSE NO. LJK-914 SIGNATURE: "M.A. RICONE."
THE SIGNATURE'S PRINTED. LOOKS LIKE THE SAME HAND. BUT WHO CAN TELL WITH PRINTING?
THE EXPERTS CAN SAY. SAME AS THEY CAN TELL YOU IF HE HAD THE SAME LIGHT TOUCH WITH THE MACHETE.
RICONE. MUST BE ITALIAN. TELL ME ABOUT THIS GUY AGAIN. TALL? SHORT? DID HE WEAR A TIE? A SUIT? FULL HEAD OF HAIR?
I DON'T KNOW. I TOLD YOU--
MOTE
THEY'LL SIT HIM DOWN WITH ONE OF OUR ARTISTS, AND HE'LL COME UP WITH SOMETHING. AND WHEN WE CATCH THIS FUCKING PSYCHO RIPPER HE'LL LOOK AS MUCH LIKE THE POLICE ARTIST'S SKETCH AS I LOOK LIKE SARA FUCKING BLAUSTEIN. SHE LOOKED LIKE A WOMAN, DIDN'T SHE?
MOSTLY SHE LOOKED DEAD.

MAYBE COOKIE WAS A SMOKESCREEN.

HOW'S THAT?

MAYBE HE KILLED HER TO TAKE THE HEAT OFF. MAKE IT LOOK LIKE A TRAIN OF RANDOM MURDERS. TO HIDE HIS MOTIVE FOR KILLING DAKKINEN.

WHAT HEAT, FOR CHRIST'S SAKE? THERE'S BEEN NO FUCKING HEAT. THERE'LL BE ENOUGH HEAT NOW TO SCORCH HIS ASS FOR HIM. NOTHING TURNS THE PRESS ON LIKE A SERIES OF RANDOM KILLINGS. THE READERS EAT IT UP, THEY POUR IT ON THEIR CORN FLAKES.

I SUPPOSE.

YOU KNOW WHAT YOU ARE, SCUDDER? YOU'RE STUBBORN.

MAYBE.

YOUR PROBLEM IS YOU WORK PRIVATE AND YOU CARRY ONE CASE AT A TIME. I GOT SO MUCH SHIT ON MY DESK IT'S A PLEASURE WHEN I GET TO LET GO OF SOMETHING, BUT WITH YOU IT'S JUST THE OPPOSITE. YOU WANT TO HANG ONTO IT AS LONG AS YOU CAN.

IS THAT WHAT THAT IS?

I DON'T KNOW. SOUNDS LIKE IT.

I went upstairs to bed. Ten minutes later, I got up again.

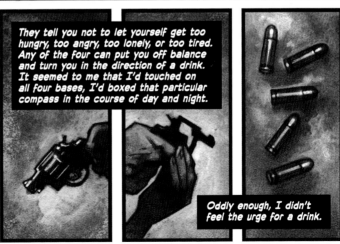

They tell you not to let yourself get too hungry, too angry, too lonely, or too tired. Any of the four can put you off balance and turn you in the direction of a drink. It seemed to me that I'd touched on all four bases, I'd boxed that particular compass in the course of day and night.

Oddly enough, I didn't feel the urge for a drink.

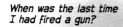
When was the last time I had fired a gun?

It had been that night in Washington Heights when I chased two holdup men into the street, shot them down and killed the little girl in the process.

In the time that I remained on the force after that incident, I never had the occasion to draw the service revolver, let alone discharge it.

CLICK!

And tonight I had been unable to do it. I had frozen.

CLICK!

I reloaded the .32 and put it back in the drawer.

I was glad I hadn't shot anyone and frightened of the implications of not shooting, and my mind went a few hard rounds with that particular conundrum.

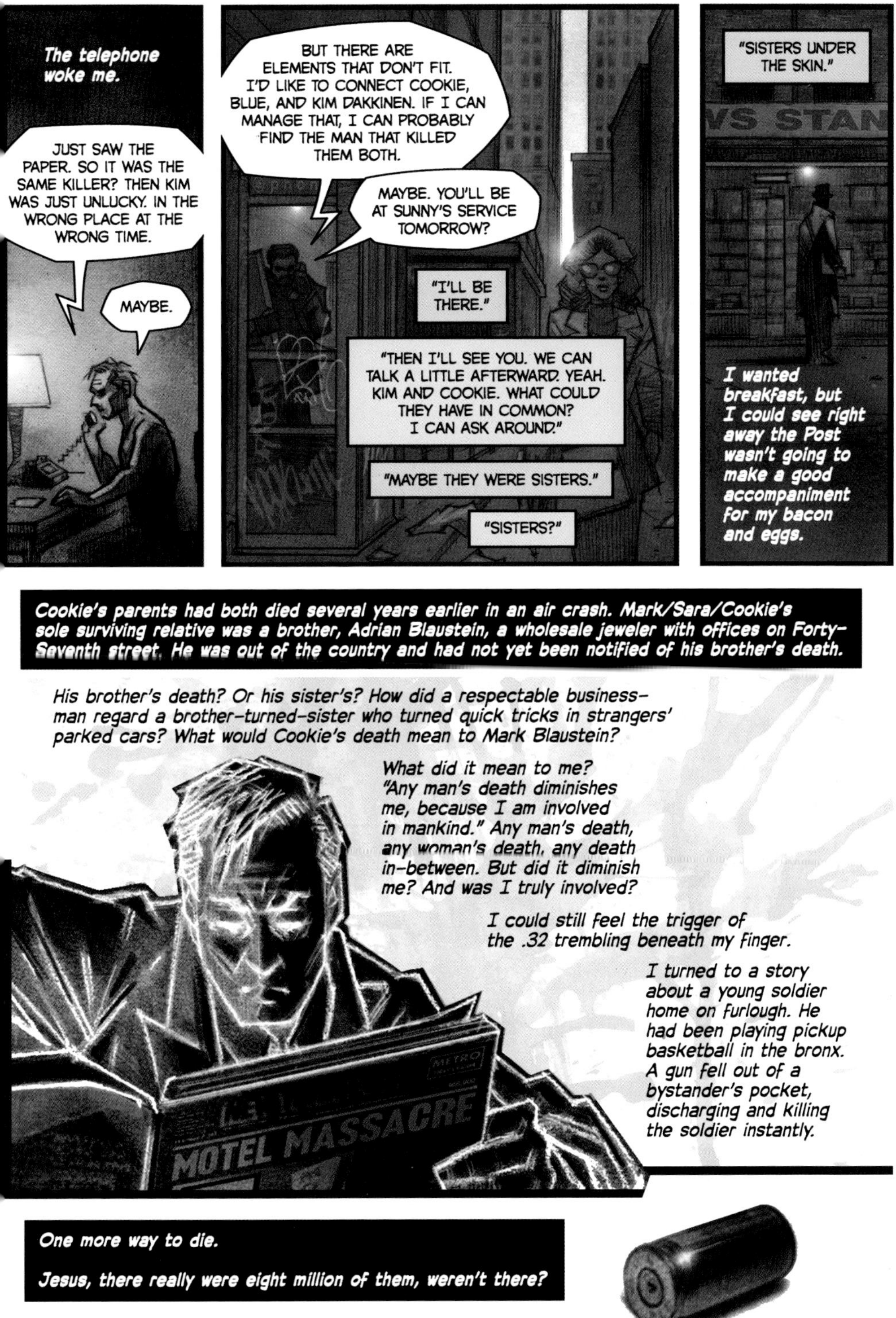
The telephone woke me.
JUST SAW THE PAPER. SO IT WAS THE SAME KILLER? THEN KIM WAS JUST UNLUCKY. IN THE WRONG PLACE AT THE WRONG TIME.
MAYBE.
BUT THERE ARE ELEMENTS THAT DON'T FIT. I'D LIKE TO CONNECT COOKIE, BLUE, AND KIM DAKKINEN. IF I CAN MANAGE THAT, I CAN PROBABLY FIND THE MAN THAT KILLED THEM BOTH.
MAYBE. YOU'LL BE AT SUNNY'S SERVICE TOMORROW?
"I'LL BE THERE."
"THEN I'LL SEE YOU. WE CAN TALK A LITTLE AFTERWARD. YEAH. KIM AND COOKIE. WHAT COULD THEY HAVE IN COMMON? I CAN ASK AROUND."
"MAYBE THEY WERE SISTERS."
"SISTERS?"
"SISTERS UNDER THE SKIN."
VS STAN
I wanted breakfast, but I could see right away the Post wasn't going to make a good accompaniment for my bacon and eggs.
Cookie's parents had both died several years earlier in an air crash. Mark/Sara/Cookie's sole surviving relative was a brother, Adrian Blaustein, a wholesale jeweler with offices on Forty-Seventh street. He was out of the country and had not yet been notified of his brother's death.
His brother's death? Or his sister's? How did a respectable businessman regard a brother-turned-sister who turned quick tricks in strangers' parked cars? What would Cookie's death mean to Mark Blaustein?
What did it mean to me? "Any man's death diminishes me, because I am involved in mankind." Any man's death, any woman's death, any death in-between. But did it diminish me? And was I truly involved?
I could still feel the trigger of the .32 trembling beneath my finger.
I turned to a story about a young soldier home on furlough. He had been playing pickup basketball in the bronx. A gun fell out of a bystander's pocket, discharging and killing the soldier instantly.
METRO
MOTEL MASSACRE
One more way to die.
Jesus, there really were eight million of them, weren't there?

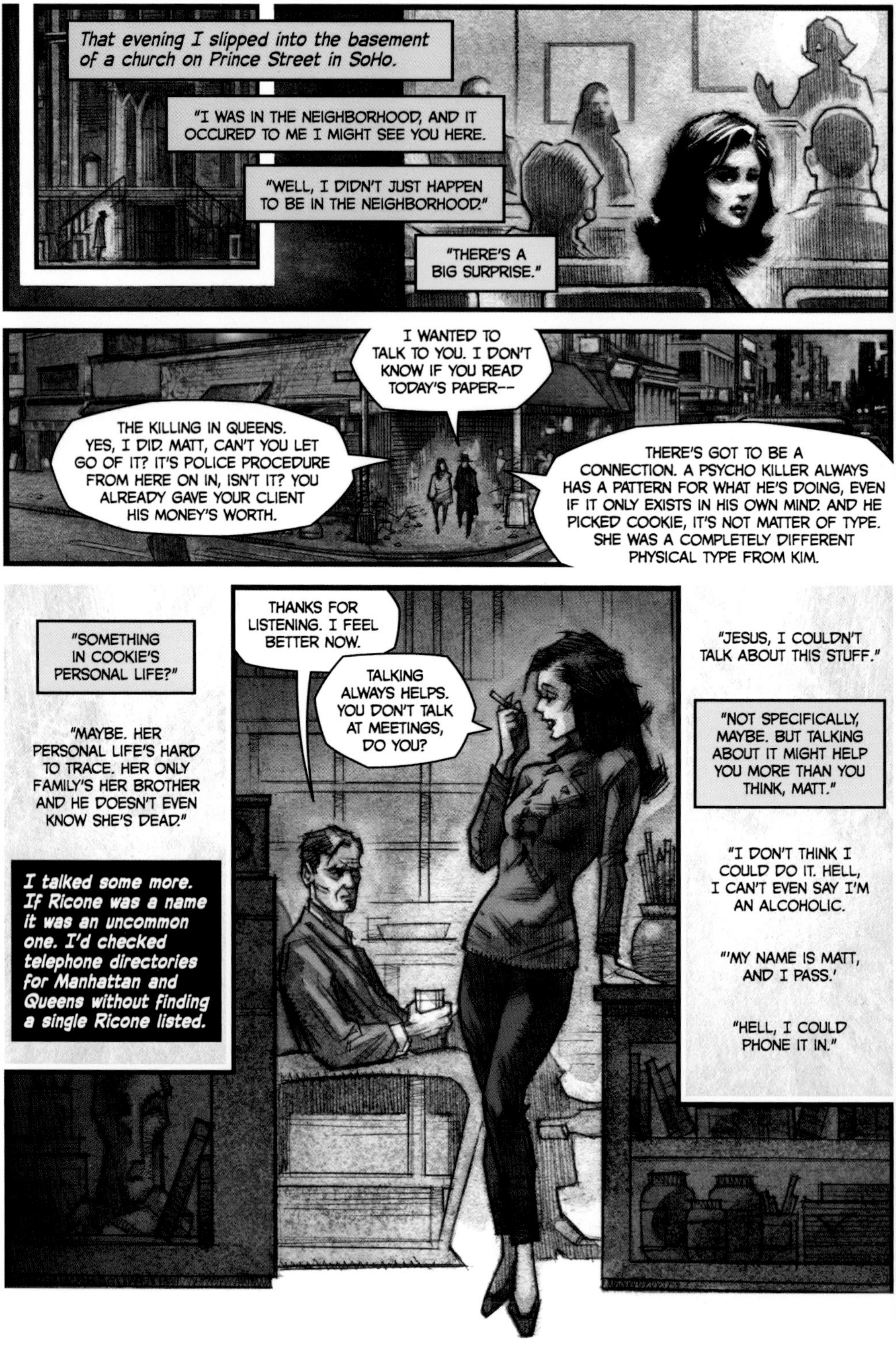
That evening I slipped into the basement of a church on Prince Street in SoHo.
"I WAS IN THE NEIGHBORHOOD, AND IT OCCURED TO ME I MIGHT SEE YOU HERE.
"WELL, I DIDN'T JUST HAPPEN TO BE IN THE NEIGHBORHOOD."
"THERE'S A BIG SURPRISE."
I WANTED TO TALK TO YOU. I DON'T KNOW IF YOU READ TODAY'S PAPER--
THE KILLING IN QUEENS. YES, I DID. MATT, CAN'T YOU LET GO OF IT? IT'S POLICE PROCEDURE FROM HERE ON IN, ISN'T IT? YOU ALREADY GAVE YOUR CLIENT HIS MONEY'S WORTH.
THERE'S GOT TO BE A CONNECTION. A PSYCHO KILLER ALWAYS HAS A PATTERN FOR WHAT HE'S DOING, EVEN IF IT ONLY EXISTS IN HIS OWN MIND. AND HE PICKED COOKIE, IT'S NOT MATTER OF TYPE. SHE WAS A COMPLETELY DIFFERENT PHYSICAL TYPE FROM KIM.
"SOMETHING IN COOKIE'S PERSONAL LIFE?"
"MAYBE. HER PERSONAL LIFE'S HARD TO TRACE. HER ONLY FAMILY'S HER BROTHER AND HE DOESN'T EVEN KNOW SHE'S DEAD."
I talked some more. If Ricone was a name it was an uncommon one. I'd checked telephone directories for Manhattan and Queens without finding a single Ricone listed.
THANKS FOR LISTENING. I FEEL BETTER NOW.
TALKING ALWAYS HELPS. YOU DON'T TALK AT MEETINGS, DO YOU?
"JESUS, I COULDN'T TALK ABOUT THIS STUFF."
"NOT SPECIFICALLY, MAYBE. BUT TALKING ABOUT IT MIGHT HELP YOU MORE THAN YOU THINK, MATT."
"I DON'T THINK I COULD DO IT. HELL, I CAN'T EVEN SAY I'M AN ALCOHOLIC.
"'MY NAME IS MATT, AND I PASS.'
"HELL, I COULD PHONE IT IN."

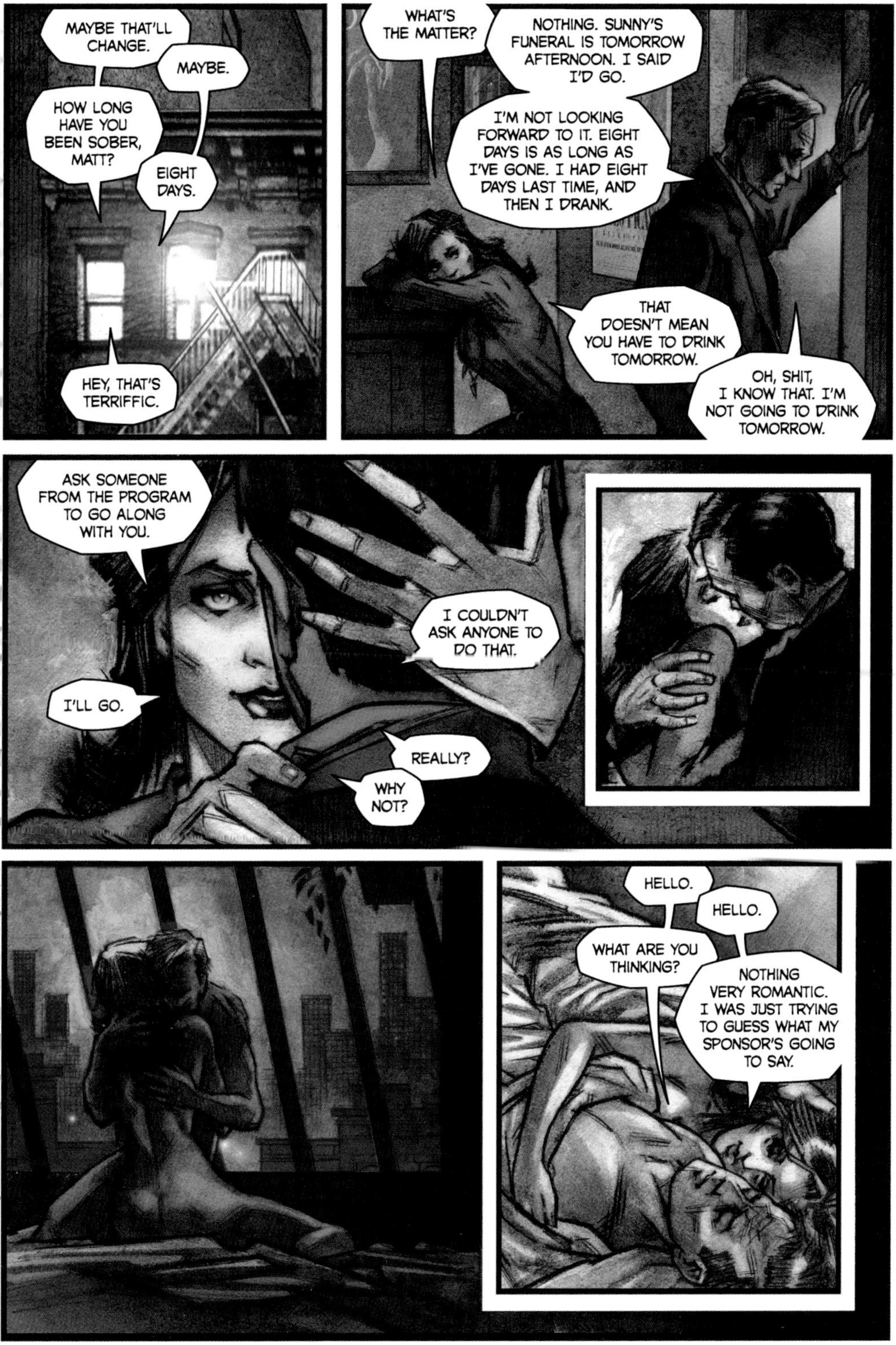
MAYBE THAT'LL CHANGE.
MAYBE.
HOW LONG HAVE YOU BEEN SOBER, MATT?
EIGHT DAYS.
HEY, THAT'S TERRIFFIC.
WHAT'S THE MATTER?
NOTHING. SUNNY'S FUNERAL IS TOMORROW AFTERNOON. I SAID I'D GO.
I'M NOT LOOKING FORWARD TO IT. EIGHT DAYS IS AS LONG AS I'VE GONE. I HAD EIGHT DAYS LAST TIME, AND THEN I DRANK.
THAT DOESN'T MEAN YOU HAVE TO DRINK TOMORROW.
OH, SHIT, I KNOW THAT. I'M NOT GOING TO DRINK TOMORROW.
ASK SOMEONE FROM THE PROGRAM TO GO ALONG WITH YOU.
I COULDN'T ASK ANYONE TO DO THAT.
I'LL GO.
REALLY?
WHY NOT?
HELLO.
HELLO.
WHAT ARE YOU THINKING?
NOTHING VERY ROMANTIC. I WAS JUST TRYING TO GUESS WHAT MY SPONSOR'S GOING TO SAY.

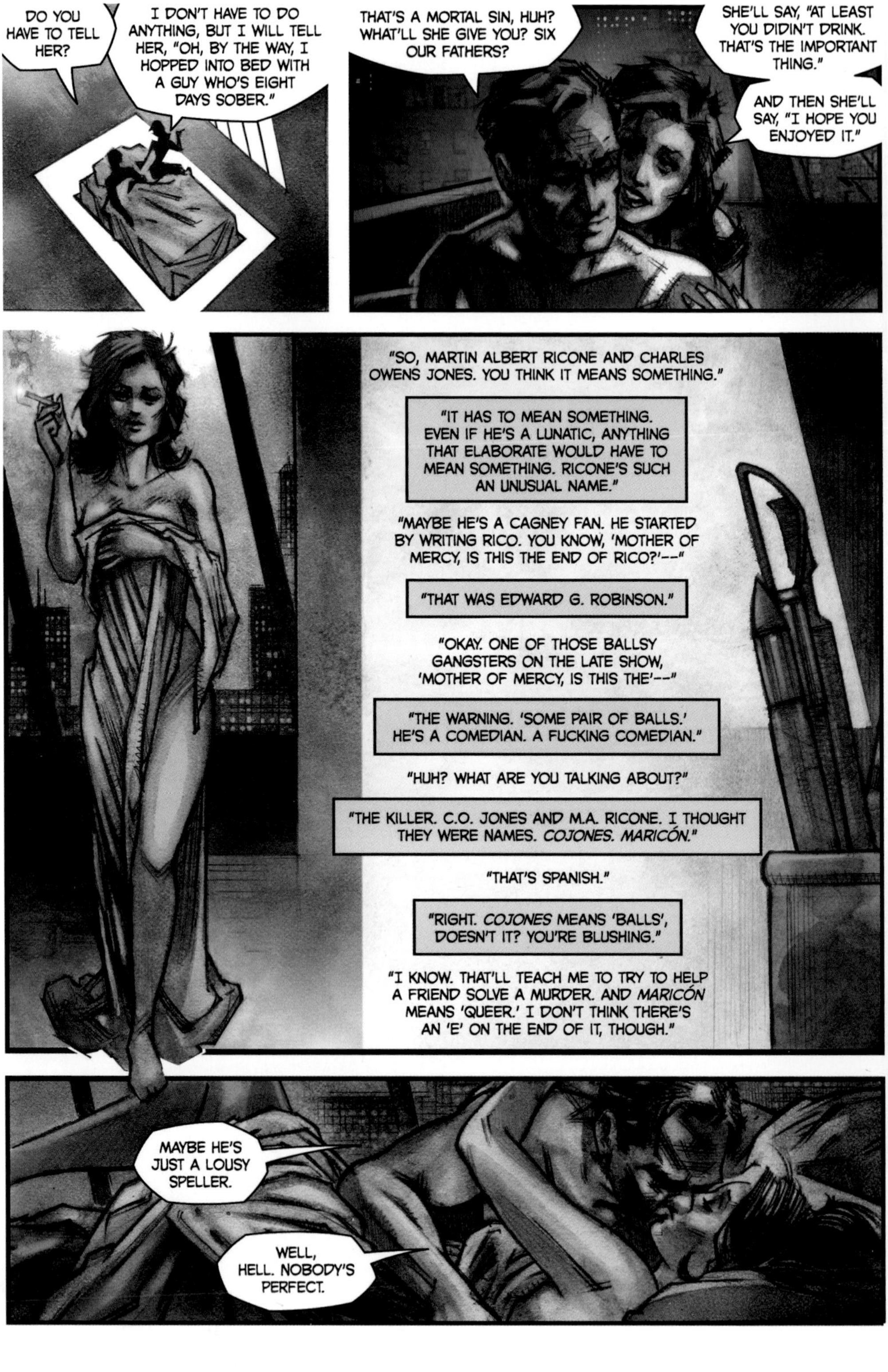
DO YOU HAVE TO TELL HER?
I DON'T HAVE TO DO ANYTHING, BUT I WILL TELL HER, "OH, BY THE WAY, I HOPPED INTO BED WITH A GUY WHO'S EIGHT DAYS SOBER."
THAT'S A MORTAL SIN, HUH? WHAT'LL SHE GIVE YOU? SIX OUR FATHERS?
SHE'LL SAY, "AT LEAST YOU DIDIN'T DRINK. THAT'S THE IMPORTANT THING."
AND THEN SHE'LL SAY, "I HOPE YOU ENJOYED IT."
"SO, MARTIN ALBERT RICONE AND CHARLES OWENS JONES. YOU THINK IT MEANS SOMETHING."
"IT HAS TO MEAN SOMETHING. EVEN IF HE'S A LUNATIC, ANYTHING THAT ELABORATE WOULD HAVE TO MEAN SOMETHING. RICONE'S SUCH AN UNUSUAL NAME."
"MAYBE HE'S A CAGNEY FAN. HE STARTED BY WRITING RICO. YOU KNOW, 'MOTHER OF MERCY, IS THIS THE END OF RICO?'--"
"THAT WAS EDWARD G. ROBINSON."
"OKAY. ONE OF THOSE BALLSY GANGSTERS ON THE LATE SHOW, 'MOTHER OF MERCY, IS THIS THE'--"
"THE WARNING. 'SOME PAIR OF BALLS.' HE'S A COMEDIAN. A FUCKING COMEDIAN."
"HUH? WHAT ARE YOU TALKING ABOUT?"
"THE KILLER. C.O. JONES AND M.A. RICONE. I THOUGHT THEY WERE NAMES. *COJONES. MARICÓN.*"
"THAT'S SPANISH."
"RIGHT. *COJONES* MEANS 'BALLS', DOESN'T IT? YOU'RE BLUSHING."
"I KNOW. THAT'LL TEACH ME TO TRY TO HELP A FRIEND SOLVE A MURDER. AND *MARICÓN* MEANS 'QUEER.' I DON'T THINK THERE'S AN 'E' ON THE END OF IT, THOUGH."
MAYBE HE'S JUST A LOUSY SPELLER.
WELL, HELL. NOBODY'S PERFECT.

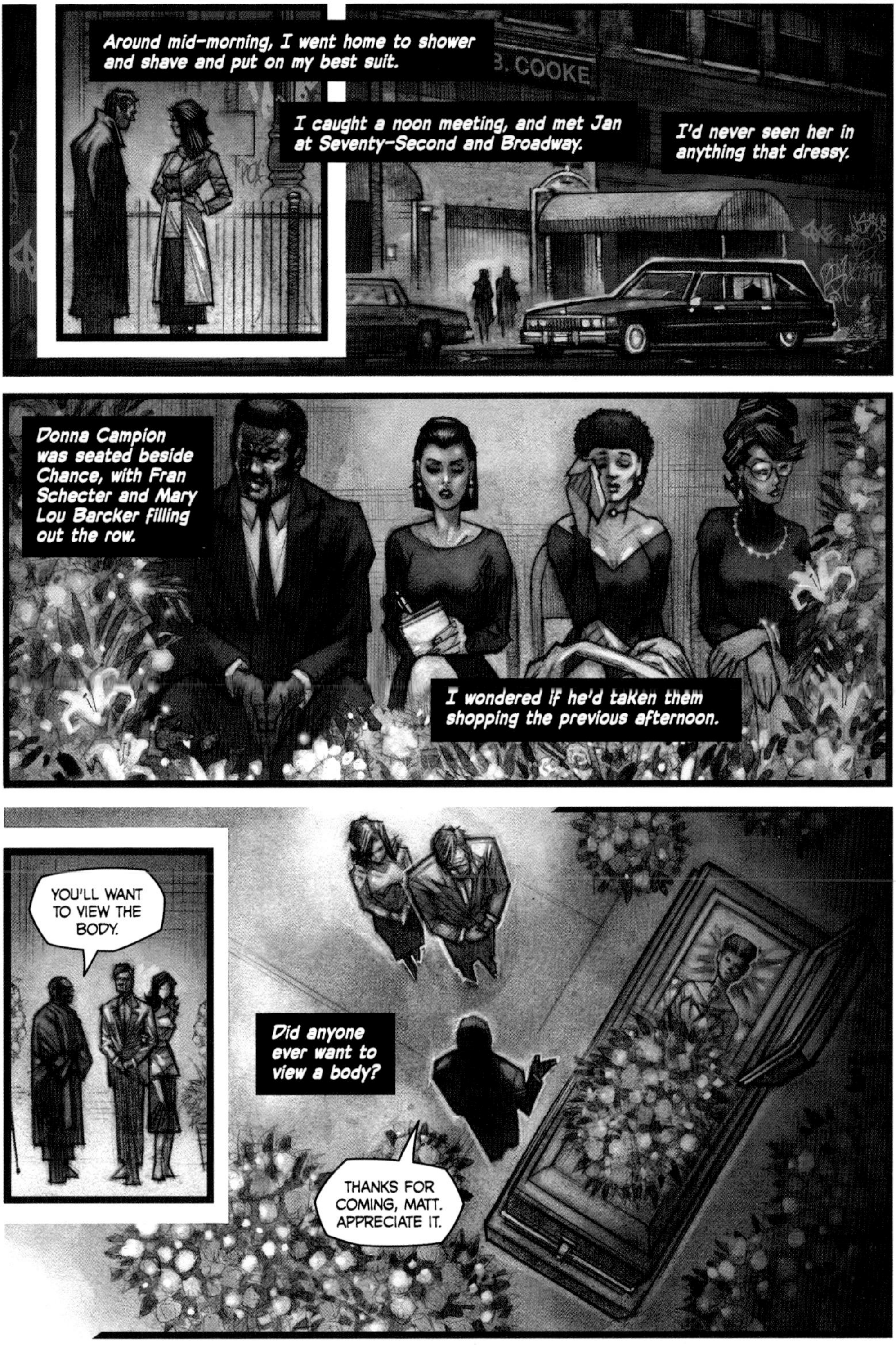
Around mid-morning, I went home to shower and shave and put on my best suit.
I caught a noon meeting, and met Jan at Seventy-Second and Broadway.
I'd never seen her in anything that dressy.
Donna Campion was seated beside Chance, with Fran Schecter and Mary Lou Barcker filling out the row.
I wondered if he'd taken them shopping the previous afternoon.
YOU'LL WANT TO VIEW THE BODY.
Did anyone ever want to view a body?
THANKS FOR COMING, MATT. APPRECIATE IT.

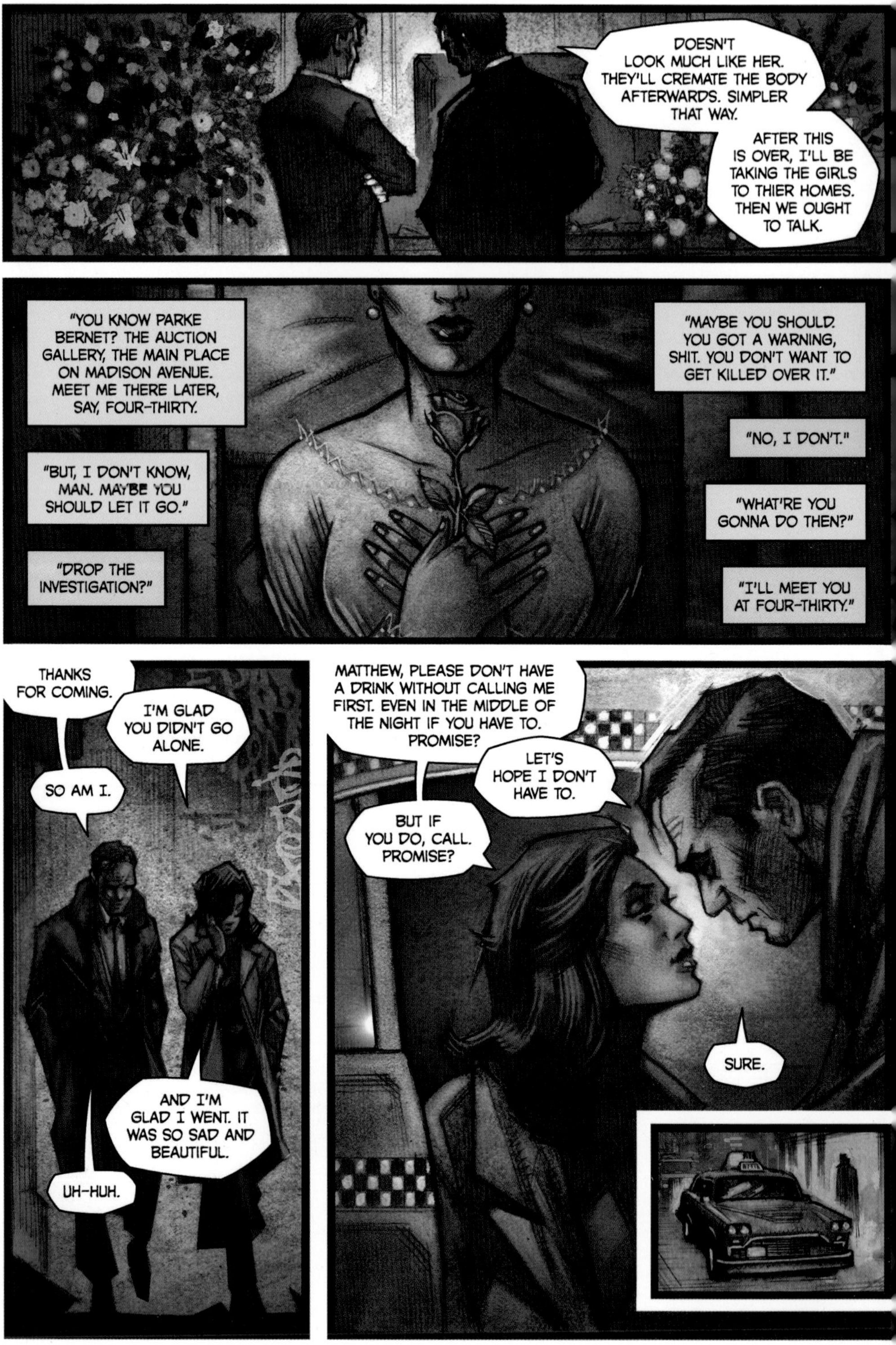
DOESN'T LOOK MUCH LIKE HER. THEY'LL CREMATE THE BODY AFTERWARDS. SIMPLER THAT WAY.
AFTER THIS IS OVER, I'LL BE TAKING THE GIRLS TO THIER HOMES. THEN WE OUGHT TO TALK.
"YOU KNOW PARKE BERNET? THE AUCTION GALLERY, THE MAIN PLACE ON MADISON AVENUE. MEET ME THERE LATER, SAY, FOUR-THIRTY.
"BUT, I DON'T KNOW, MAN. MAYBE YOU SHOULD LET IT GO."
"DROP THE INVESTIGATION?"
"MAYBE YOU SHOULD. YOU GOT A WARNING, SHIT. YOU DON'T WANT TO GET KILLED OVER IT."
"NO, I DON'T."
"WHAT'RE YOU GONNA DO THEN?"
"I'LL MEET YOU AT FOUR-THIRTY."
THANKS FOR COMING.
I'M GLAD YOU DIDN'T GO ALONE.
SO AM I.
AND I'M GLAD I WENT. IT WAS SO SAD AND BEAUTIFUL.
UH-HUH.
MATTHEW, PLEASE DON'T HAVE A DRINK WITHOUT CALLING ME FIRST. EVEN IN THE MIDDLE OF THE NIGHT IF YOU HAVE TO. PROMISE?
LET'S HOPE I DON'T HAVE TO.
BUT IF YOU DO, CALL. PROMISE?
SURE.

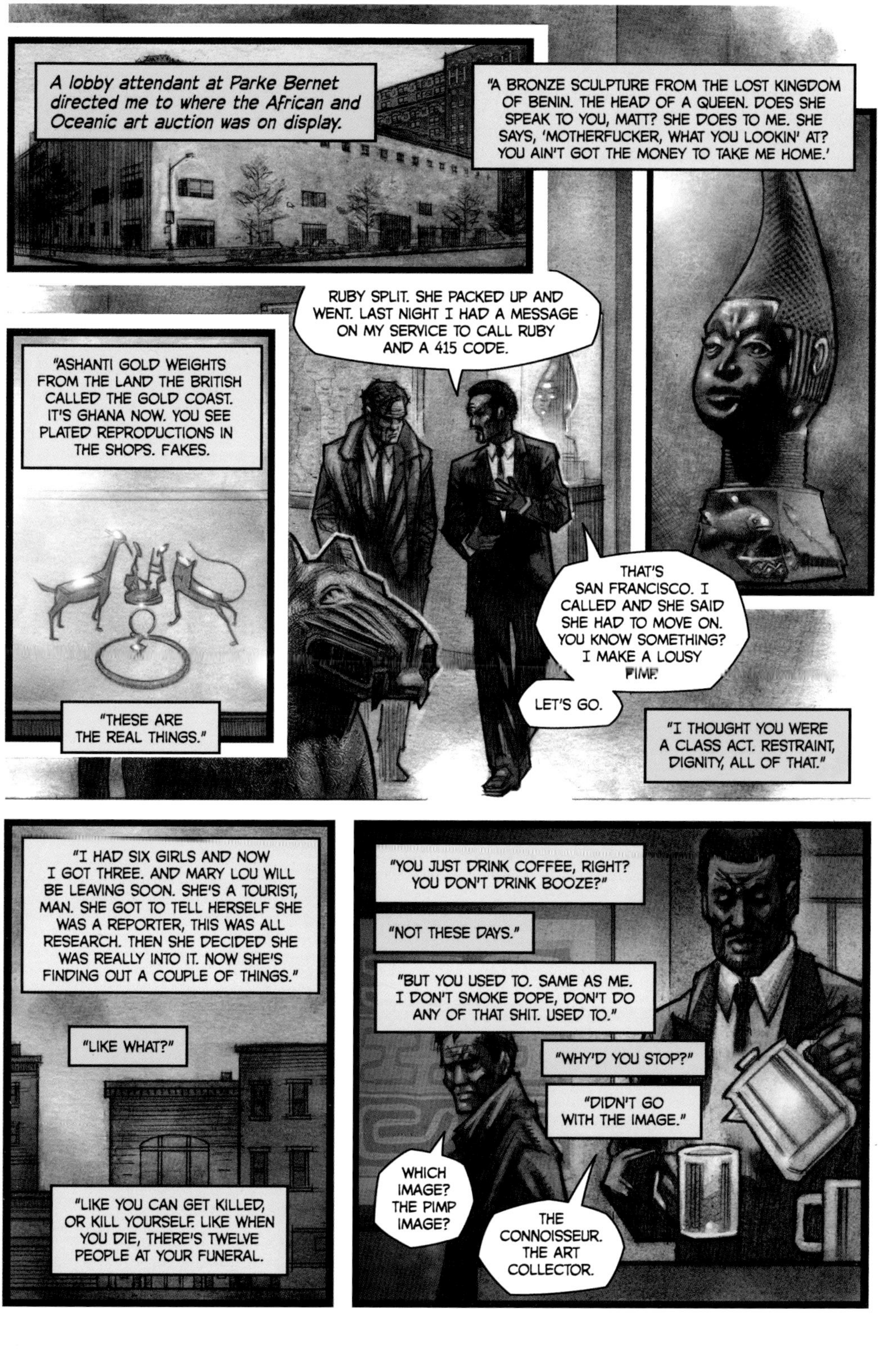
A lobby attendant at Parke Bernet directed me to where the African and Oceanic art auction was on display.
"A BRONZE SCULPTURE FROM THE LOST KINGDOM OF BENIN. THE HEAD OF A QUEEN. DOES SHE SPEAK TO YOU, MATT? SHE DOES TO ME. SHE SAYS, 'MOTHERFUCKER, WHAT YOU LOOKIN' AT? YOU AIN'T GOT THE MONEY TO TAKE ME HOME.'
"ASHANTI GOLD WEIGHTS FROM THE LAND THE BRITISH CALLED THE GOLD COAST. IT'S GHANA NOW. YOU SEE PLATED REPRODUCTIONS IN THE SHOPS. FAKES.
"THESE ARE THE REAL THINGS."
RUBY SPLIT. SHE PACKED UP AND WENT. LAST NIGHT I HAD A MESSAGE ON MY SERVICE TO CALL RUBY AND A 415 CODE.
THAT'S SAN FRANCISCO. I CALLED AND SHE SAID SHE HAD TO MOVE ON. YOU KNOW SOMETHING? I MAKE A LOUSY PIMP.
LET'S GO.
"I THOUGHT YOU WERE A CLASS ACT. RESTRAINT, DIGNITY, ALL OF THAT."
"I HAD SIX GIRLS AND NOW I GOT THREE. AND MARY LOU WILL BE LEAVING SOON. SHE'S A TOURIST, MAN. SHE GOT TO TELL HERSELF SHE WAS A REPORTER, THIS WAS ALL RESEARCH. THEN SHE DECIDED SHE WAS REALLY INTO IT. NOW SHE'S FINDING OUT A COUPLE OF THINGS."
"LIKE WHAT?"
"LIKE YOU CAN GET KILLED, OR KILL YOURSELF. LIKE WHEN YOU DIE, THERE'S TWELVE PEOPLE AT YOUR FUNERAL.
"YOU JUST DRINK COFFEE, RIGHT? YOU DON'T DRINK BOOZE?"
"NOT THESE DAYS."
"BUT YOU USED TO. SAME AS ME. I DON'T SMOKE DOPE, DON'T DO ANY OF THAT SHIT. USED TO."
"WHY'D YOU STOP?"
"DIDN'T GO WITH THE IMAGE."
WHICH IMAGE? THE PIMP IMAGE?
THE CONNOISSEUR. THE ART COLLECTOR.

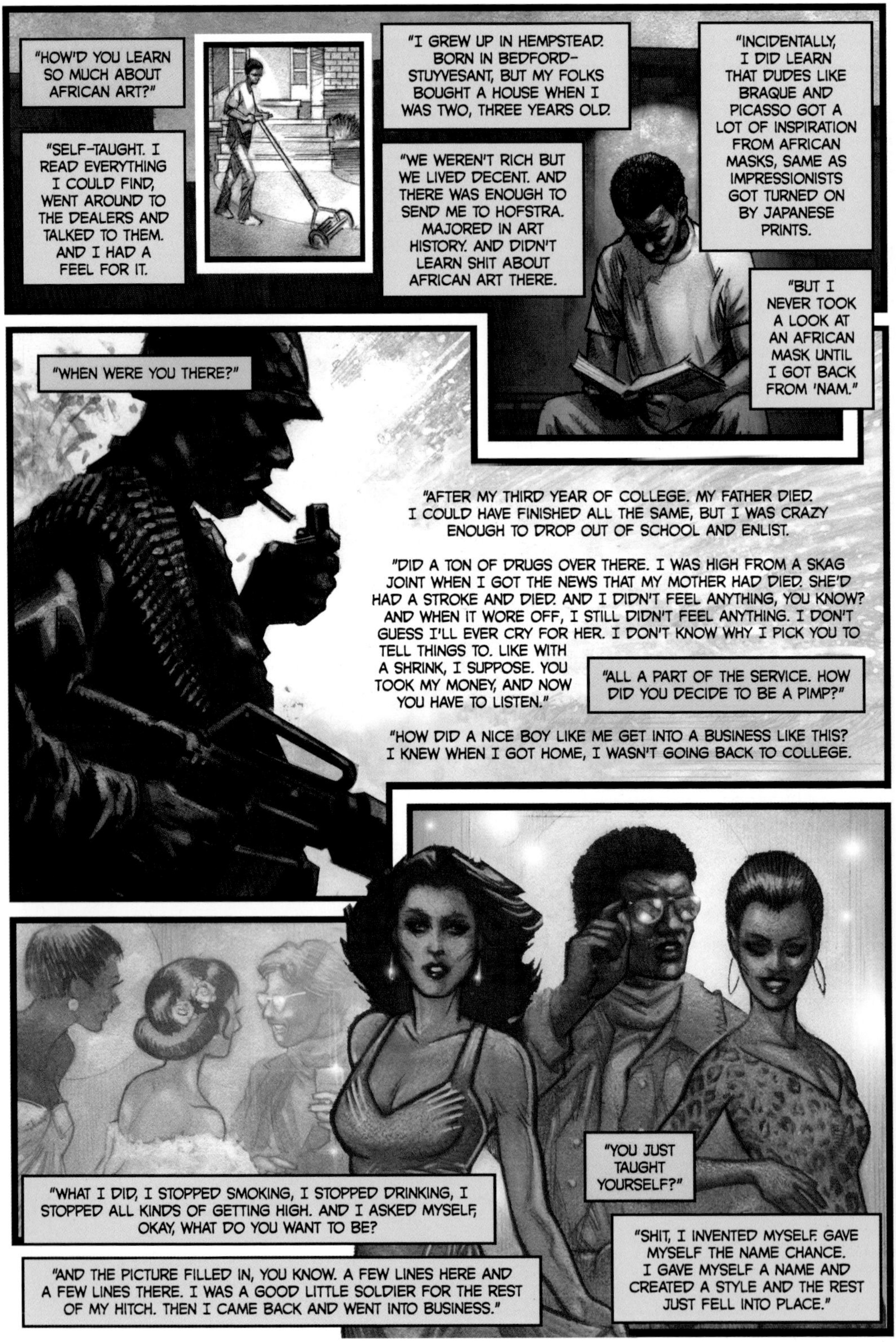
"HOW'D YOU LEARN SO MUCH ABOUT AFRICAN ART?"
"SELF-TAUGHT. I READ EVERYTHING I COULD FIND, WENT AROUND TO THE DEALERS AND TALKED TO THEM. AND I HAD A FEEL FOR IT.
"I GREW UP IN HEMPSTEAD. BORN IN BEDFORD-STUYVESANT, BUT MY FOLKS BOUGHT A HOUSE WHEN I WAS TWO, THREE YEARS OLD.
"WE WEREN'T RICH BUT WE LIVED DECENT. AND THERE WAS ENOUGH TO SEND ME TO HOFSTRA. MAJORED IN ART HISTORY. AND DIDN'T LEARN SHIT ABOUT AFRICAN ART THERE.
"INCIDENTALLY, I DID LEARN THAT DUDES LIKE BRAQUE AND PICASSO GOT A LOT OF INSPIRATION FROM AFRICAN MASKS, SAME AS IMPRESSIONISTS GOT TURNED ON BY JAPANESE PRINTS.
"BUT I NEVER TOOK A LOOK AT AN AFRICAN MASK UNTIL I GOT BACK FROM 'NAM."
"WHEN WERE YOU THERE?"
"AFTER MY THIRD YEAR OF COLLEGE. MY FATHER DIED. I COULD HAVE FINISHED ALL THE SAME, BUT I WAS CRAZY ENOUGH TO DROP OUT OF SCHOOL AND ENLIST.
"DID A TON OF DRUGS OVER THERE. I WAS HIGH FROM A SKAG JOINT WHEN I GOT THE NEWS THAT MY MOTHER HAD DIED. SHE'D HAD A STROKE AND DIED. AND I DIDN'T FEEL ANYTHING, YOU KNOW? AND WHEN IT WORE OFF, I STILL DIDN'T FEEL ANYTHING. I DON'T GUESS I'LL EVER CRY FOR HER. I DON'T KNOW WHY I PICK YOU TO TELL THINGS TO. LIKE WITH A SHRINK, I SUPPOSE. YOU TOOK MY MONEY, AND NOW YOU HAVE TO LISTEN."
"ALL A PART OF THE SERVICE. HOW DID YOU DECIDE TO BE A PIMP?"
"HOW DID A NICE BOY LIKE ME GET INTO A BUSINESS LIKE THIS? I KNEW WHEN I GOT HOME, I WASN'T GOING BACK TO COLLEGE.
"WHAT I DID, I STOPPED SMOKING, I STOPPED DRINKING, I STOPPED ALL KINDS OF GETTING HIGH. AND I ASKED MYSELF, OKAY, WHAT DO YOU WANT TO BE?
"AND THE PICTURE FILLED IN, YOU KNOW. A FEW LINES HERE AND A FEW LINES THERE. I WAS A GOOD LITTLE SOLDIER FOR THE REST OF MY HITCH. THEN I CAME BACK AND WENT INTO BUSINESS."
"YOU JUST TAUGHT YOURSELF?"
"SHIT, I INVENTED MYSELF. GAVE MYSELF THE NAME CHANCE. I GAVE MYSELF A NAME AND CREATED A STYLE AND THE REST JUST FELL INTO PLACE."

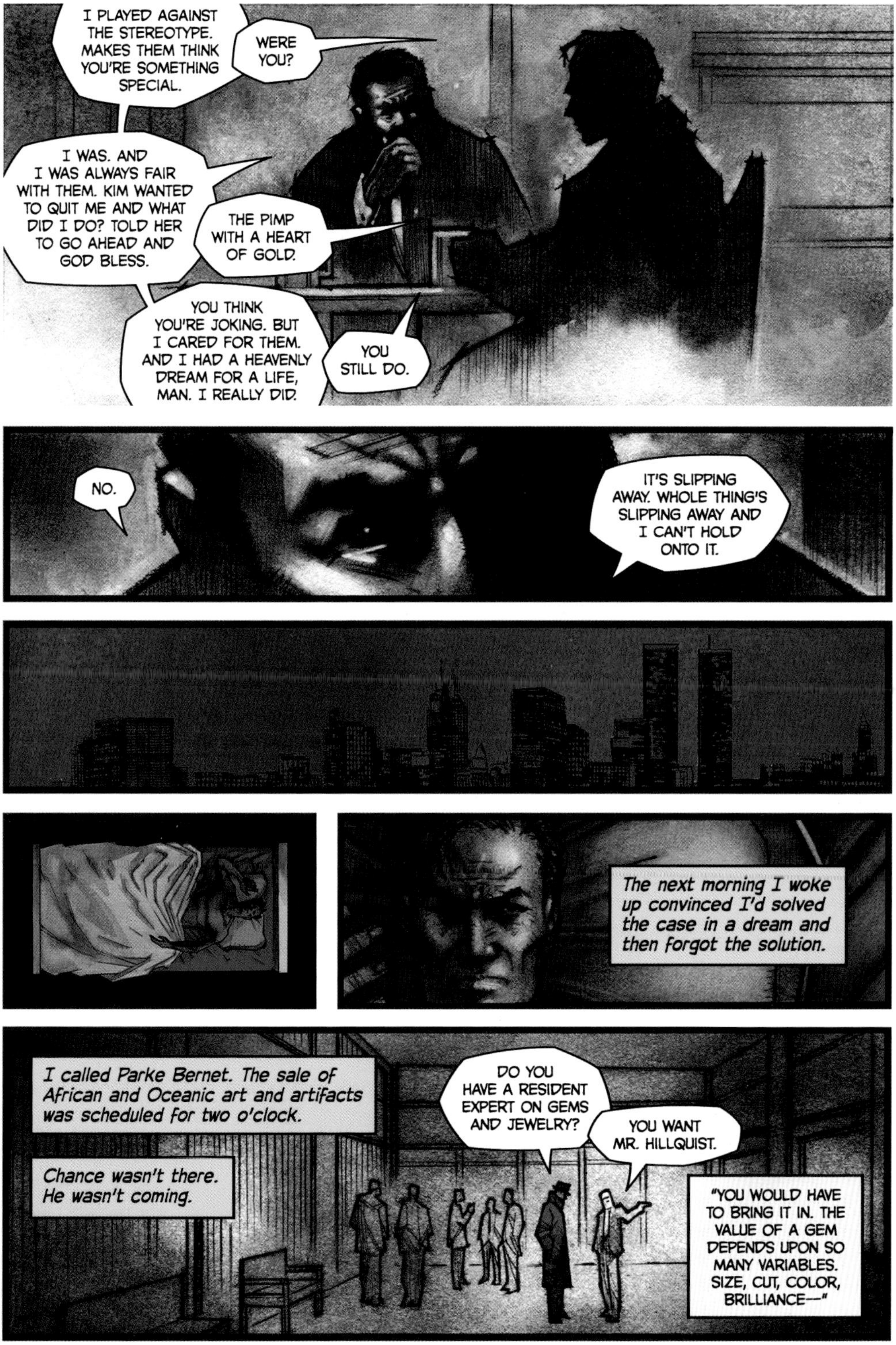
I PLAYED AGAINST THE STEREOTYPE. MAKES THEM THINK YOU'RE SOMETHING SPECIAL.
WERE YOU?
I WAS. AND I WAS ALWAYS FAIR WITH THEM. KIM WANTED TO QUIT ME AND WHAT DID I DO? TOLD HER TO GO AHEAD AND GOD BLESS.
THE PIMP WITH A HEART OF GOLD.
YOU THINK YOU'RE JOKING. BUT I CARED FOR THEM. AND I HAD A HEAVENLY DREAM FOR A LIFE, MAN. I REALLY DID.
YOU STILL DO.
NO.
IT'S SLIPPING AWAY. WHOLE THING'S SLIPPING AWAY AND I CAN'T HOLD ONTO IT.
The next morning I woke up convinced I'd solved the case in a dream and then forgot the solution.
I called Parke Bernet. The sale of African and Oceanic art and artifacts was scheduled for two o'clock.
Chance wasn't there. He wasn't coming.
DO YOU HAVE A RESIDENT EXPERT ON GEMS AND JEWELRY?
YOU WANT MR. HILLQUIST.
"YOU WOULD HAVE TO BRING IT IN. THE VALUE OF A GEM DEPENDS UPON SO MANY VARIABLES. SIZE, CUT, COLOR, BRILLIANCE—"

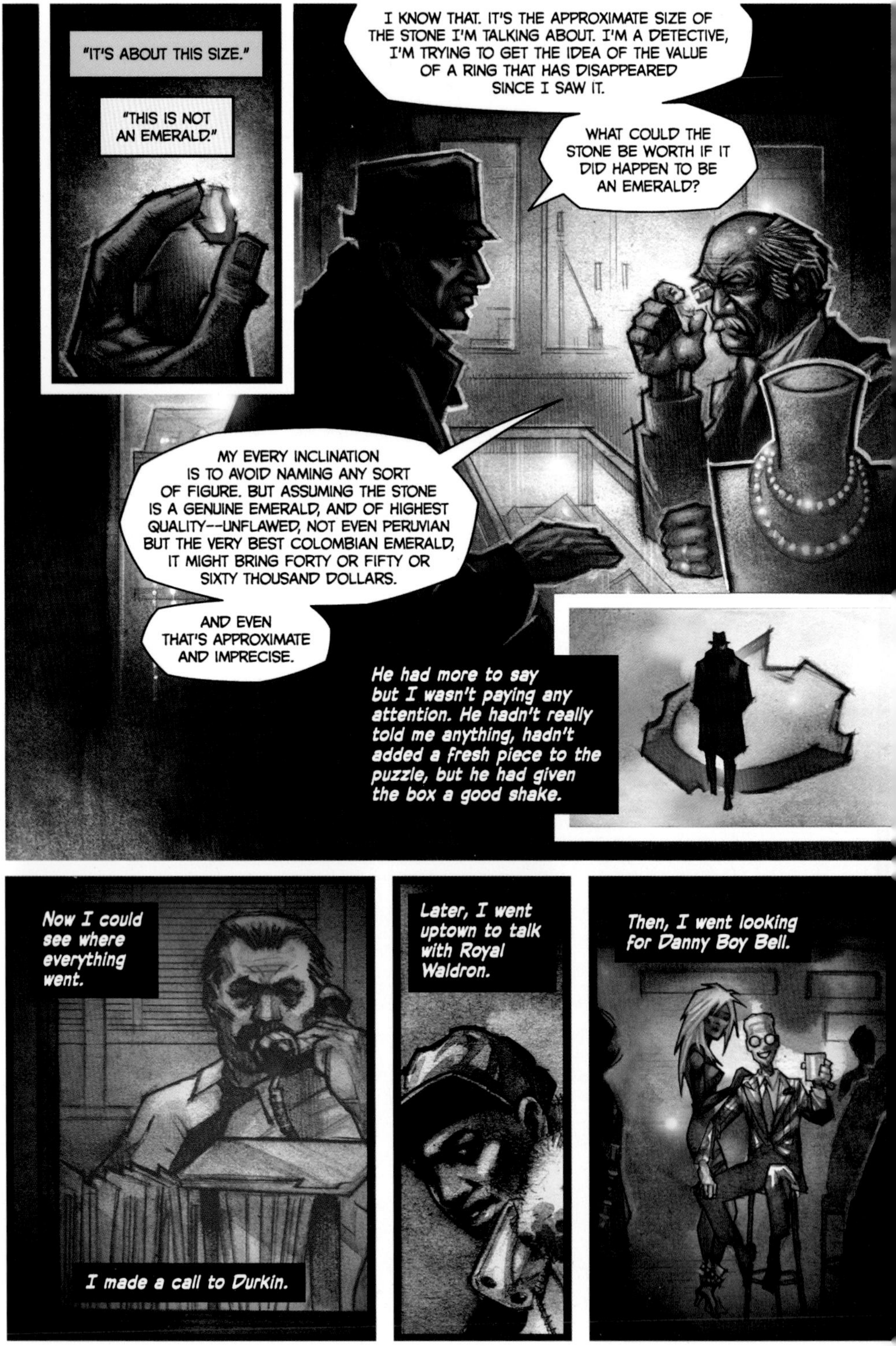
"IT'S ABOUT THIS SIZE."
"THIS IS NOT AN EMERALD."
I KNOW THAT. IT'S THE APPROXIMATE SIZE OF THE STONE I'M TALKING ABOUT. I'M A DETECTIVE, I'M TRYING TO GET THE IDEA OF THE VALUE OF A RING THAT HAS DISAPPEARED SINCE I SAW IT.
WHAT COULD THE STONE BE WORTH IF IT DID HAPPEN TO BE AN EMERALD?
MY EVERY INCLINATION IS TO AVOID NAMING ANY SORT OF FIGURE. BUT ASSUMING THE STONE IS A GENUINE EMERALD, AND OF HIGHEST QUALITY--UNFLAWED, NOT EVEN PERUVIAN BUT THE VERY BEST COLOMBIAN EMERALD, IT MIGHT BRING FORTY OR FIFTY OR SIXTY THOUSAND DOLLARS.
AND EVEN THAT'S APPROXIMATE AND IMPRECISE.
He had more to say but I wasn't paying any attention. He hadn't really told me anything, hadn't added a fresh piece to the puzzle, but he had given the box a good shake.
Now I could see where everything went.
I made a call to Durkin.
Later, I went uptown to talk with Royal Waldron.
Then, I went looking for Danny Boy Bell.

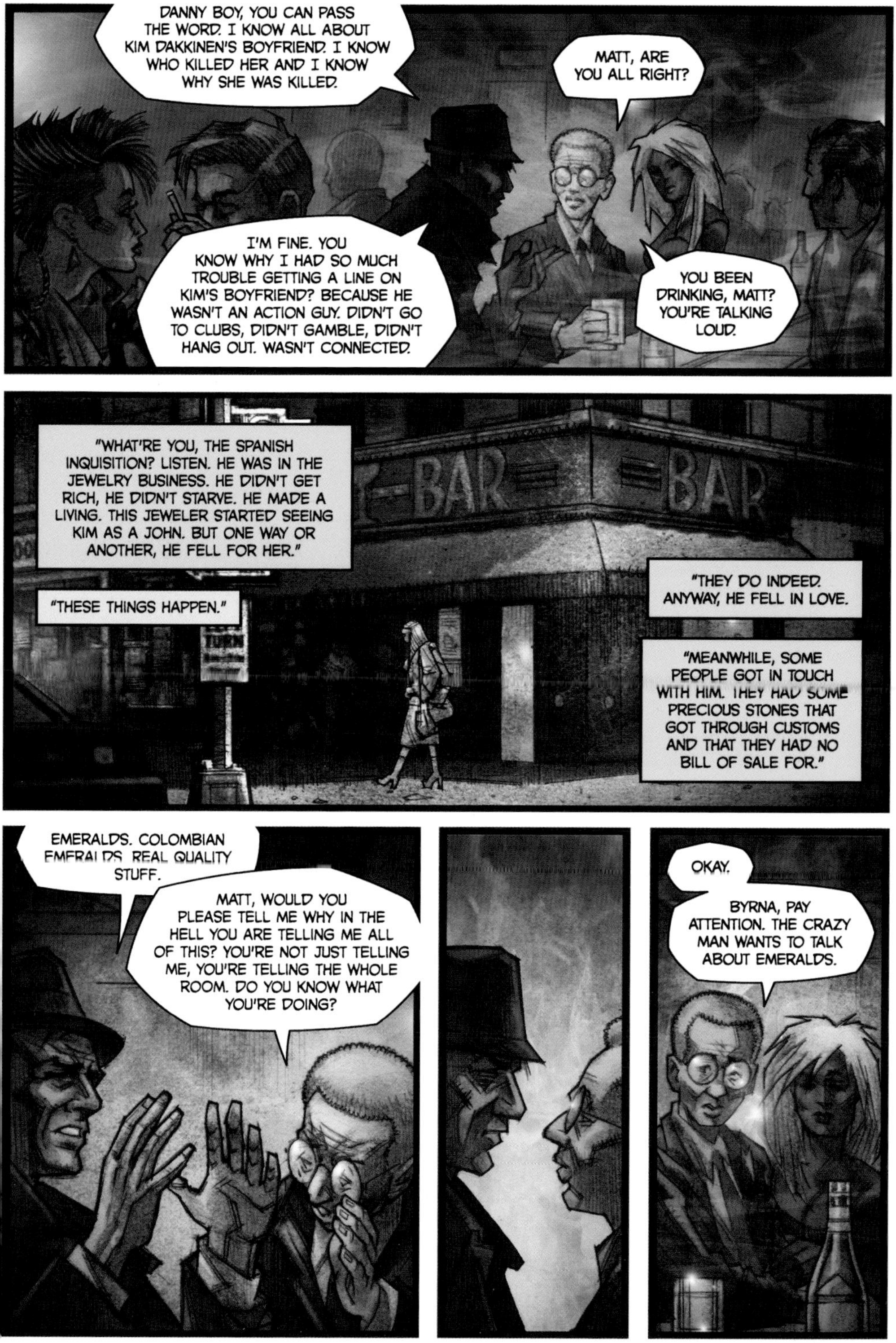
DANNY BOY, YOU CAN PASS THE WORD. I KNOW ALL ABOUT KIM DAKKINEN'S BOYFRIEND. I KNOW WHO KILLED HER AND I KNOW WHY SHE WAS KILLED.
MATT, ARE YOU ALL RIGHT?
I'M FINE. YOU KNOW WHY I HAD SO MUCH TROUBLE GETTING A LINE ON KIM'S BOYFRIEND? BECAUSE HE WASN'T AN ACTION GUY. DIDN'T GO TO CLUBS, DIDN'T GAMBLE, DIDN'T HANG OUT. WASN'T CONNECTED.
YOU BEEN DRINKING, MATT? YOU'RE TALKING LOUD.
"WHAT'RE YOU, THE SPANISH INQUISITION? LISTEN. HE WAS IN THE JEWELRY BUSINESS. HE DIDN'T GET RICH, HE DIDN'T STARVE. HE MADE A LIVING. THIS JEWELER STARTED SEEING KIM AS A JOHN. BUT ONE WAY OR ANOTHER, HE FELL FOR HER."
BAR
BAR
"THESE THINGS HAPPEN."
"THEY DO INDEED. ANYWAY, HE FELL IN LOVE.
"MEANWHILE, SOME PEOPLE GOT IN TOUCH WITH HIM. THEY HAD SOME PRECIOUS STONES THAT GOT THROUGH CUSTOMS AND THAT THEY HAD NO BILL OF SALE FOR."
EMERALDS. COLOMBIAN EMERALDS. REAL QUALITY STUFF.
MATT, WOULD YOU PLEASE TELL ME WHY IN THE HELL YOU ARE TELLING ME ALL OF THIS? YOU'RE NOT JUST TELLING ME, YOU'RE TELLING THE WHOLE ROOM. DO YOU KNOW WHAT YOU'RE DOING?
OKAY.
BYRNA, PAY ATTENTION. THE CRAZY MAN WANTS TO TALK ABOUT EMERALDS.

"KIM'S BOYFRIEND WAS GOING TO BE THE MIDDLEMAN. HE DID THIS SORT OF THING BEFORE, BUT NOW HE WAS IN LOVE WITH AN EXPENSIVE LADY AND HE HAD A REASON TO WANT SOME REAL MONEY. SO HE TRIED A CROSS."

"HOW?"

"IF I WERE GOING TO GUESS, I'D SAY HE DID A SWITCH AND WENT OUT OF THE COUNTRY TO UNLOAD THE GOOD STUFF. KIM GOT HERSELF FREE OF CHANCE WHILE HE WAS GONE, AND WHEN HE GOT BACK IT WAS GOING TO BE HAPPILY EVER AFTER TIME. BUT HE NEVER CAME BACK."

"IF HE NEVER CAME BACK, WHO KILLED HER?"

"THE PEOPLE HE CROSSED. THEY DECOYED HER TO THAT ROOM AT THE GALAXY DOWNTOWNER. SUPPOSE SHE GETS A CALL FROM SOMEBODY WHO SAYS HE'S A FRIEND AND THE BOYFRIEND'S AFRAID TO COME TO HER PLACE, HE THINKS HE'S BEING FOLLOWED, SO WOULD SHE PLEASE COME TO THE HOTEL?

"AND SHE WENT. SHE WORE THE PRESENTS HE GAVE HER, THE MINK JACKET AND THE EMERALD RING. THE JACKET WASN'T WORTH A FORTUNE BECAUSE THE GUY WASN'T RICH, BUT HE COULD GIVE HER A TERRIFIC EMERALD BECAUSE THE EMERALDS DIDN'T COST HIM ANYTHING. HE COULD TAKE ONE OF THOSE SMUGGLED STONES AND HAVE IT SET IN A RING FOR HER."

"SO YOU FIGURE SHE WENT OVER AND GOT KILLED. WHY? THEY KILLED HER TO GET THE RING BACK?"

"THEY KILLED HER TO KILL HER. BECAUSE THEY WERE COLOMBIANS, AND THAT'S HOW THEY DO IT. WHEN THEY HAVE A REASON TO HIT SOMEONE THEY GO FOR THE WHOLE FAMILY."

"JESUS."

"KIM'S BOYFRIEND WASN'T A MARRIED GUY. HE WAS A BACHELOR. NO WIFE, NO KIDS, NO LIVING PARENTS. YOU WANT TO RUB OUT HIS FAMILY, WHAT DO YOU DO? YOU KILL HIS GIRLFRIEND.

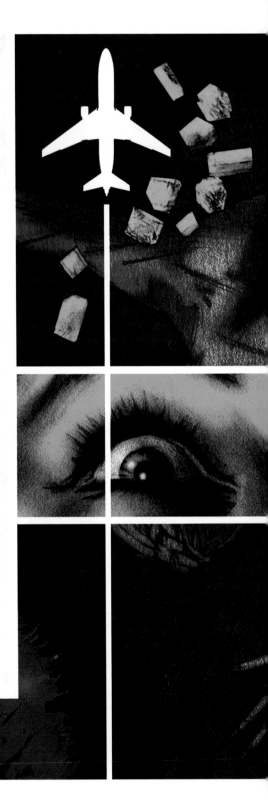

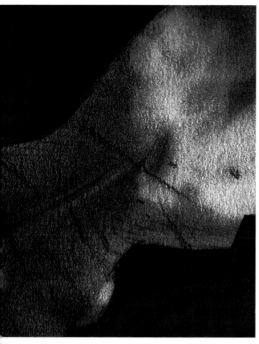

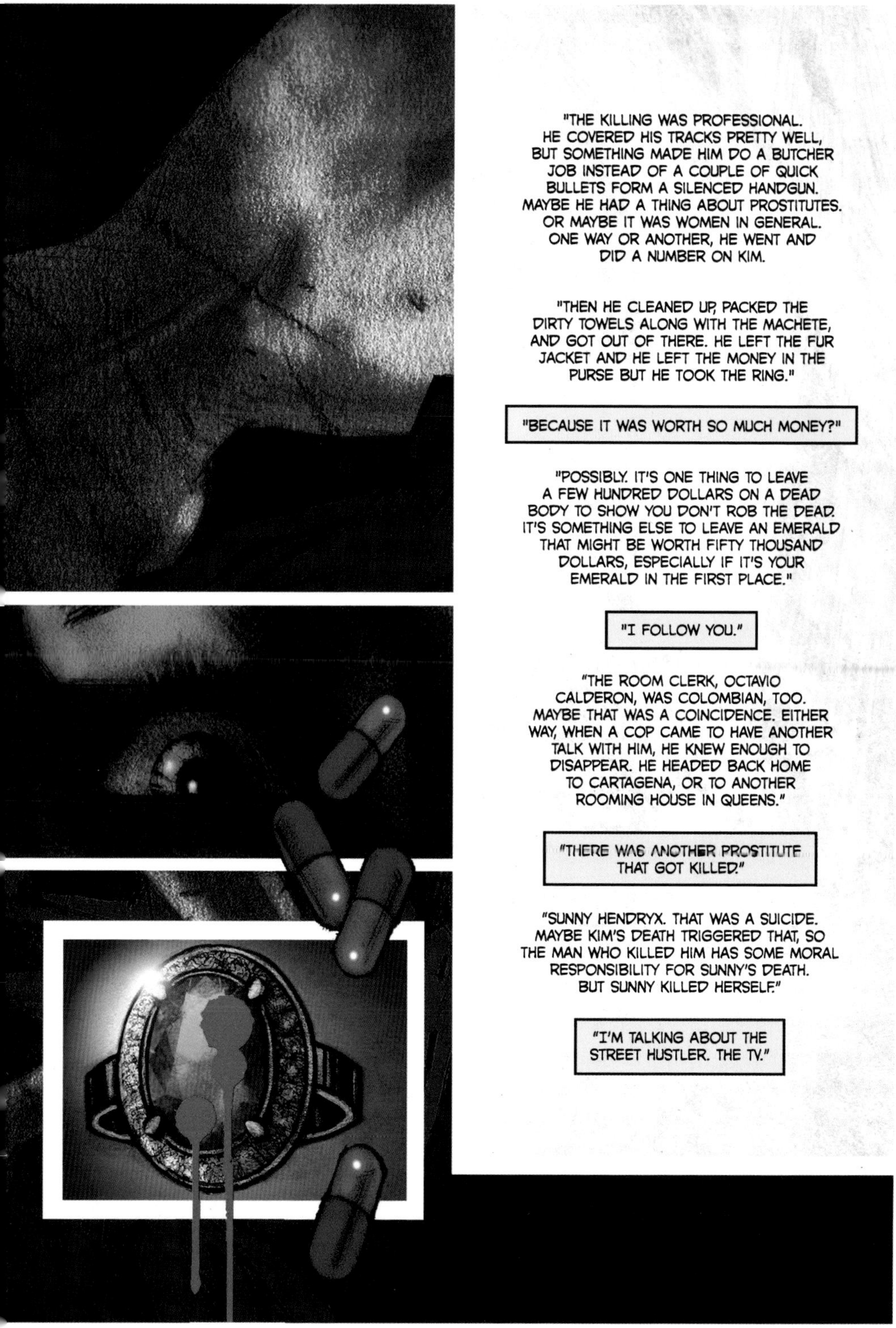

"THE KILLING WAS PROFESSIONAL. HE COVERED HIS TRACKS PRETTY WELL, BUT SOMETHING MADE HIM DO A BUTCHER JOB INSTEAD OF A COUPLE OF QUICK BULLETS FORM A SILENCED HANDGUN. MAYBE HE HAD A THING ABOUT PROSTITUTES. OR MAYBE IT WAS WOMEN IN GENERAL. ONE WAY OR ANOTHER, HE WENT AND DID A NUMBER ON KIM.

"THEN HE CLEANED UP, PACKED THE DIRTY TOWELS ALONG WITH THE MACHETE, AND GOT OUT OF THERE. HE LEFT THE FUR JACKET AND HE LEFT THE MONEY IN THE PURSE BUT HE TOOK THE RING."

"BECAUSE IT WAS WORTH SO MUCH MONEY?"

"POSSIBLY. IT'S ONE THING TO LEAVE A FEW HUNDRED DOLLARS ON A DEAD BODY TO SHOW YOU DON'T ROB THE DEAD. IT'S SOMETHING ELSE TO LEAVE AN EMERALD THAT MIGHT BE WORTH FIFTY THOUSAND DOLLARS, ESPECIALLY IF IT'S YOUR EMERALD IN THE FIRST PLACE."

"I FOLLOW YOU."

"THE ROOM CLERK, OCTAVIO CALDERON, WAS COLOMBIAN, TOO. MAYBE THAT WAS A COINCIDENCE. EITHER WAY, WHEN A COP CAME TO HAVE ANOTHER TALK WITH HIM, HE KNEW ENOUGH TO DISAPPEAR. HE HEADED BACK HOME TO CARTAGENA, OR TO ANOTHER ROOMING HOUSE IN QUEENS."

"THERE WAS ANOTHER PROSTITUTE THAT GOT KILLED."

"SUNNY HENDRYX. THAT WAS A SUICIDE. MAYBE KIM'S DEATH TRIGGERED THAT, SO THE MAN WHO KILLED HIM HAS SOME MORAL RESPONSIBILITY FOR SUNNY'S DEATH. BUT SUNNY KILLED HERSELF."

"I'M TALKING ABOUT THE STREET HUSTLER. THE TV."

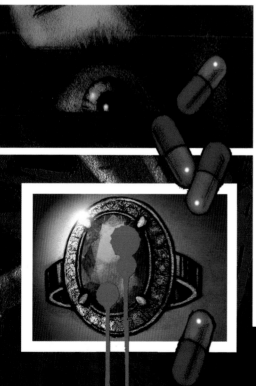

"COOKIE BLUE."

"THAT'S THE ONE. WHY DID SHE GET KILLED? TO THROW YOU OFF THE TRACK? EXCEPT YOU WEREN'T ON THE TRACK TO BEGIN WITH."

"NO."

"THEN WHY? YOU THINK THE FIRST KILLING TURNED THE KILLER NUTS? SOMETHING IN HIM THAT MADE HIM WANT TO DO IT AGAIN?"

"I THINK THAT'S PART OF IT. NOBODY WOULD DO A SECOND BUTCHER JOB LIKE THAT UNLESS HE ENJOYED THE FIRST ONE. I DON'T KNOW IF HE HAD SEX WITH EITHER OF HIS VICTIMS, BUT THE KICK HE GOT OUT OF THE KILLINGS HAD TO BE SEXUAL."

"SO HE JUST PICKED UP COOKIE FOR THE HELL OF IT?"

"NO. COOKIE WAS KILLED FOR A SPECIFIC REASON. COOKIE WAS FAMILY. COOKIE STARTED LIFE AS MARK BLAUSTEIN. MARK HAD AN OLDER BROTHER NAMED ADRIAN WHO WENT INTO THE JEWELRY BUSINESS. ADRIAN BLAUSTEIN HAD A GIRLFRIEND NAMED KIM AND SOME BUSINESS ASSOCIATES FROM COLOMBIA."

"SO COOKIE AND KIM WERE CONNECTED."

"THEY HAD TO BE CONNECTED. I'M SURE THEY NEVER MET EACH OTHER. I DON'T THINK MARK AND ADRIAN HAD ANY CONTACT IN RECENT YEARS. THAT MAY EXPLAIN WHY IT TOOK THE KILLER SO LONG TO FIND COOKIE. BUT I KNEW THERE HAD TO BE SOME KIND OF A LINK. I TOLD SOMEONE EARLIER THEY WERE SISTERS UNDER THE SKIN. THEY WERE ALMOST SISTERS-IN-LAW."

BYRNA, PLEASE GIVE US A FEW MOMENTS ALONE. THANK YOU.

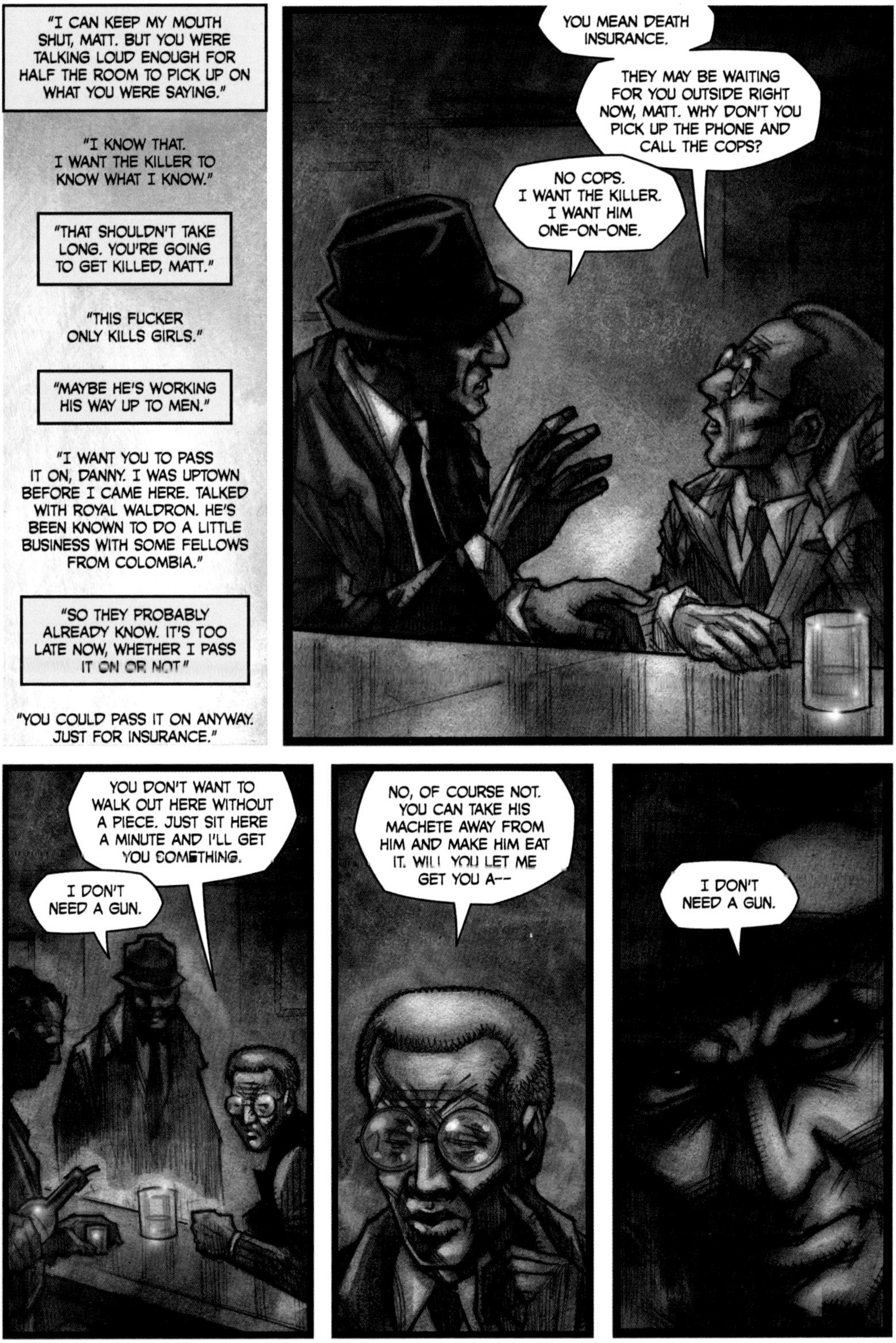
"I CAN KEEP MY MOUTH SHUT, MATT. BUT YOU WERE TALKING LOUD ENOUGH FOR HALF THE ROOM TO PICK UP ON WHAT YOU WERE SAYING."
"I KNOW THAT. I WANT THE KILLER TO KNOW WHAT I KNOW."
"THAT SHOULDN'T TAKE LONG. YOU'RE GOING TO GET KILLED, MATT."
"THIS FUCKER ONLY KILLS GIRLS."
"MAYBE HE'S WORKING HIS WAY UP TO MEN."
"I WANT YOU TO PASS IT ON, DANNY. I WAS UPTOWN BEFORE I CAME HERE. TALKED WITH ROYAL WALDRON. HE'S BEEN KNOWN TO DO A LITTLE BUSINESS WITH SOME FELLOWS FROM COLOMBIA."
"SO THEY PROBABLY ALREADY KNOW. IT'S TOO LATE NOW, WHETHER I PASS IT ON OR NOT."
"YOU COULD PASS IT ON ANYWAY. JUST FOR INSURANCE."
YOU MEAN DEATH INSURANCE.
THEY MAY BE WAITING FOR YOU OUTSIDE RIGHT NOW, MATT. WHY DON'T YOU PICK UP THE PHONE AND CALL THE COPS?
NO COPS. I WANT THE KILLER. I WANT HIM ONE-ON-ONE.
YOU DON'T WANT TO WALK OUT HERE WITHOUT A PIECE. JUST SIT HERE A MINUTE AND I'LL GET YOU SOMETHING.
I DON'T NEED A GUN.
NO, OF COURSE NOT. YOU CAN TAKE HIS MACHETE AWAY FROM HIM AND MAKE HIM EAT IT. WILL YOU LET ME GET YOU A--
I DON'T NEED A GUN.

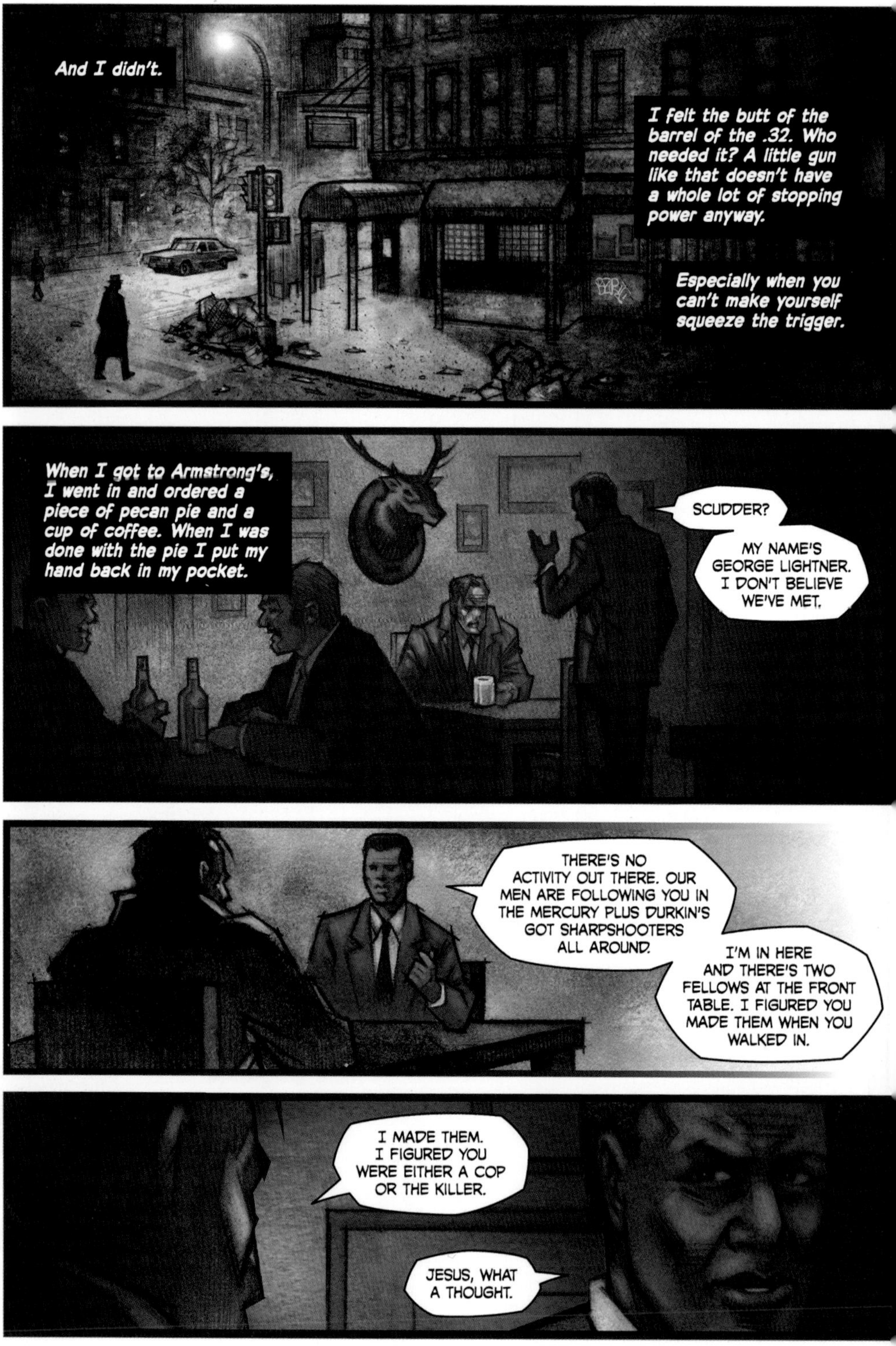

And I didn't.
I felt the butt of the barrel of the .32. Who needed it? A little gun like that doesn't have a whole lot of stopping power anyway.
Especially when you can't make yourself squeeze the trigger.
When I got to Armstrong's, I went in and ordered a piece of pecan pie and a cup of coffee. When I was done with the pie I put my hand back in my pocket.
SCUDDER?
MY NAME'S GEORGE LIGHTNER. I DON'T BELIEVE WE'VE MET.
THERE'S NO ACTIVITY OUT THERE. OUR MEN ARE FOLLOWING YOU IN THE MERCURY PLUS DURKIN'S GOT SHARPSHOOTERS ALL AROUND.
I'M IN HERE AND THERE'S TWO FELLOWS AT THE FRONT TABLE. I FIGURED YOU MADE THEM WHEN YOU WALKED IN.
I MADE THEM. I FIGURED YOU WERE EITHER A COP OR THE KILLER.
JESUS, WHAT A THOUGHT.

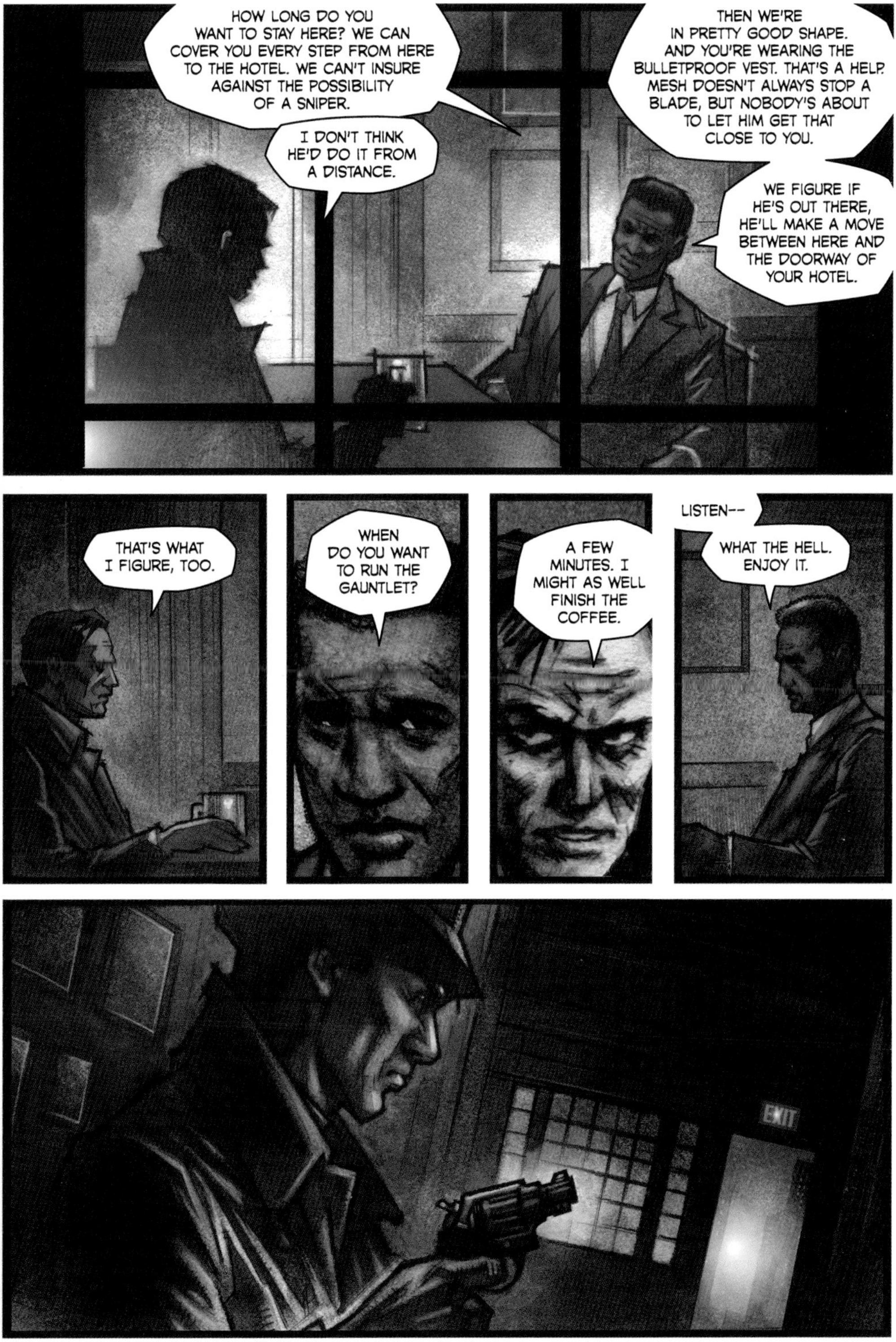
HOW LONG DO YOU WANT TO STAY HERE? WE CAN COVER YOU EVERY STEP FROM HERE TO THE HOTEL. WE CAN'T INSURE AGAINST THE POSSIBILITY OF A SNIPER.
I DON'T THINK HE'D DO IT FROM A DISTANCE.
THEN WE'RE IN PRETTY GOOD SHAPE. AND YOU'RE WEARING THE BULLETPROOF VEST. THAT'S A HELP. MESH DOESN'T ALWAYS STOP A BLADE, BUT NOBODY'S ABOUT TO LET HIM GET THAT CLOSE TO YOU.
WE FIGURE IF HE'S OUT THERE, HE'LL MAKE A MOVE BETWEEN HERE AND THE DOORWAY OF YOUR HOTEL.
THAT'S WHAT I FIGURE, TOO.
WHEN DO YOU WANT TO RUN THE GAUNTLET?
A FEW MINUTES. I MIGHT AS WELL FINISH THE COFFEE.
LISTEN--
WHAT THE HELL. ENJOY IT.
EXIT

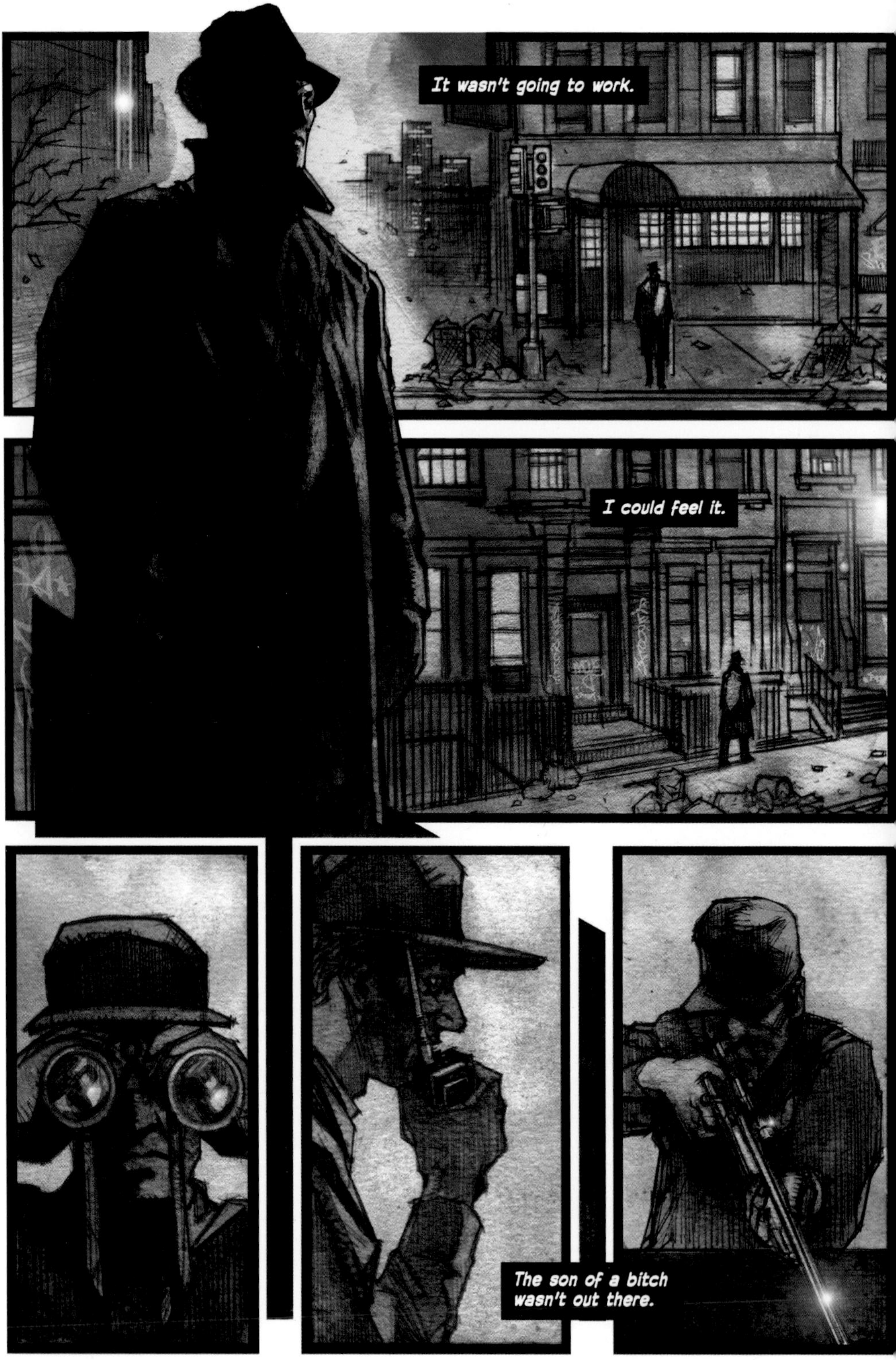
It wasn't going to work.
I could feel it.
The son of a bitch
wasn't out there.

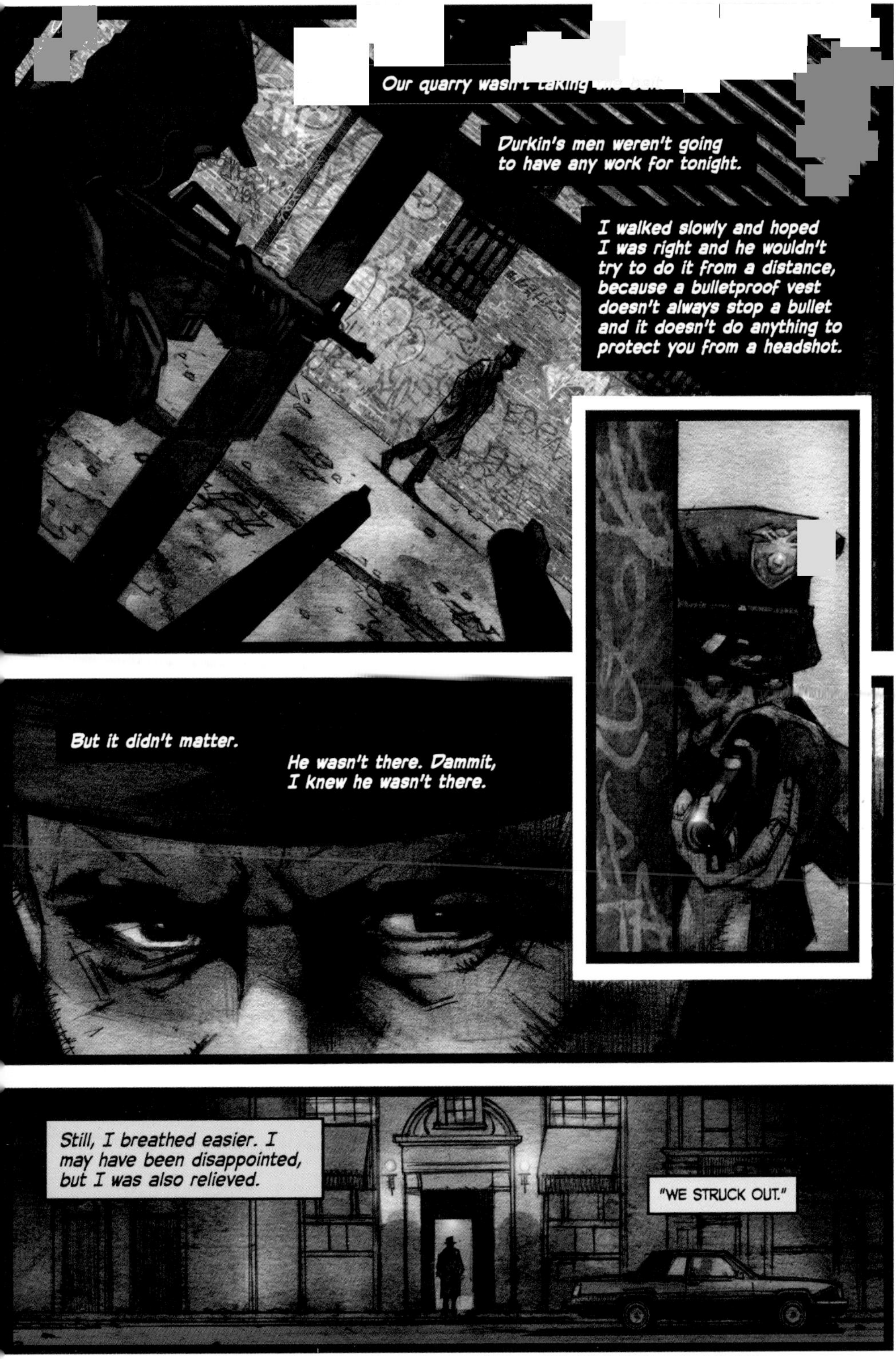
Our quarry wasn't taking
Durkin's men weren't going to have any work for tonight.
I walked slowly and hoped I was right and he wouldn't try to do it from a distance, because a bulletproof vest doesn't always stop a bullet and it doesn't do anything to protect you from a headshot.
But it didn't matter.
He wasn't there. Dammit, I knew he wasn't there.
Still, I breathed easier. I may have been disappointed, but I was also relieved.
"WE STRUCK OUT."

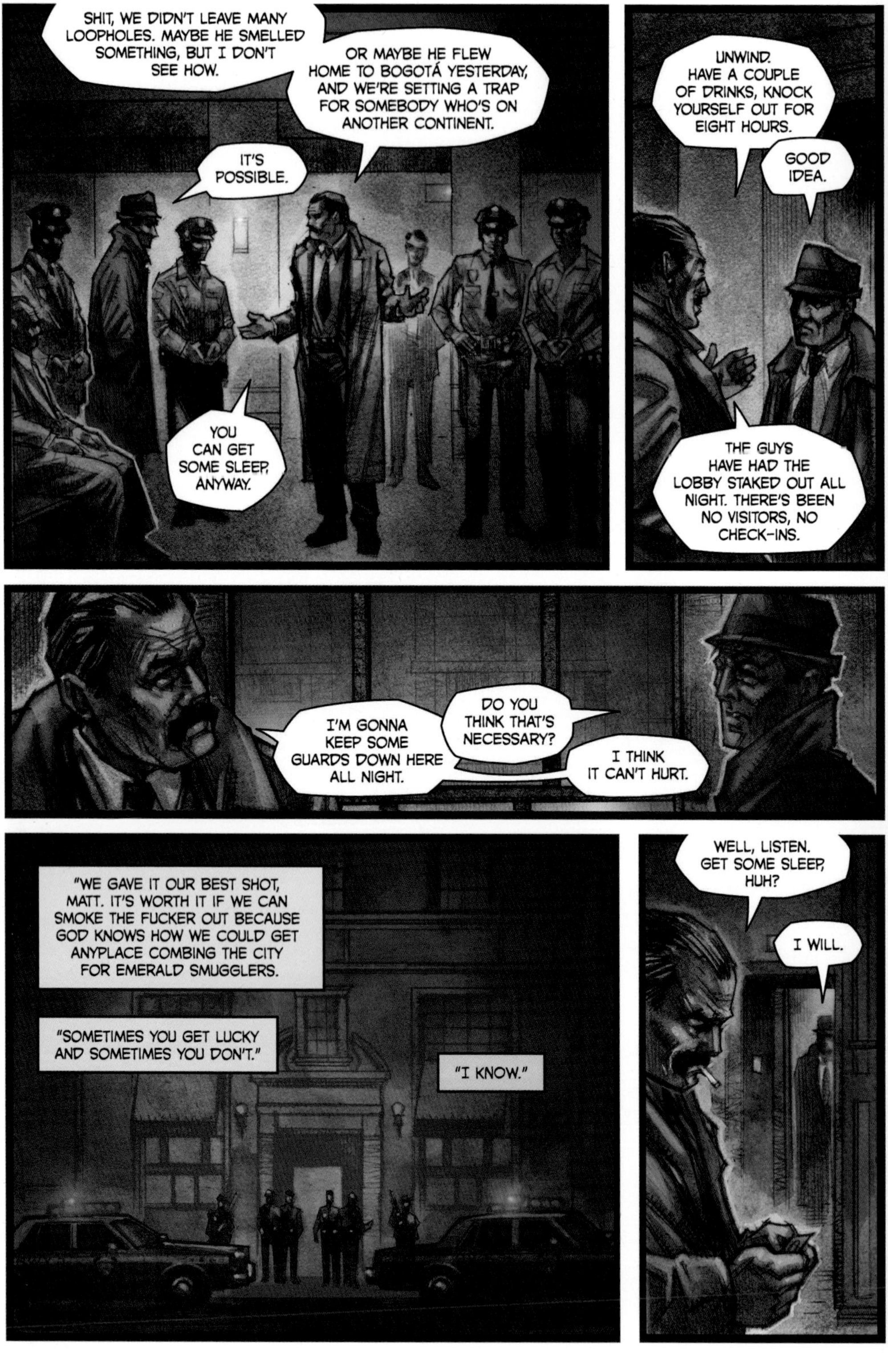
SHIT, WE DIDN'T LEAVE MANY LOOPHOLES. MAYBE HE SMELLED SOMETHING, BUT I DON'T SEE HOW.
OR MAYBE HE FLEW HOME TO BOGOTÁ YESTERDAY, AND WE'RE SETTING A TRAP FOR SOMEBODY WHO'S ON ANOTHER CONTINENT.
IT'S POSSIBLE.
YOU CAN GET SOME SLEEP, ANYWAY.
UNWIND. HAVE A COUPLE OF DRINKS, KNOCK YOURSELF OUT FOR EIGHT HOURS.
GOOD IDEA.
THE GUYS HAVE HAD THE LOBBY STAKED OUT ALL NIGHT. THERE'S BEEN NO VISITORS, NO CHECK-INS.
I'M GONNA KEEP SOME GUARDS DOWN HERE ALL NIGHT.
DO YOU THINK THAT'S NECESSARY?
I THINK IT CAN'T HURT.
"WE GAVE IT OUR BEST SHOT, MATT. IT'S WORTH IT IF WE CAN SMOKE THE FUCKER OUT BECAUSE GOD KNOWS HOW WE COULD GET ANYPLACE COMBING THE CITY FOR EMERALD SMUGGLERS.
"SOMETIMES YOU GET LUCKY AND SOMETIMES YOU DON'T."
"I KNOW."
WELL, LISTEN. GET SOME SLEEP, HUH?
I WILL.

"Have a few drinks."

I didn't even feel like a drink.

Ten days.

Just go to bed and you've got ten days.

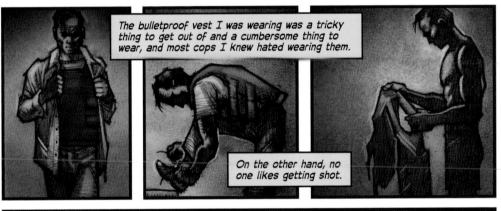

The bulletproof vest I was wearing was a tricky thing to get out of and a cumbersome thing to wear, and most cops I knew hated wearing them.

On the other hand, no one likes getting shot.

Something clicked.

Some little alarm went off.

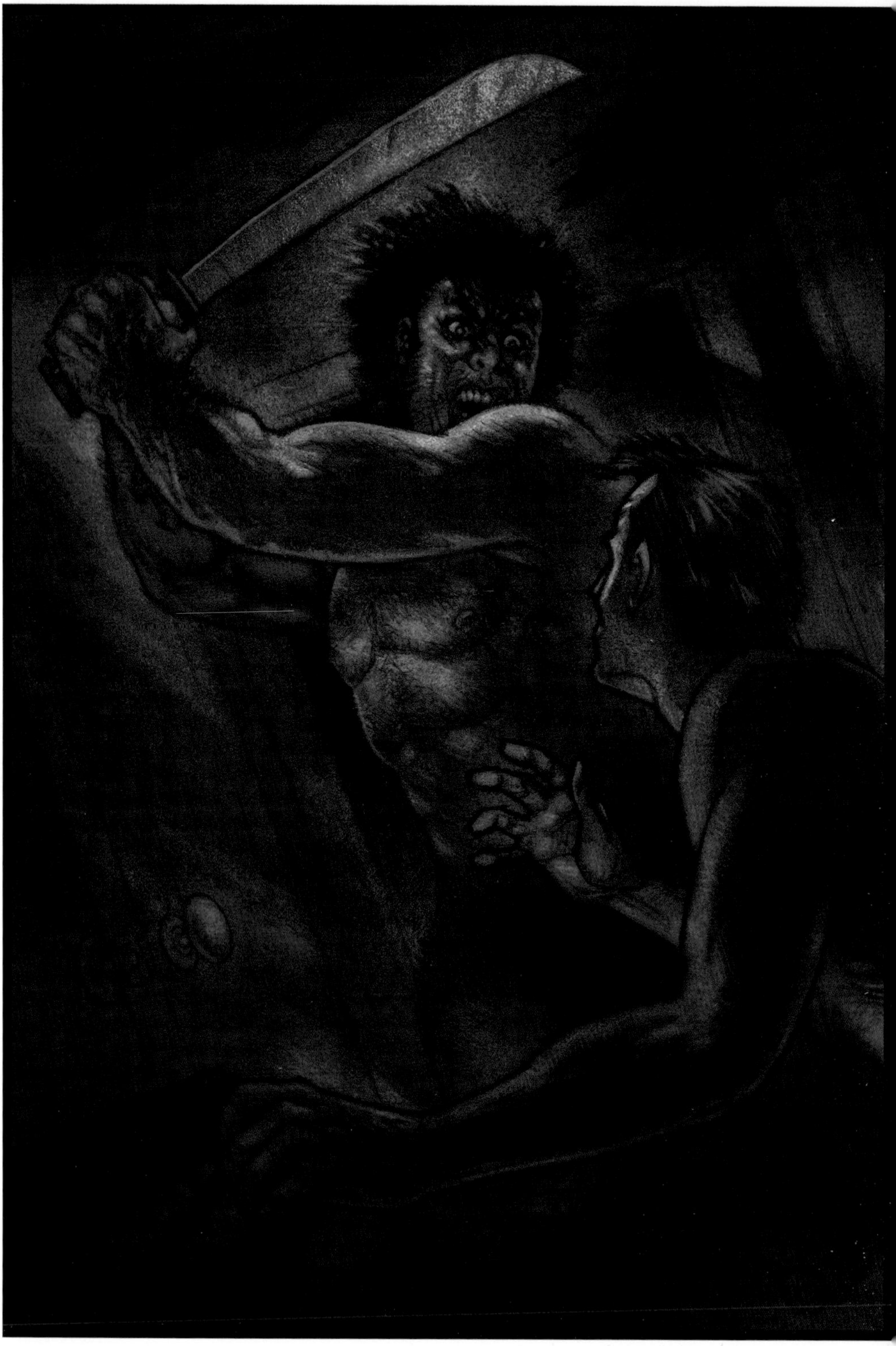

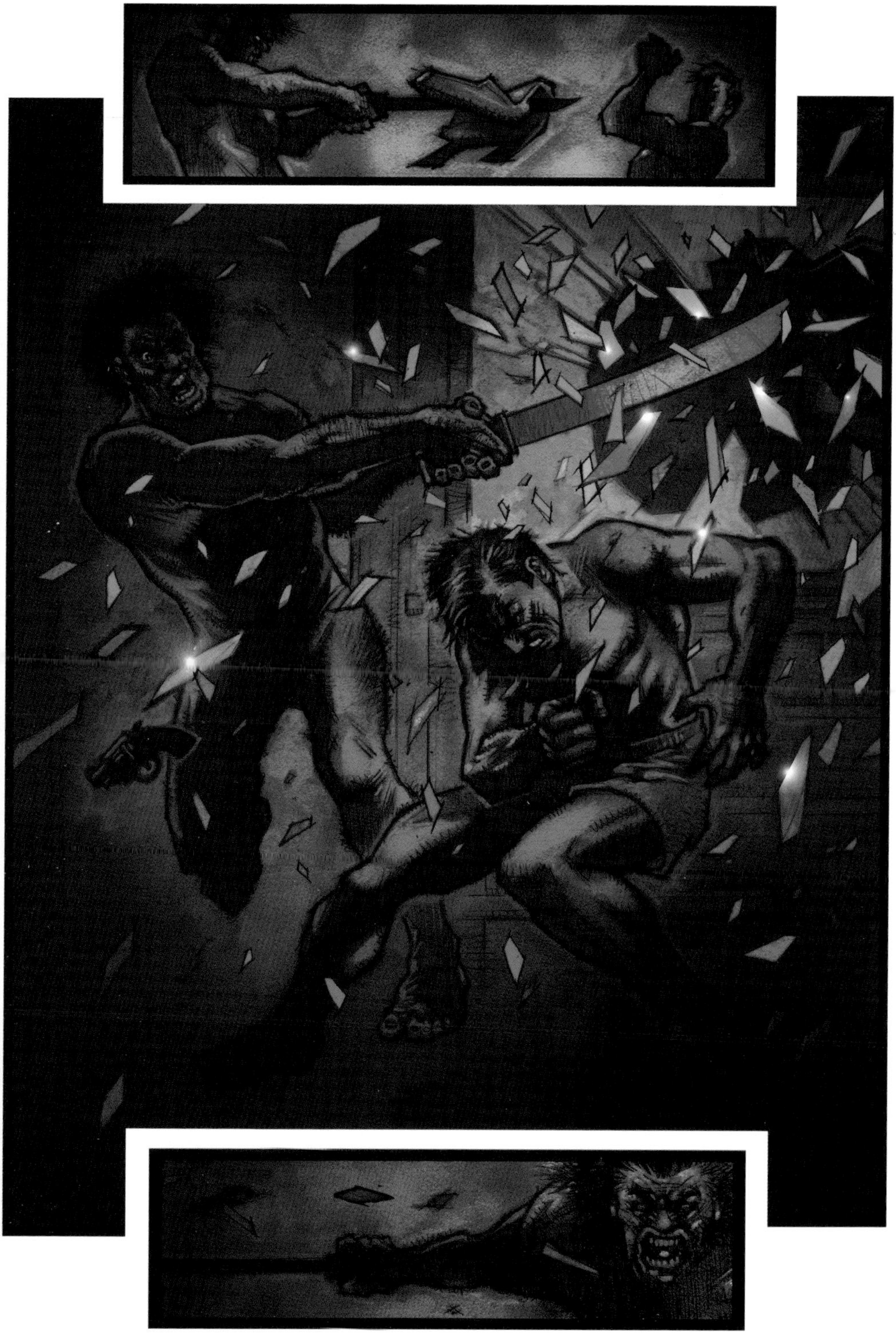

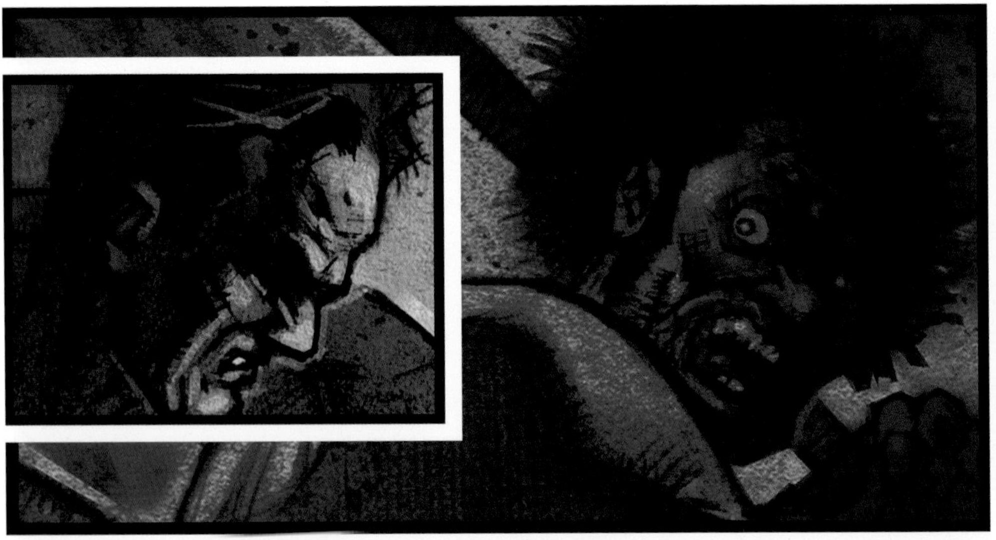

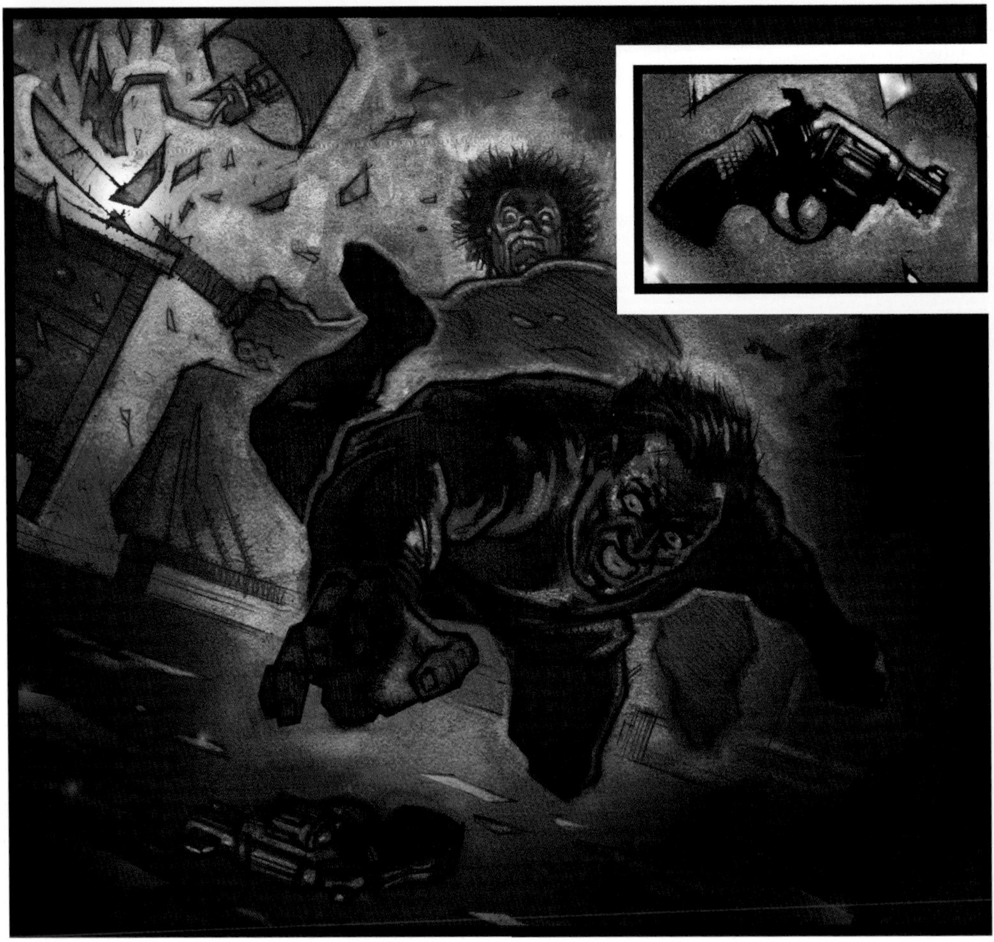

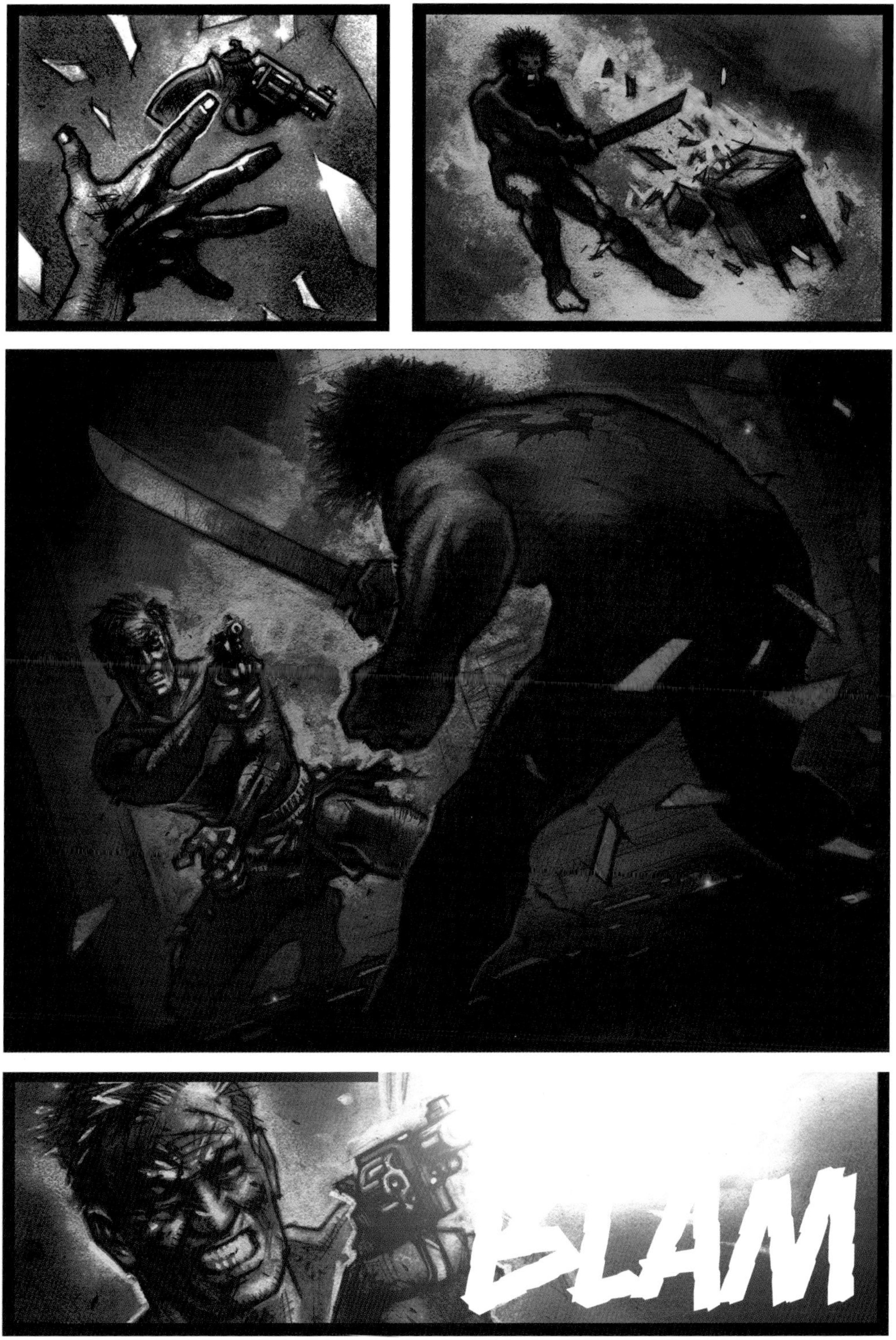
BLAM

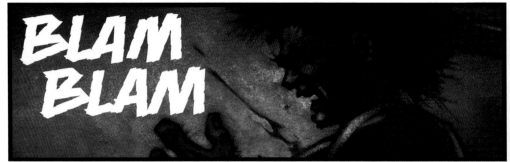

BLAM
BLAM

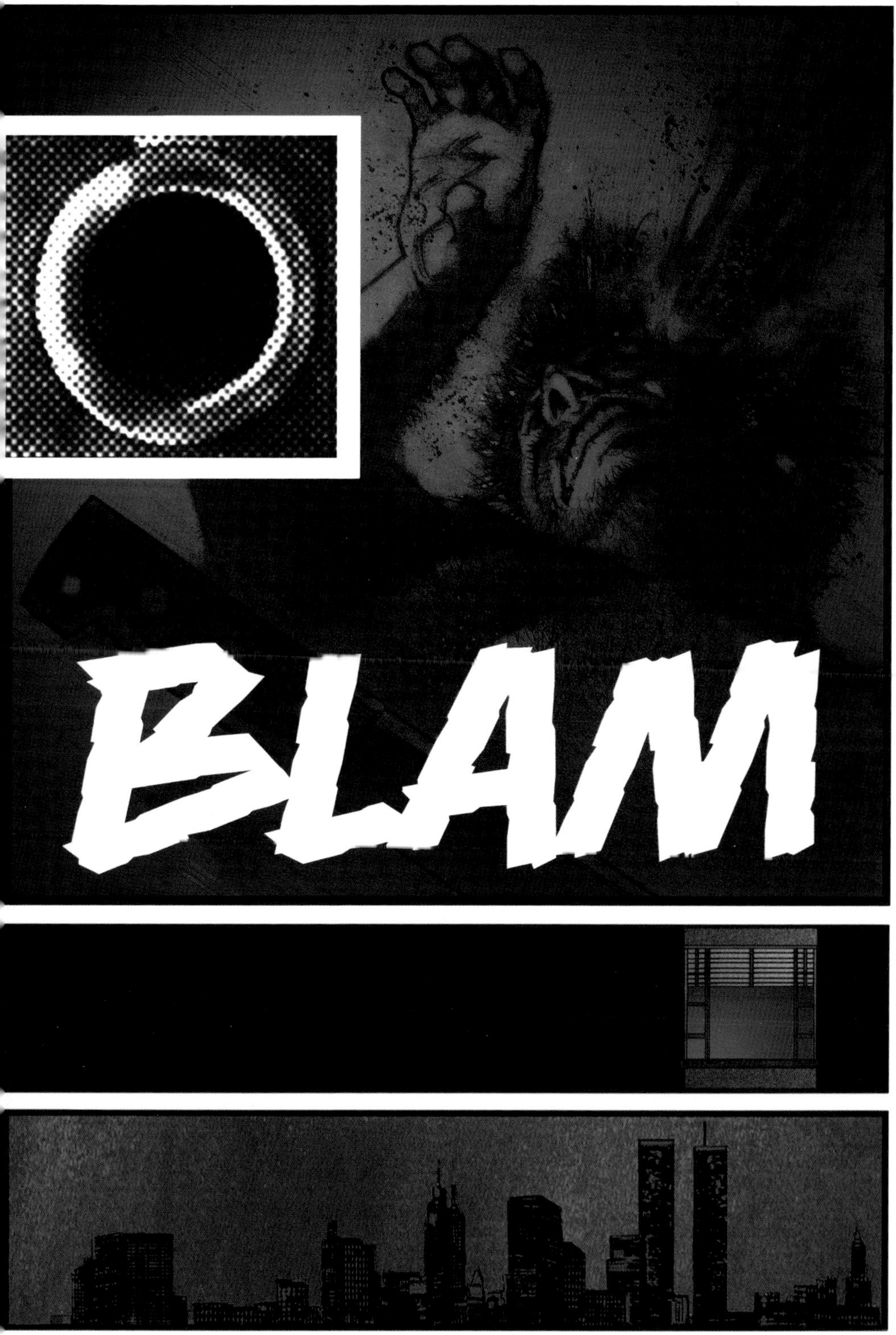
BLAM

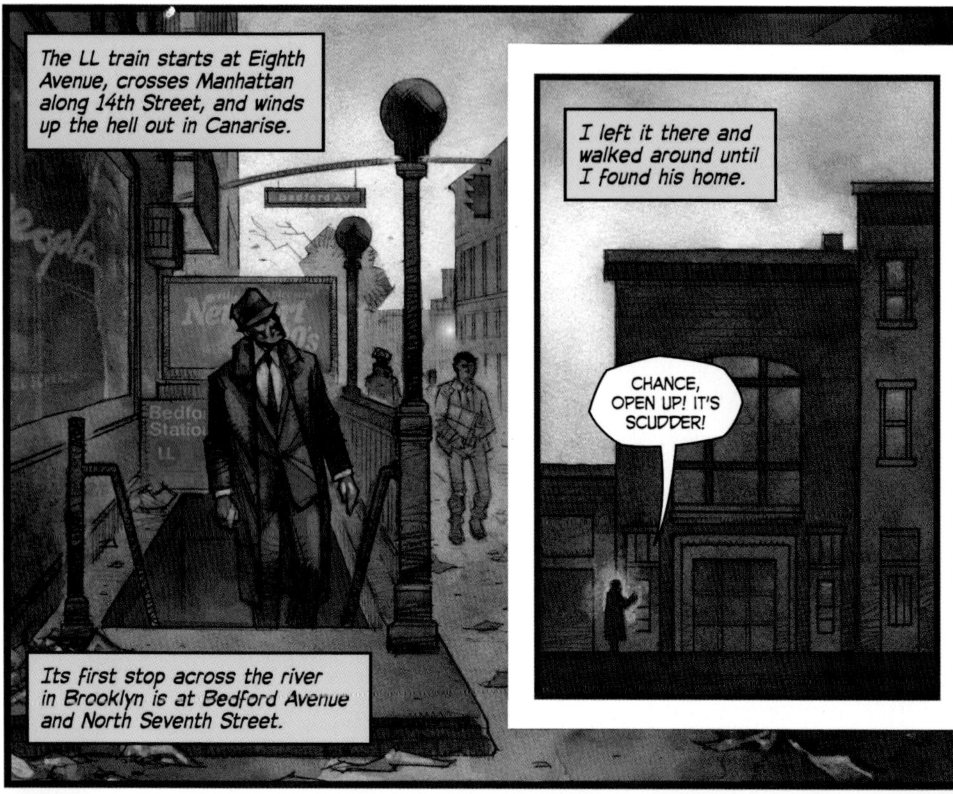
The LL train starts at Eighth Avenue, crosses Manhattan along 14th Street, and winds up the hell out in Canarise.
Its first stop across the river in Brooklyn is at Bedford Avenue and North Seventh Street.
I left it there and walked around until I found his home.
CHANCE, OPEN UP! IT'S SCUDDER!

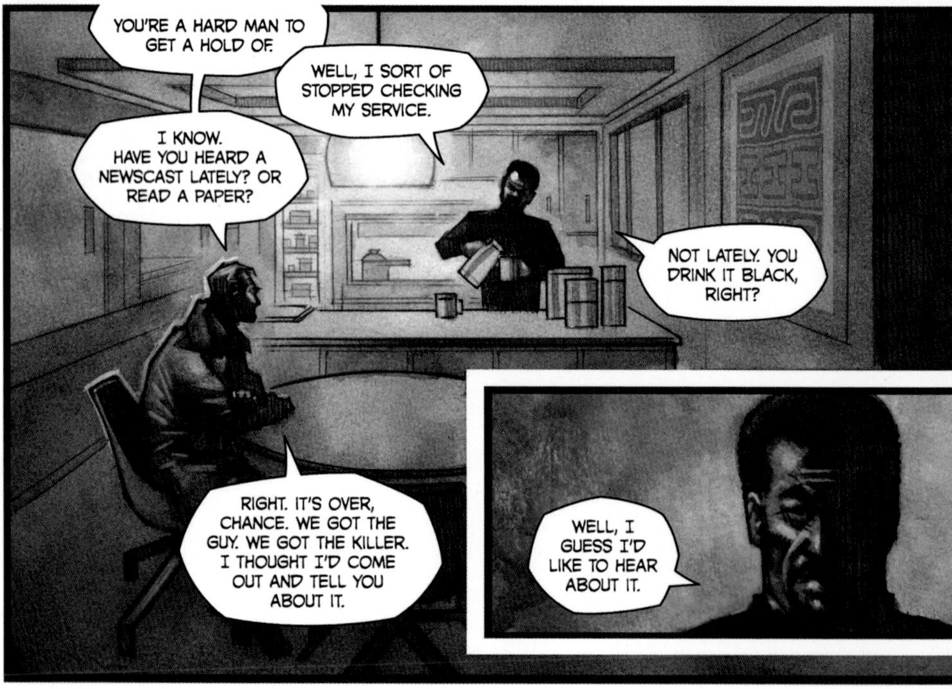
YOU'RE A HARD MAN TO GET A HOLD OF.
WELL, I SORT OF STOPPED CHECKING MY SERVICE.
I KNOW. HAVE YOU HEARD A NEWSCAST LATELY? OR READ A PAPER?
NOT LATELY. YOU DRINK IT BLACK, RIGHT?
RIGHT. IT'S OVER, CHANCE. WE GOT THE GUY. WE GOT THE KILLER. I THOUGHT I'D COME OUT AND TELL YOU ABOUT IT.
WELL, I GUESS I'D LIKE TO HEAR ABOUT IT.

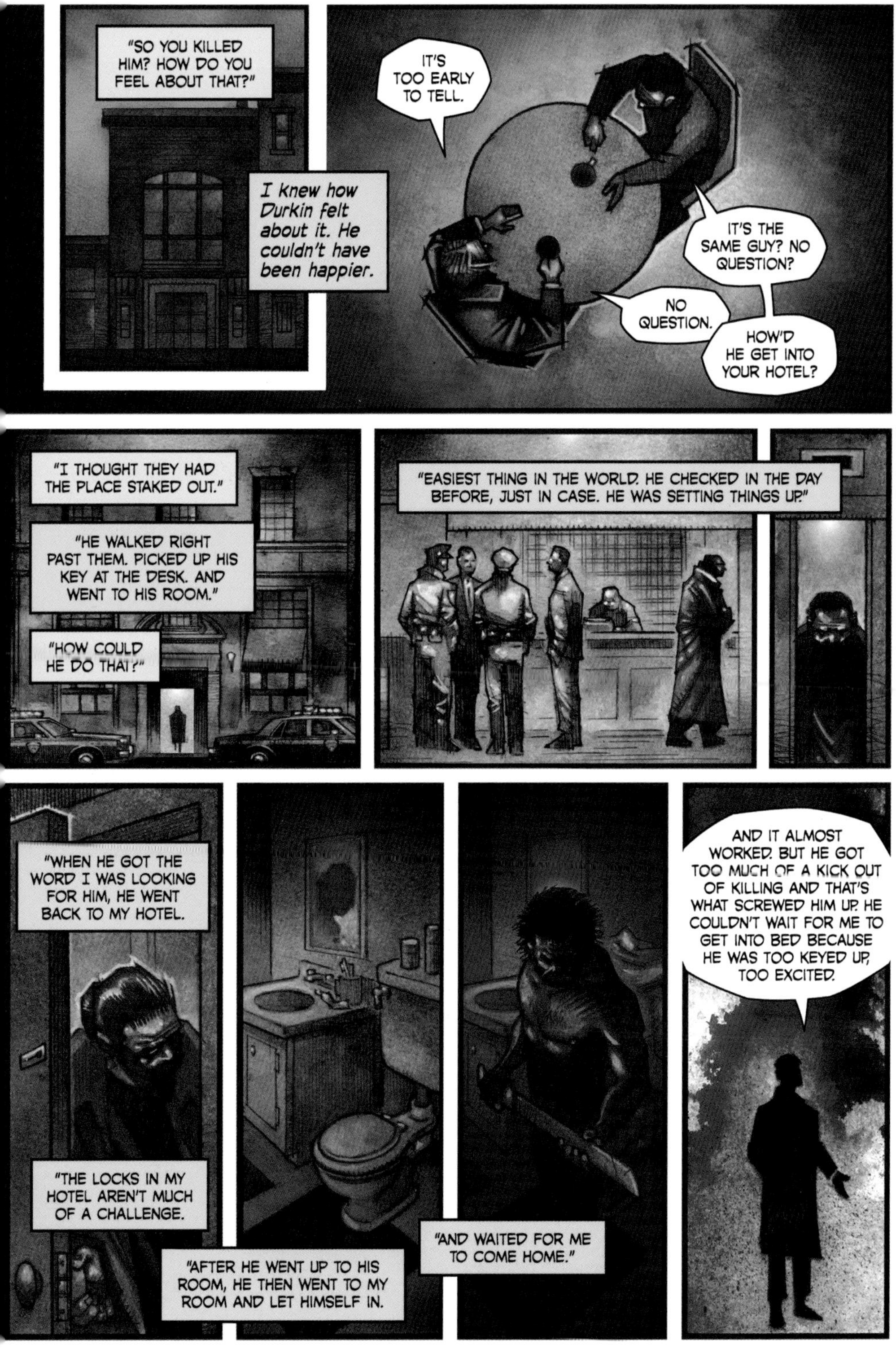
"SO YOU KILLED HIM? HOW DO YOU FEEL ABOUT THAT?"
I knew how Durkin felt about it. He couldn't have been happier.
IT'S TOO EARLY TO TELL.
IT'S THE SAME GUY? NO QUESTION?
NO QUESTION.
HOW'D HE GET INTO YOUR HOTEL?
"I THOUGHT THEY HAD THE PLACE STAKED OUT."
"HE WALKED RIGHT PAST THEM. PICKED UP HIS KEY AT THE DESK. AND WENT TO HIS ROOM."
"HOW COULD HE DO THAT?"
"EASIEST THING IN THE WORLD. HE CHECKED IN THE DAY BEFORE, JUST IN CASE. HE WAS SETTING THINGS UP."
"WHEN HE GOT THE WORD I WAS LOOKING FOR HIM, HE WENT BACK TO MY HOTEL.
"THE LOCKS IN MY HOTEL AREN'T MUCH OF A CHALLENGE.
"AFTER HE WENT UP TO HIS ROOM, HE THEN WENT TO MY ROOM AND LET HIMSELF IN.
"AND WAITED FOR ME TO COME HOME."
AND IT ALMOST WORKED. BUT HE GOT TOO MUCH OF A KICK OUT OF KILLING AND THAT'S WHAT SCREWED HIM UP. HE COULDN'T WAIT FOR ME TO GET INTO BED BECAUSE HE WAS TOO KEYED UP, TOO EXCITED.

"OF COURSE, IF I HADN'T HAD THE GUN HANDY, HE WOULD'VE KILLED ME ANYWAY."

"HE COULDN'T HAVE BEEN ALONE."

"HE WAS ALONE AS FAR AS THE KILLINGS WERE CONCERNED. HE PROBABLY HAD PARTNERS IN THE EMERALD OPERATION. EVEN IF THE COPS GET SOMEWHERE LOOKING FOR THEM, THERE'S NO REAL WAY TO MAKE A CASE AGAINST ANYBODY."

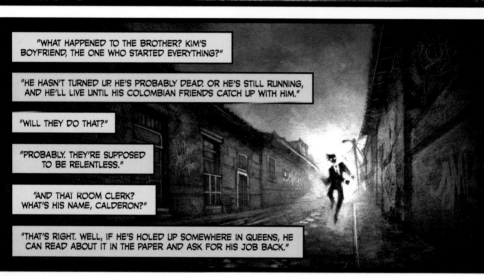

"WHAT HAPPENED TO THE BROTHER? KIM'S BOYFRIEND, THE ONE WHO STARTED EVERYTHING?"

"HE HASN'T TURNED UP. HE'S PROBABLY DEAD. OR HE'S STILL RUNNING, AND HE'LL LIVE UNTIL HIS COLOMBIAN FRIENDS CATCH UP WITH HIM."

"WILL THEY DO THAT?"

"PROBABLY. THEY'RE SUPPOSED TO BE RELENTLESS."

"AND THAT ROOM CLERK? WHAT'S HIS NAME, CALDERON?"

"THAT'S RIGHT. WELL, IF HE'S HOLED UP SOMEWHERE IN QUEENS, HE CAN READ ABOUT IT IN THE PAPER AND ASK FOR HIS JOB BACK."

YOU WERE UP LATE.

ALL NIGHT.

YOU BEEN TO SLEEP YET?

NOT YET. YOU STOPPED CALLING YOUR SERVICE.

I STOPPED CALLING MY SERVICE. I STOPPED LEAVING THE HOUSE. KIM'S DEAD AND THIS COOKIE'S DEAD, AND MAYBE THE BROTHER'S DEAD, AND WHAT'S-HIS-NAME IS DEAD, THE ONE YOU SHOT--

MARQUEZ.

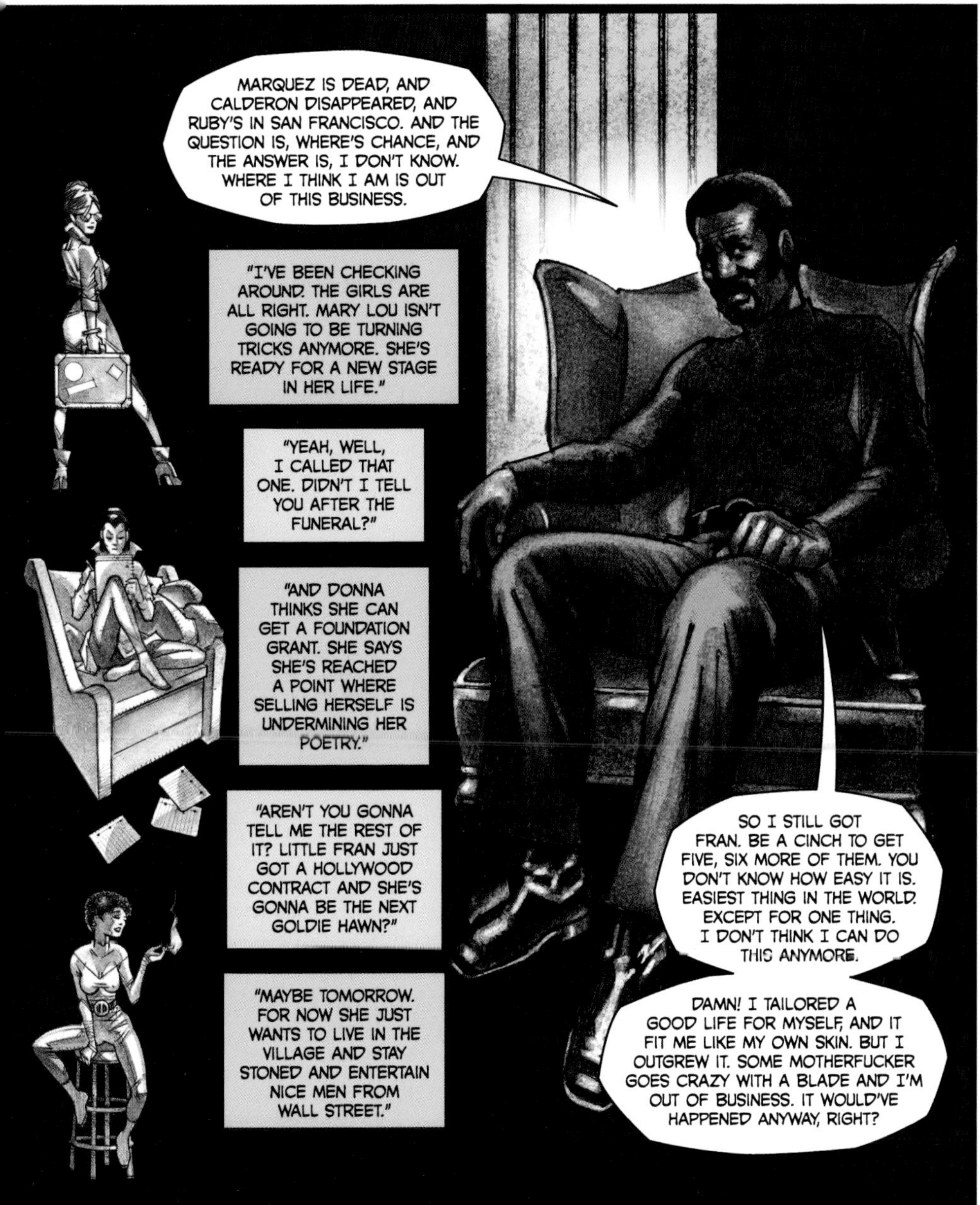
MARQUEZ IS DEAD, AND CALDERON DISAPPEARED, AND RUBY'S IN SAN FRANCISCO. AND THE QUESTION IS, WHERE'S CHANCE, AND THE ANSWER IS, I DON'T KNOW. WHERE I THINK I AM IS OUT OF THIS BUSINESS.
"I'VE BEEN CHECKING AROUND. THE GIRLS ARE ALL RIGHT. MARY LOU ISN'T GOING TO BE TURNING TRICKS ANYMORE. SHE'S READY FOR A NEW STAGE IN HER LIFE."
"YEAH, WELL, I CALLED THAT ONE. DIDN'T I TELL YOU AFTER THE FUNERAL?"
"AND DONNA THINKS SHE CAN GET A FOUNDATION GRANT. SHE SAYS SHE'S REACHED A POINT WHERE SELLING HERSELF IS UNDERMINING HER POETRY."
"AREN'T YOU GONNA TELL ME THE REST OF IT? LITTLE FRAN JUST GOT A HOLLYWOOD CONTRACT AND SHE'S GONNA BE THE NEXT GOLDIE HAWN?"
"MAYBE TOMORROW. FOR NOW SHE JUST WANTS TO LIVE IN THE VILLAGE AND STAY STONED AND ENTERTAIN NICE MEN FROM WALL STREET."
SO I STILL GOT FRAN. BE A CINCH TO GET FIVE, SIX MORE OF THEM. YOU DON'T KNOW HOW EASY IT IS. EASIEST THING IN THE WORLD. EXCEPT FOR ONE THING. I DON'T THINK I CAN DO THIS ANYMORE.
DAMN! I TAILORED A GOOD LIFE FOR MYSELF, AND IT FIT ME LIKE MY OWN SKIN. BUT I OUTGREW IT. SOME MOTHERFUCKER GOES CRAZY WITH A BLADE AND I'M OUT OF BUSINESS. IT WOULD'VE HAPPENED ANYWAY, RIGHT?

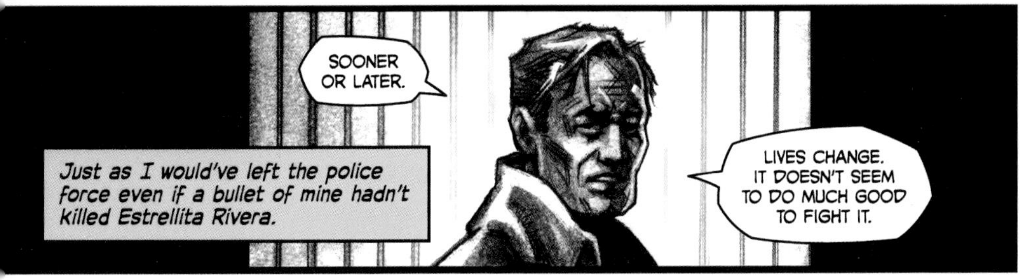
SOONER OR LATER.
Just as I would've left the police force even if a bullet of mine hadn't killed Estrellita Rivera.
LIVES CHANGE. IT DOESN'T SEEM TO DO MUCH GOOD TO FIGHT IT.

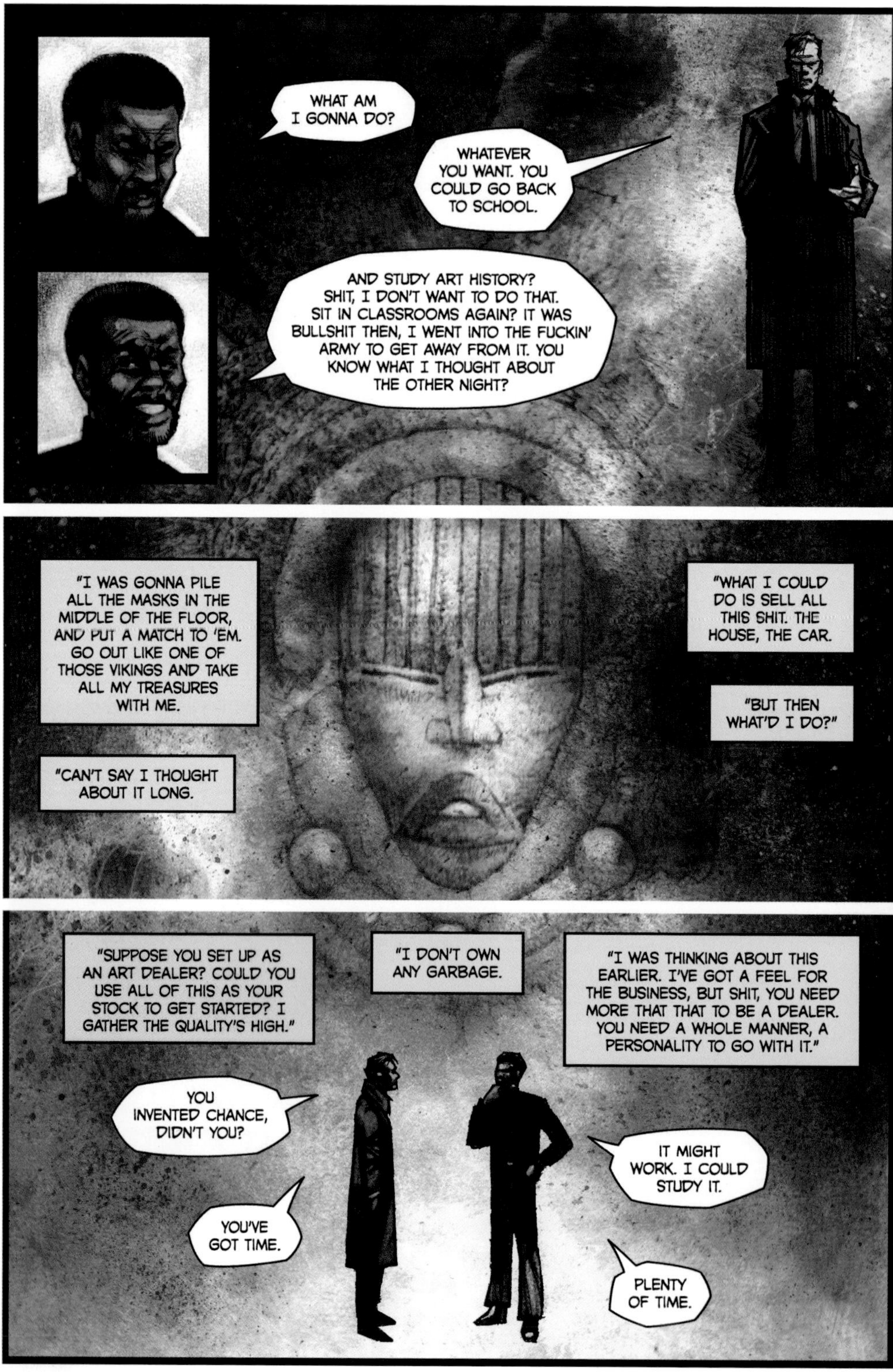
WHAT AM I GONNA DO?
WHATEVER YOU WANT. YOU COULD GO BACK TO SCHOOL.
AND STUDY ART HISTORY? SHIT, I DON'T WANT TO DO THAT. SIT IN CLASSROOMS AGAIN? IT WAS BULLSHIT THEN, I WENT INTO THE FUCKIN' ARMY TO GET AWAY FROM IT. YOU KNOW WHAT I THOUGHT ABOUT THE OTHER NIGHT?
"I WAS GONNA PILE ALL THE MASKS IN THE MIDDLE OF THE FLOOR, AND PUT A MATCH TO 'EM. GO OUT LIKE ONE OF THOSE VIKINGS AND TAKE ALL MY TREASURES WITH ME.
"CAN'T SAY I THOUGHT ABOUT IT LONG.
"WHAT I COULD DO IS SELL ALL THIS SHIT. THE HOUSE, THE CAR.
"BUT THEN WHAT'D I DO?"
"SUPPOSE YOU SET UP AS AN ART DEALER? COULD YOU USE ALL OF THIS AS YOUR STOCK TO GET STARTED? I GATHER THE QUALITY'S HIGH."
"I DON'T OWN ANY GARBAGE.
"I WAS THINKING ABOUT THIS EARLIER. I'VE GOT A FEEL FOR THE BUSINESS, BUT SHIT, YOU NEED MORE THAT THAT TO BE A DEALER. YOU NEED A WHOLE MANNER, A PERSONALITY TO GO WITH IT."
YOU INVENTED CHANCE, DIDN'T YOU?
IT MIGHT WORK. I COULD STUDY IT.
YOU'VE GOT TIME.
PLENTY OF TIME.

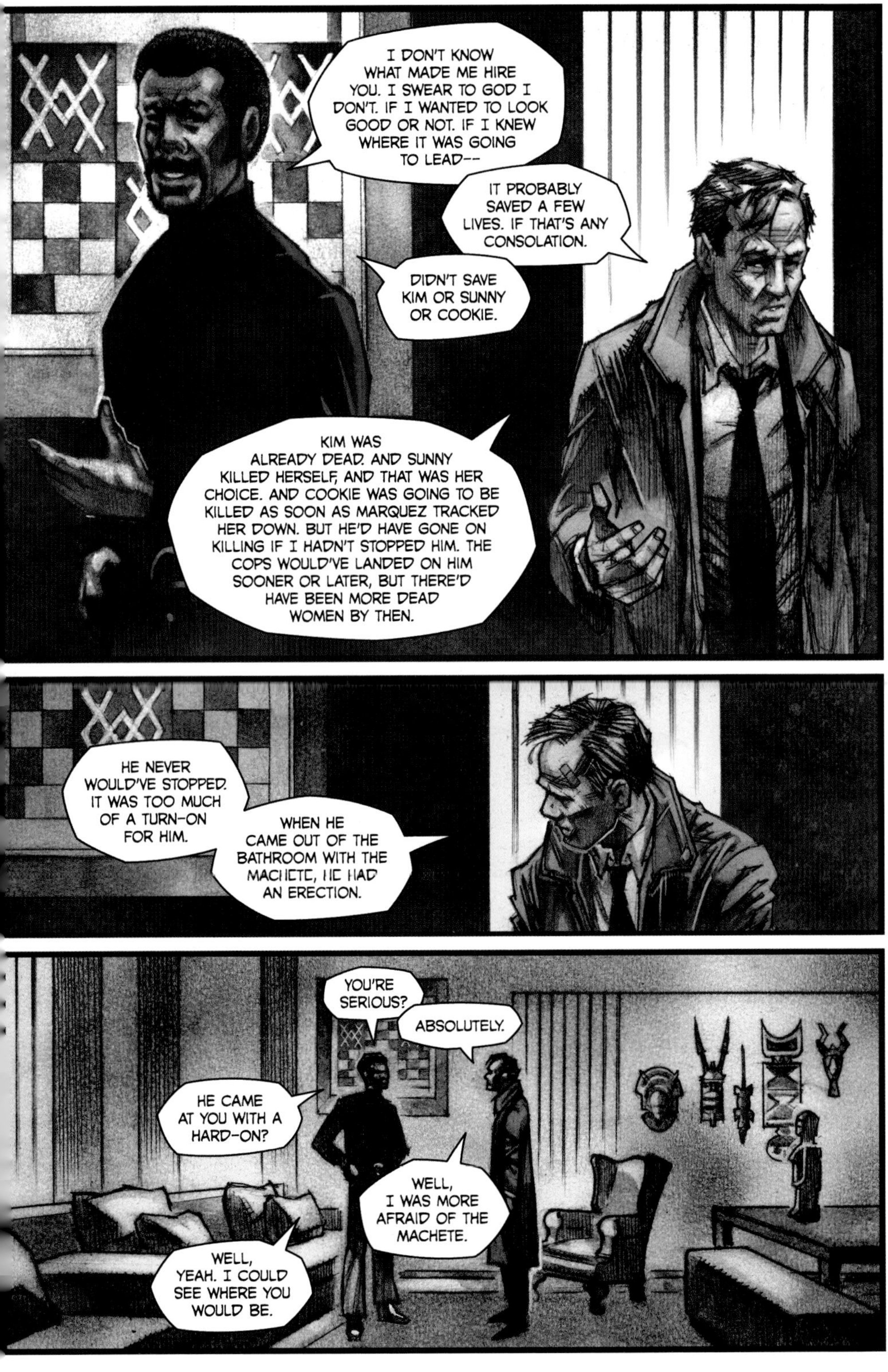
I DON'T KNOW WHAT MADE ME HIRE YOU. I SWEAR TO GOD I DON'T. IF I WANTED TO LOOK GOOD OR NOT. IF I KNEW WHERE IT WAS GOING TO LEAD--
IT PROBABLY SAVED A FEW LIVES. IF THAT'S ANY CONSOLATION.
DIDN'T SAVE KIM OR SUNNY OR COOKIE.
KIM WAS ALREADY DEAD. AND SUNNY KILLED HERSELF, AND THAT WAS HER CHOICE. AND COOKIE WAS GOING TO BE KILLED AS SOON AS MARQUEZ TRACKED HER DOWN. BUT HE'D HAVE GONE ON KILLING IF I HADN'T STOPPED HIM. THE COPS WOULD'VE LANDED ON HIM SOONER OR LATER, BUT THERE'D HAVE BEEN MORE DEAD WOMEN BY THEN.
HE NEVER WOULD'VE STOPPED. IT WAS TOO MUCH OF A TURN-ON FOR HIM.
WHEN HE CAME OUT OF THE BATHROOM WITH THE MACHETE, HE HAD AN ERECTION.
YOU'RE SERIOUS?
ABSOLUTELY.
HE CAME AT YOU WITH A HARD-ON?
WELL, I WAS MORE AFRAID OF THE MACHETE.
WELL, YEAH. I COULD SEE WHERE YOU WOULD BE.

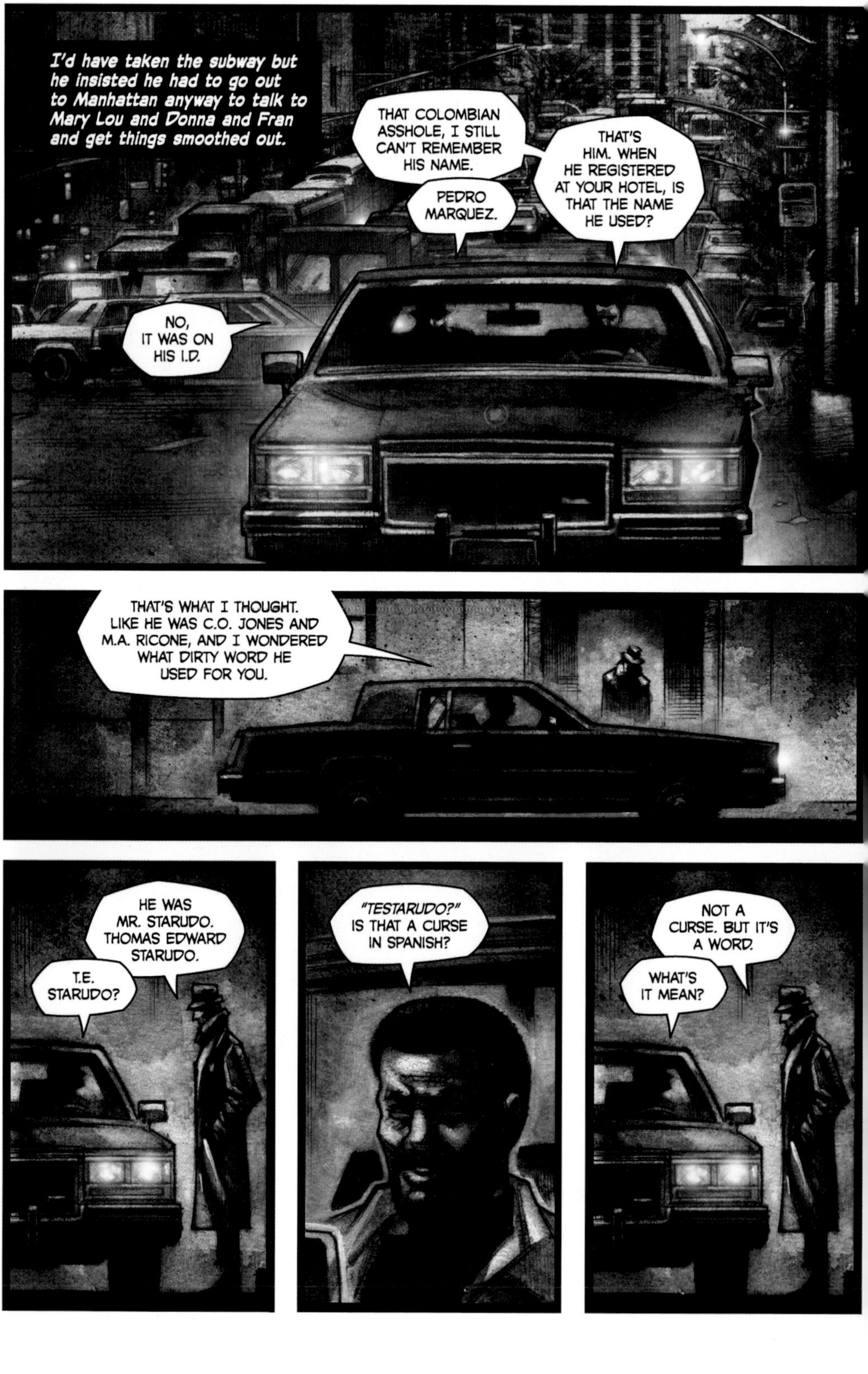
I'd have taken the subway but he insisted he had to go out to Manhattan anyway to talk to Mary Lou and Donna and Fran and get things smoothed out.
THAT COLOMBIAN ASSHOLE, I STILL CAN'T REMEMBER HIS NAME.
PEDRO MARQUEZ.
THAT'S HIM. WHEN HE REGISTERED AT YOUR HOTEL, IS THAT THE NAME HE USED?
NO, IT WAS ON HIS I.D.
THAT'S WHAT I THOUGHT. LIKE HE WAS C.O. JONES AND M.A. RICONE, AND I WONDERED WHAT DIRTY WORD HE USED FOR YOU.
HE WAS MR. STARUDO. THOMAS EDWARD STARUDO.
T.E. STARUDO?
"TESTARUDO?" IS THAT A CURSE IN SPANISH?
NOT A CURSE. BUT IT'S A WORD.
WHAT'S IT MEAN?

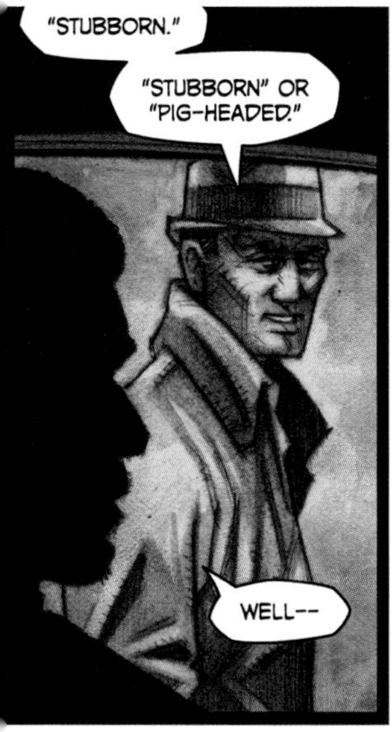
"STUBBORN."
"STUBBORN" OR "PIG-HEADED."
WELL--

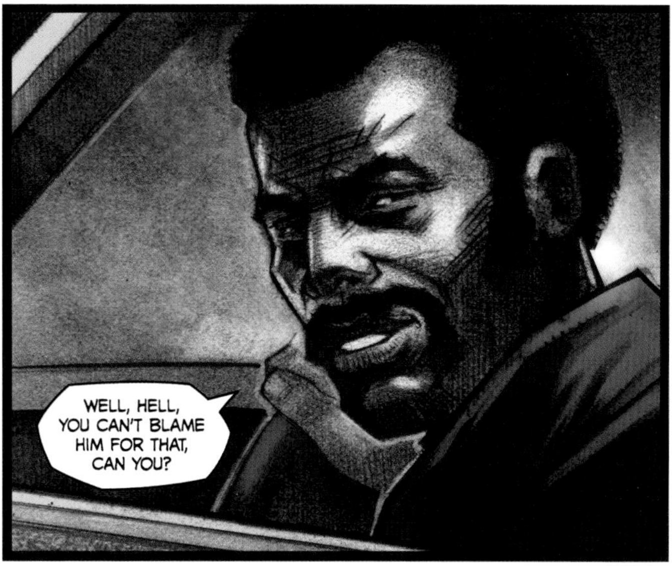
WELL, HELL, YOU CAN'T BLAME HIM FOR THAT, CAN YOU?

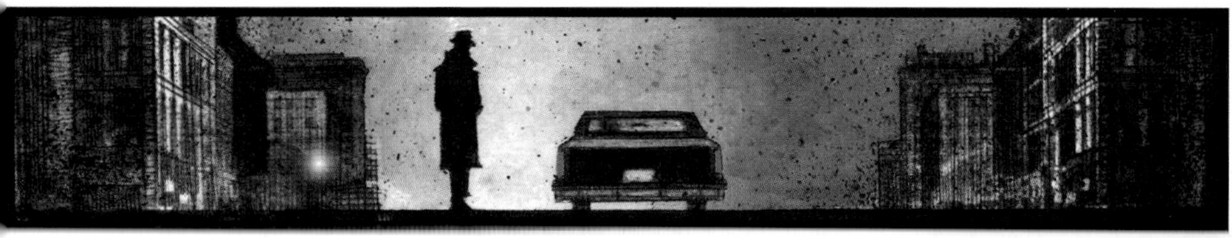

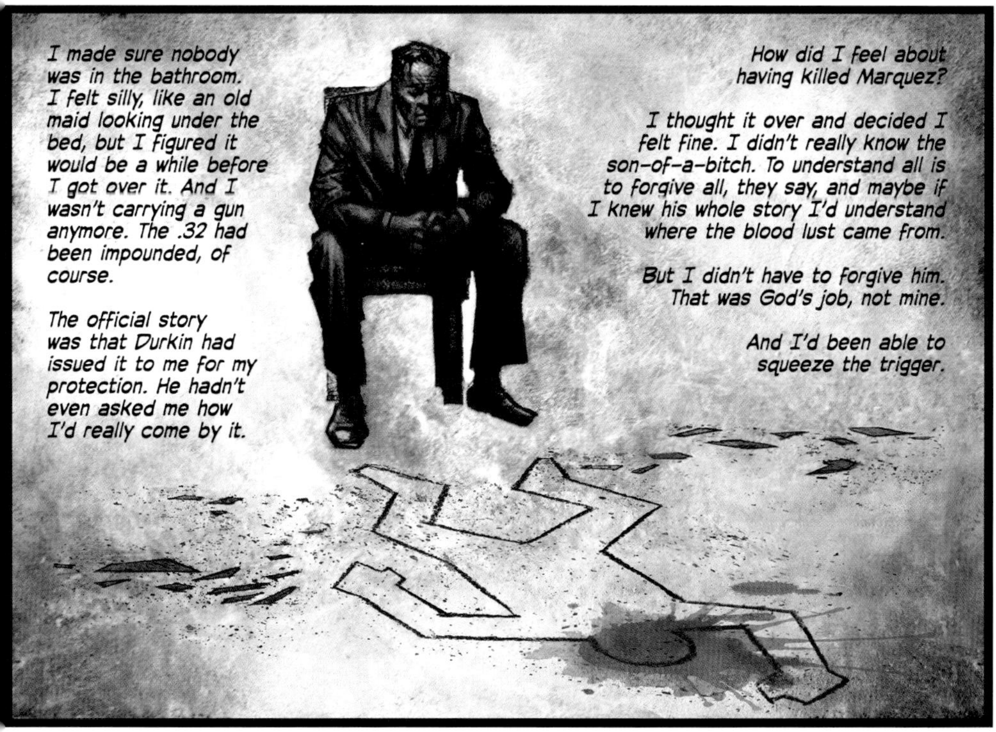
I made sure nobody was in the bathroom. I felt silly, like an old maid looking under the bed, but I figured it would be a while before I got over it. And I wasn't carrying a gun anymore. The .32 had been impounded, of course.
The official story was that Durkin had issued it to me for my protection. He hadn't even asked me how I'd really come by it.
How did I feel about having killed Marquez?
I thought it over and decided I felt fine. I didn't really know the son-of-a-bitch. To understand all is to forgive all, they say, and maybe if I knew his whole story I'd understand where the blood lust came from.
But I didn't have to forgive him. That was God's job, not mine.
And I'd been able to squeeze the trigger.

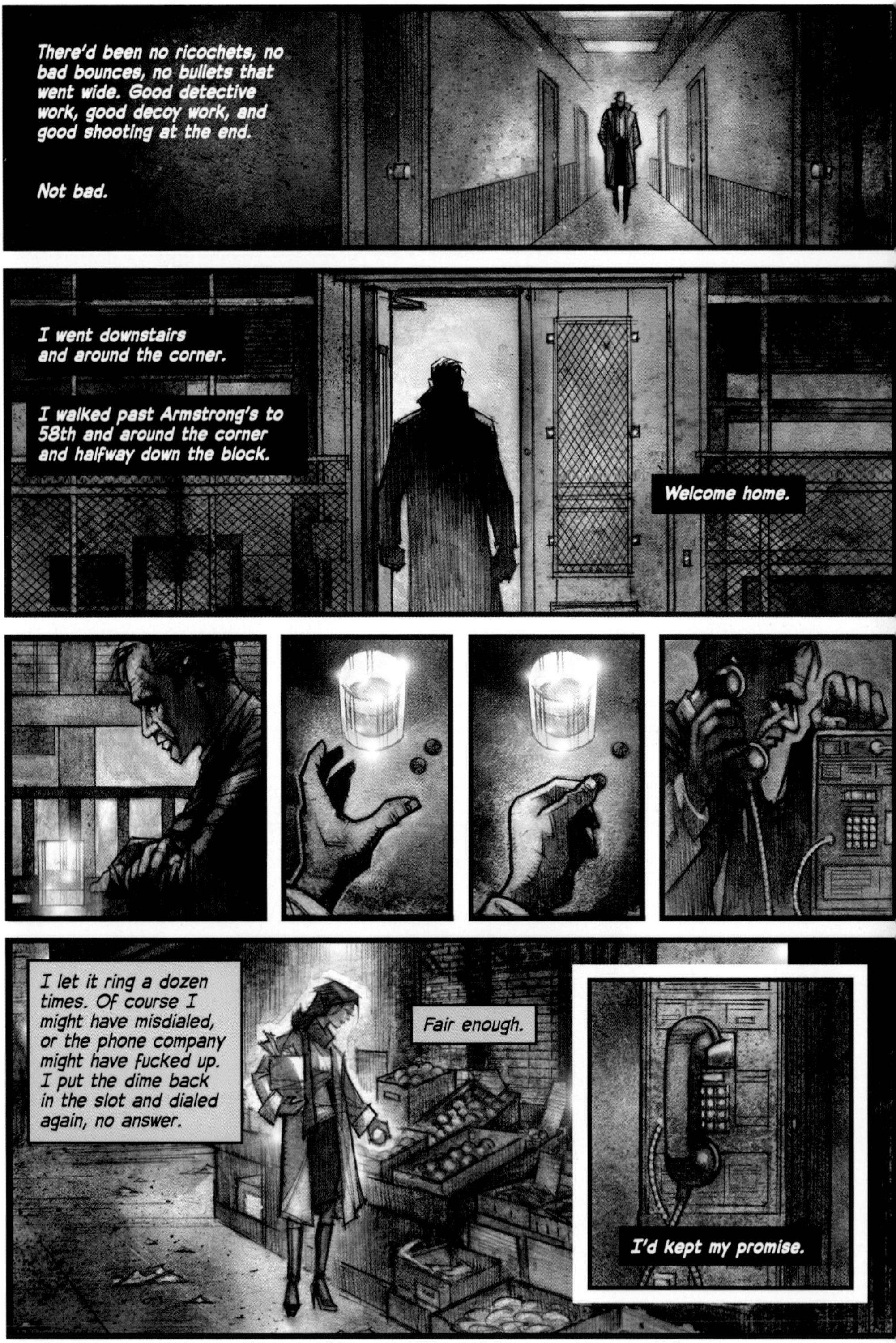
There'd been no ricochets, no bad bounces, no bullets that went wide. Good detective work, good decoy work, and good shooting at the end.
Not bad.
I went downstairs and around the corner.
I walked past Armstrong's to 58th and around the corner and halfway down the block.
Welcome home.
I let it ring a dozen times. Of course I might have misdialed, or the phone company might have fucked up. I put the dime back in the slot and dialed again, no answer.
Fair enough.
I'd kept my promise.

I returned to the bar.

Why?

The case was finished, solved, wrapped up. The killer would never kill anyone again.

I had done a whole lot of things right, and felt very good about my role in the proceedings.

I wasn't nervous, I wasn't anxious, I wasn't depressed.

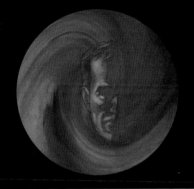

I was fine, for Christ's sake.

I hadn't wanted a drink, I hadn't even thought of a drink, and here I was with a drink in front of me and I was going to swallow it.

Why? What the hell was wrong with me?

If I drank the fucking drink, I would wind up dead or in the hospital. It might take a day or a week or a month, but that was how it would play. I knew that. But here I was, in a gin joint with a drink in front of me.

Why?

Because--

Because what?

Because--

I got out of there.

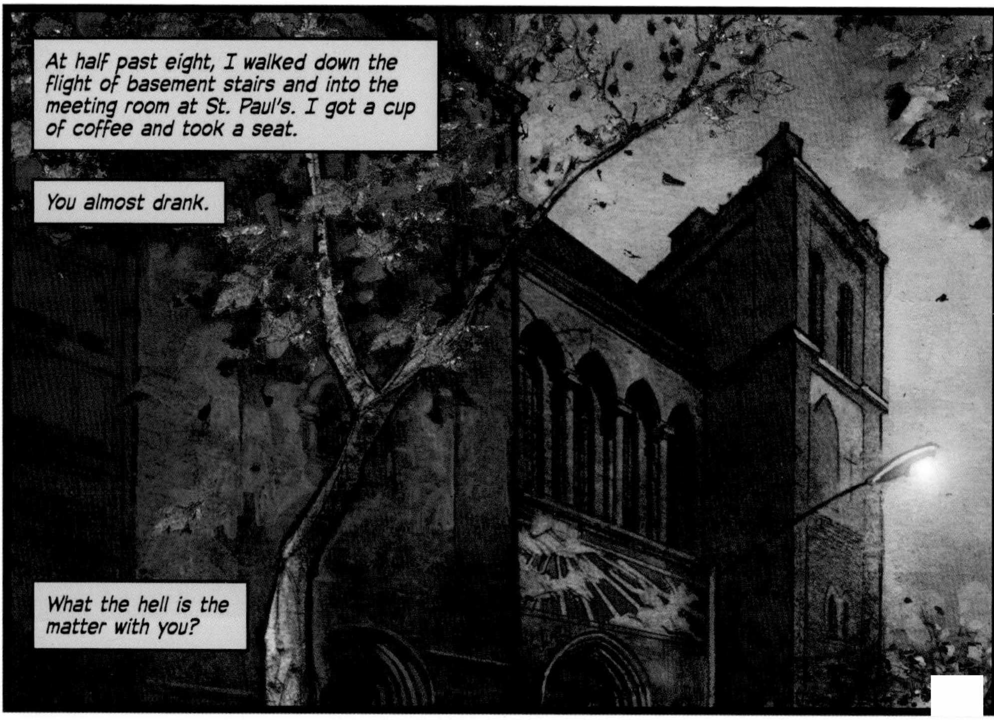
At half past eight, I walked down the flight of basement stairs and into the meeting room at St. Paul's. I got a cup of coffee and took a seat.
You almost drank.
What the hell is the matter with you?

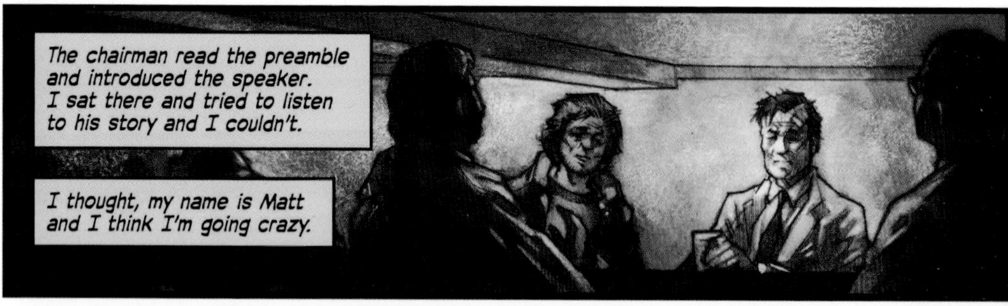
The chairman read the preamble and introduced the speaker. I sat there and tried to listen to his story and I couldn't.
I thought, my name is Matt and I think I'm going crazy.

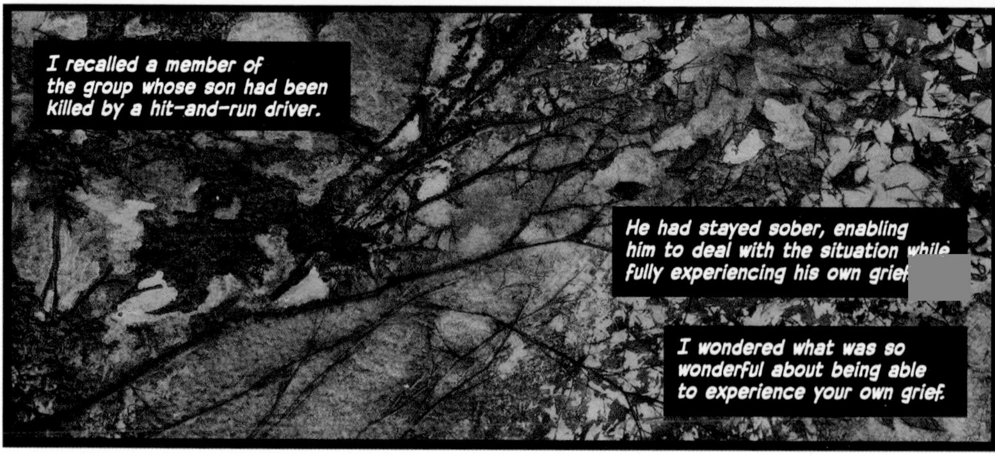
I recalled a member of the group whose son had been killed by a hit-and-run driver.
He had stayed sober, enabling him to deal with the situation while fully experiencing his own grief.
I wondered what was so wonderful about being able to experience your own grief.

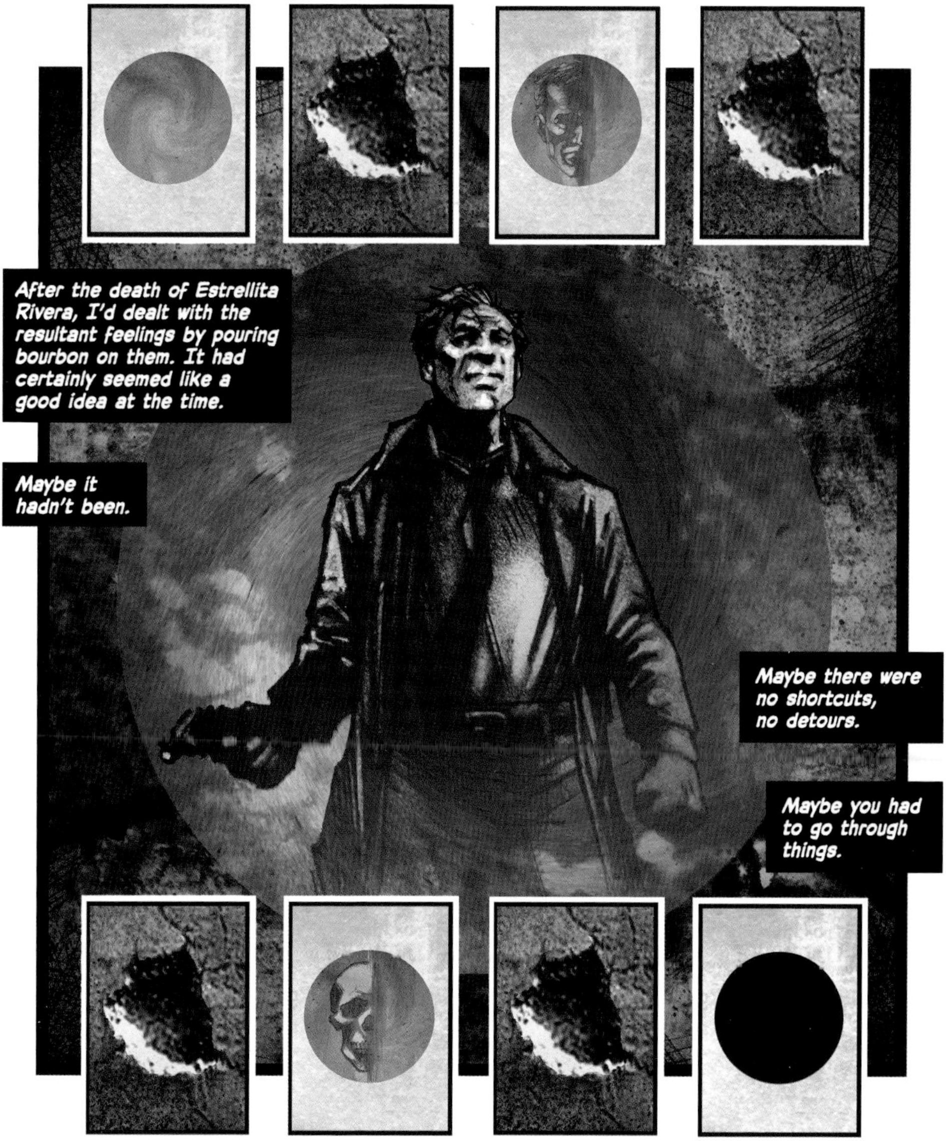
After the death of Estrellita Rivera, I'd dealt with the resultant feelings by pouring bourbon on them. It had certainly seemed like a good idea at the time.
Maybe it hadn't been.
Maybe there were no shortcuts, no detours.
Maybe you had to go through things.

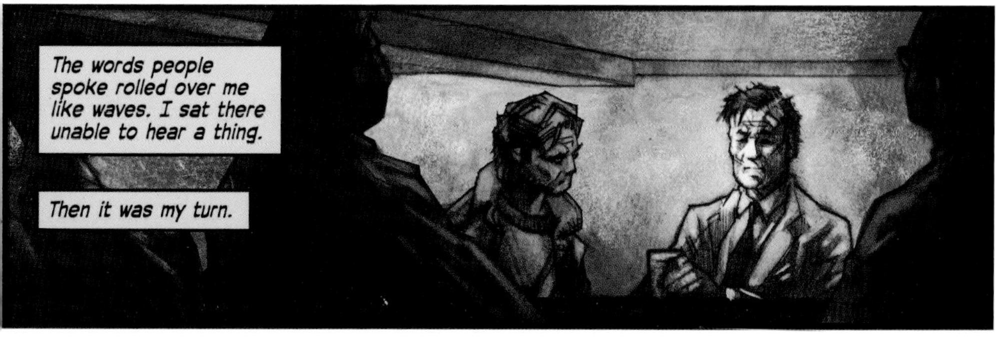
The words people spoke rolled over me like waves. I sat there unable to hear a thing.
Then it was my turn.

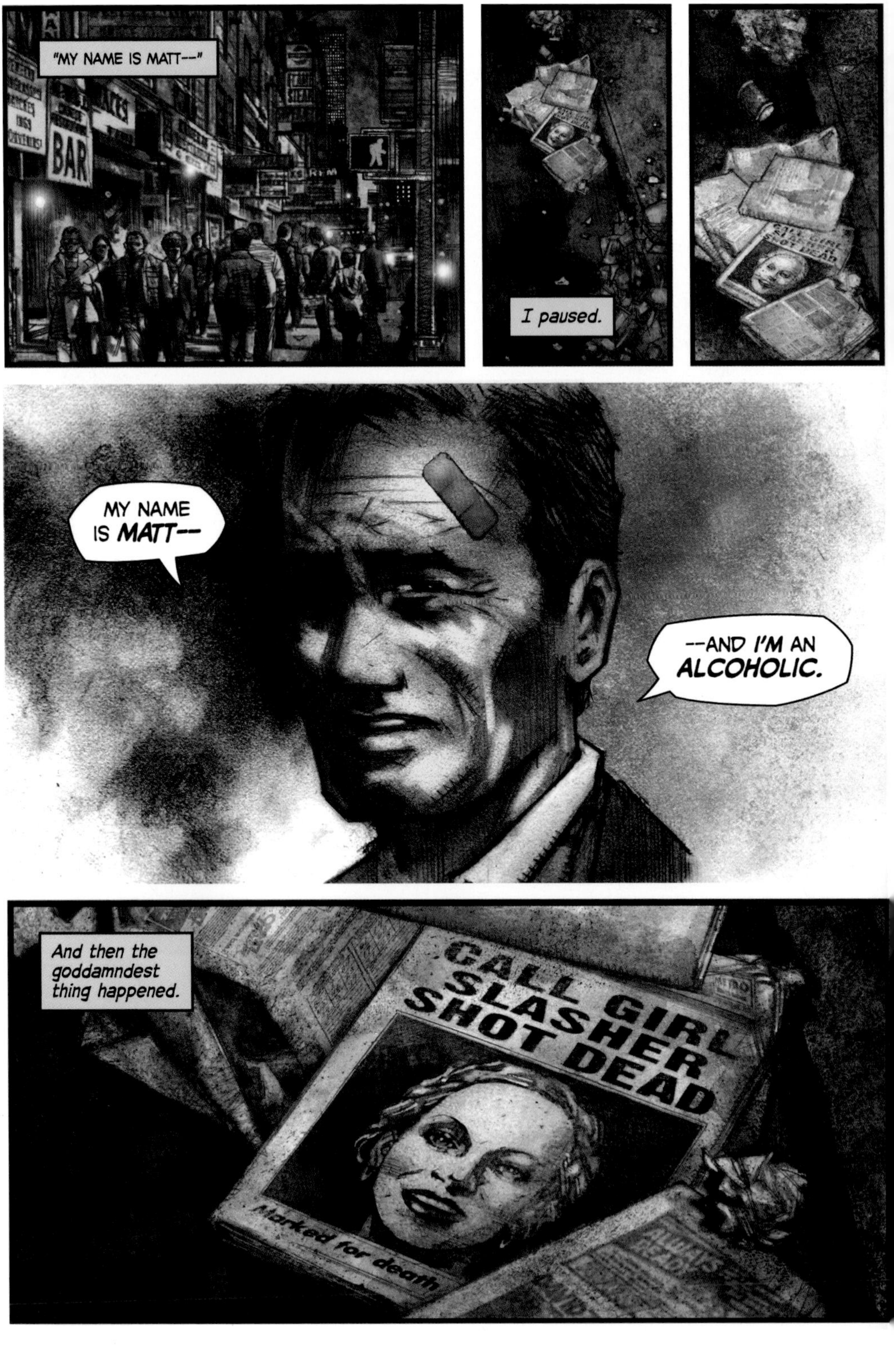
"MY NAME IS MATT--"
BAR
I paused.
MY NAME IS MATT--
--AND I'M AN ALCOHOLIC.
And then the goddamndest thing happened.
CALL GIRL SLASHER SHOT DEAD
Marked for death

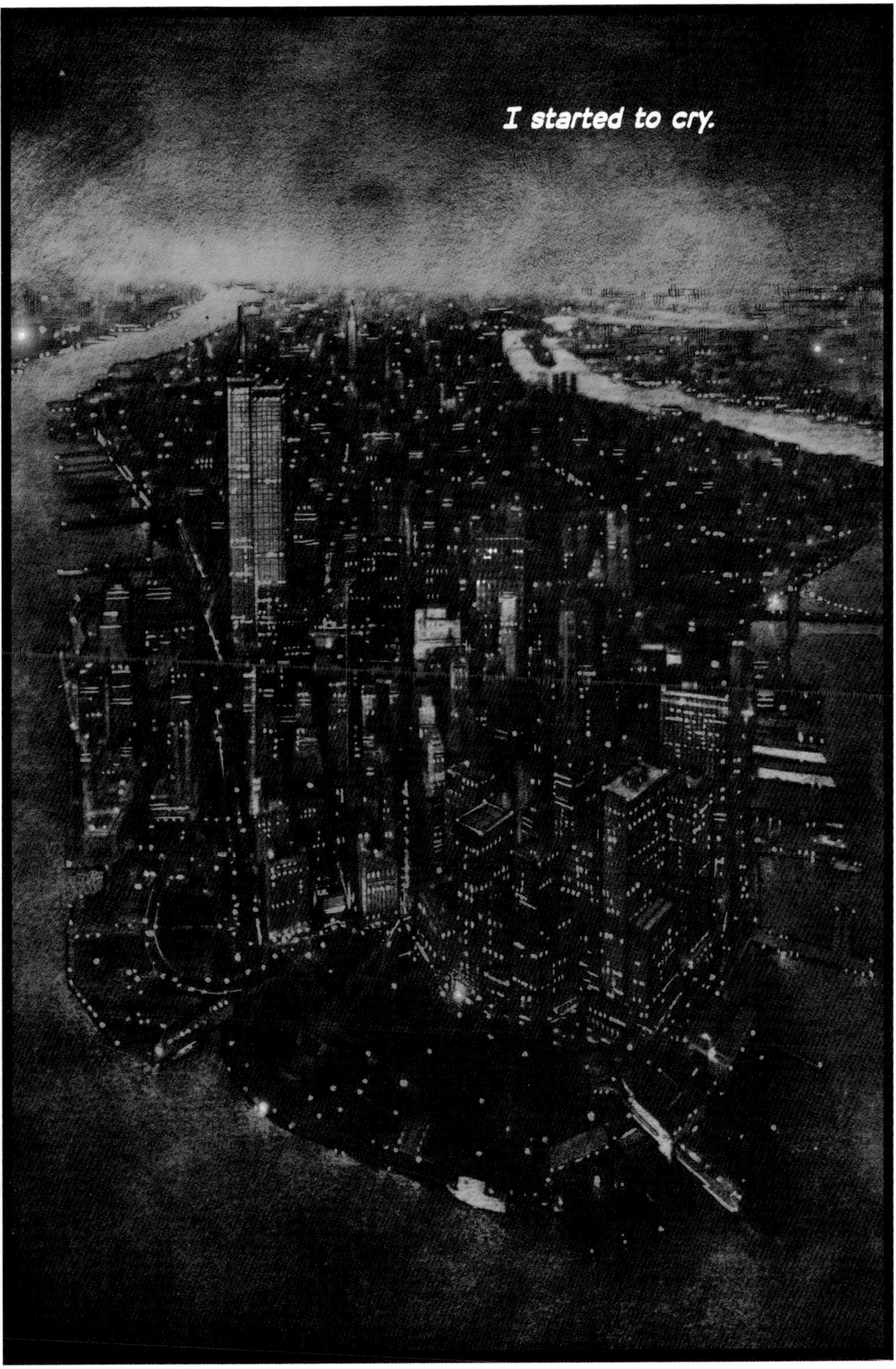
I started to cry.

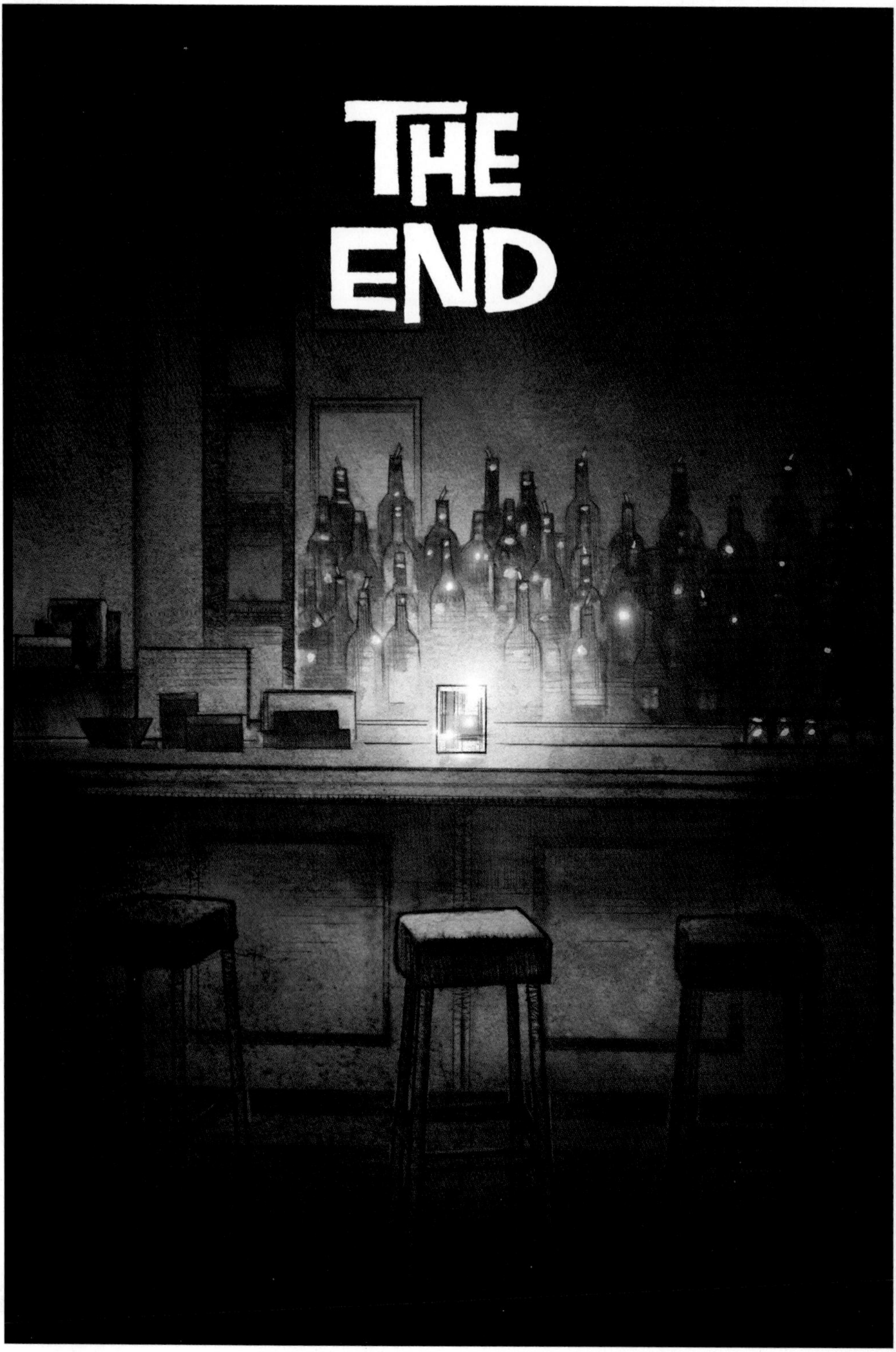
THE END

SPECIAL THANKS TO:

Lawrence Block
David Trevor
Danny Baror
Heather Baror
Ted Adams
Greg Goldstein
Chris Ryall
Justin Eisinger
Alonzo Simon
My gracious editor,
Tom Waltz
and everyone at IDW
for making it all come together
and family, friends, and
colleagues for their
support and encouragement
all along the way

Dedicated to the works of:

Arnold Drake, Leslie Waller, and Matt Baker,
Jim Steranko
Don McGregor, Marshall Rogers, and Gene Colan
Darwyn Cooke
and
Hal Ashby

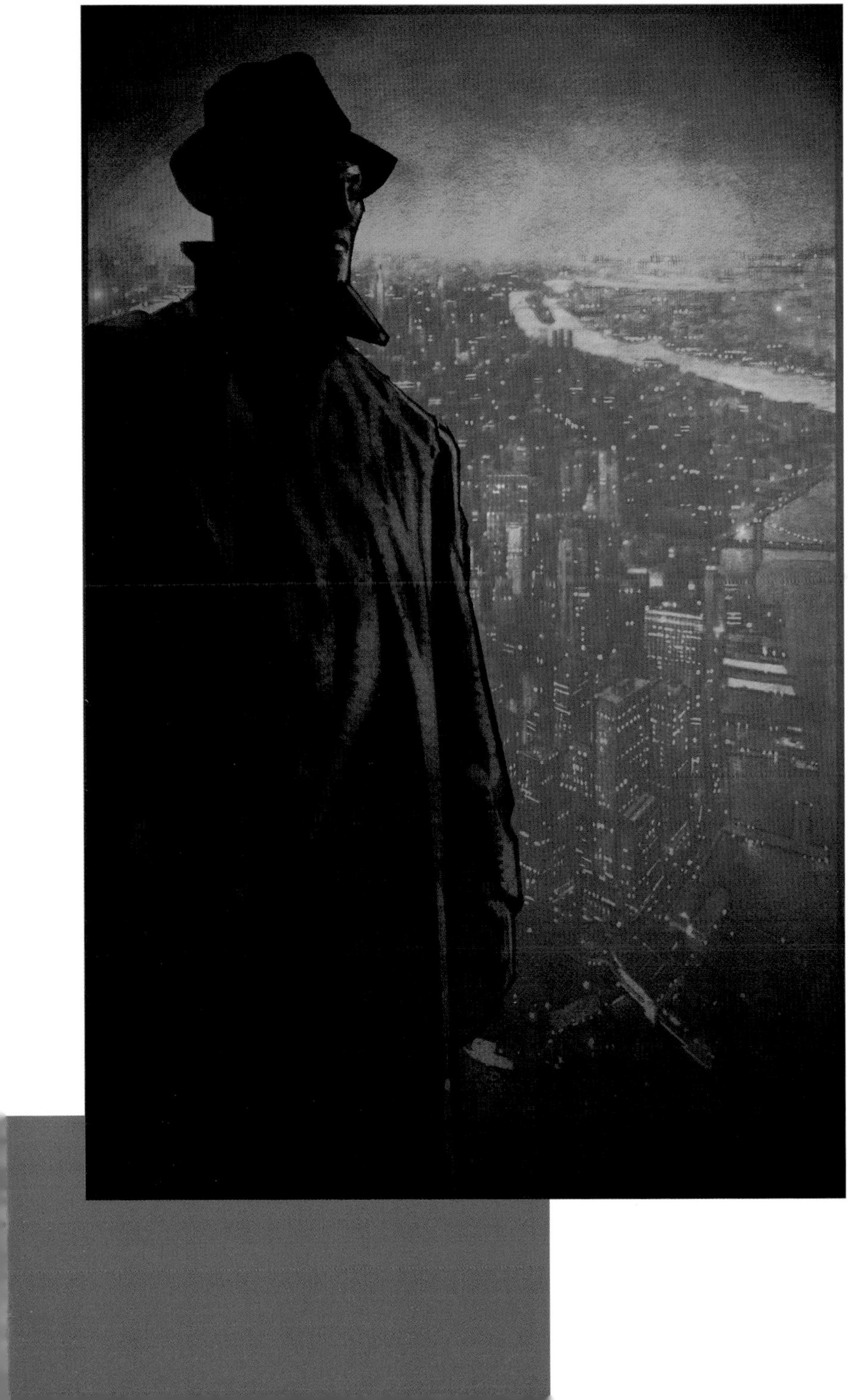